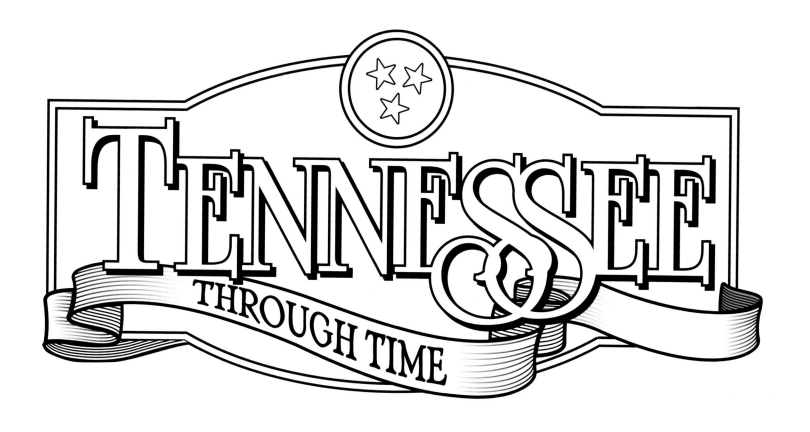

THE EARLY YEARS

Gibbs Smith, Publisher
Salt Lake City

Published by
Gibbs Smith, Publisher
P.O. Box 667
Layton, UT 84041
800-748-5439
www.gibbs-smith.com/textbooks

Managing Editor: Valerie Thursby Hatch
Editorial Assistants: Jennifer Petersen, Kris Brunson, Erin Flinders, Aimee Stoddard
Education Editor: Rachel Pike
Photo Editor: Janis Hansen
Photo Research Assistant: Wendy Knight
Cover Design: Alan Connell, John Vehar
Book Design: Alan Connell
Maps and Graphs: Alan Connell

Printed and bound in China.
ISBN 1-58685-804-1

15 14 13 12 11 10 09 08   10 9 8 7 6 5 4 3 2 1

ABOUT THE AUTHOR

Carole Stanford Bucy is a professor of history at Volunteer State Community College in Gallatin, Tennessee. As a native of Bonham, Texas, Bucy earned a B.A. in history from Baylor University, an M.A. in American history from George Peabody College for Teachers, and a Ph.D. in American history from Vanderbilt University.

Professor Bucy speaks frequently on both Tennessee and American history to community groups and professional organizations. She is the author of several articles and books, including *Women Helping Women: The YWCA of Nashville*, *The Nashville City Cemetery–History Carved in Stone* and *The Civil War Years in Tennessee*. Bucy is also the project director of TEACH (Tennessee Educators' Active Colloquia for History), a program funded by the United States Department of American History to provide professional development opportunities for teachers.

Despite her many responsibilities and assignments, Bucy's first love is teaching. She began her career 30 years ago in Atlanta, Georgia, and is still inspiring her students through storytelling and her love of Tennessee history.

CONTRIBUTORS & REVIEWERS

After receiving an M.A. and Ph.D. from Emory University, **Edwin S. Gleaves** pursued two career paths. For 20 years, he served as Director of the School of Library and Information Science at Peabody College, Vanderbilt University. He then served 18 years as the State Librarian and Archivist of Tennessee. In addition to publishing widely in the field of library and information science, Gleaves has served on a number of boards and contributed to the *Tennessee Historical Quarterly* and the *Tennessee Encyclopedia of History and Culture*. Since retiring in 2005, Gleaves has taught English and Tennessee history at Lipscomb University in Nashville and continues to serve on the board of the Disciples of Christ Historical Society.

As Curator of Education with the East Tennessee Historical Society (ETHS), **Lisa N. Oakley** is responsible for all aspects of student and teacher programming. Oakley also serves as project director for a number of grant projects, including the Tennessee River Valley Consortium's Teaching of American History Grant. Oakley received a B.A. in history from the University of Tennessee and holds an M.A. in history with an emphasis in historic preservation from Middle Tennessee State University.

Carol Farrar Kaplan received her education from George Peabody College. She has worked for The Hermitage (home of President Andrew Jackson) and as the first registrar at the Tennessee State Museum. Kaplan has co-authored two books, *Remember the Ladies: Mt. Olivet Cemetery* and *The Nashville City Cemetery –History Carved in Stone*. Kaplan recently retired after working 25 years in the local history division (Nashville Room) of the Nashville Public Library. She is a 7th generation Tennessean.

Contents

Maps & Charts

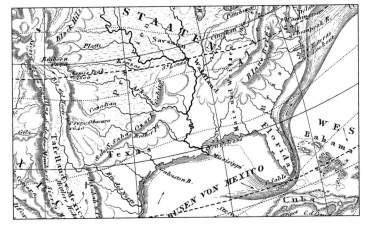

Portraits

Passport to History

Explore Tennessee!

Chapter Review

> "*Perhaps the history of no State in the Union contains more events of romantic interest than that of Tennessee.*"
>
> —*W. H. Carpenter, 1854*

Your Tennessee Adventure Begins

Chapter 1

Learning about history is an adventure! It is kind of like a treasure hunt. As you read, you will follow clues that will lead you to secrets about the past. Soon you will begin your adventure into Tennessee's past. What do you think you will discover?

This is Shiloh National Military Park. It was the site of the largest Civil War battle in Tennessee.

WORDS TO UNDERSTAND

glossary
index
table of contents
technology
timeline

What Do You Think❓

Why do you think a place's history has so much to do with its location?

The best way to begin learning about a place's history is to study its location in the world.

Let's Begin

Welcome to *Tennessee Through Time: The Early Years!* In this book, you will learn all about our state. You will find its place in our country and in the world. You will study our land. You will learn about Tennessee's past and how people lived. You will learn about the people who live in our state today and how the past influenced them. You will think about things you can do to create a better future for Tennessee.

Taking a Trip

Have you ever taken a car trip with your family? Did you go to a fun place? You probably saw signs along the way. Road signs help people know where they are going.

Signs Along the Way

This book has signs too! The signs point you to tools that help you study Tennessee's history.

Pictures

Every chapter starts with a big picture about Tennessee. Look at the picture carefully. It gives you clues about what you will read in the chapter. Try to imagine yourself in the picture. What do you see around you? What are you doing?

Timelines

At the beginning of most chapters, you will see a *timeline.* It shows the dates of important events. If you study the timeline before you begin reading the chapter, you will have a good idea of what you are about to learn. Timelines show the order of events through time. They help us see how some events led to other events.

Lessons

Each chapter is divided into lessons. Each lesson has a name and these important lists:

People to Know   Places to Locate   Words to Understand

Read the lists at the beginning of each lesson. See if you know any of the names of the People to Know. Find the Places to Locate on a map. Read the Words to Understand. Are any of them new to you? If so, look them up in the glossary. Watch for the names, places, and words as you read each lesson.

What Do You Think?

Some questions do not have right or wrong answers. "What Do You Think?" questions are like that. They give you a chance to think more and to share your opinion about certain things.

Linking the Present to the Past

Many of the events that happened in the past still affect your life today. How has modern Tennessee been shaped by things that happened long ago? Look for this sign to learn about the ways past events continue to affect your life today.

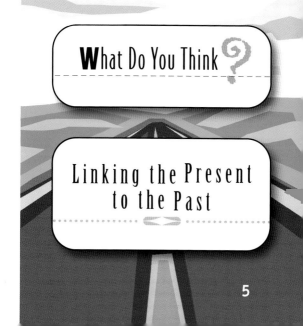

Passport to History

Passport to History activities are very special. Only one appears in each chapter. After you complete this activity, ask your teacher for a stamp in your very own passport to history.

Our Land, Our Lives

Where we live affects how we live and work. Many things about your life would change if you lived in another place. The land had a great deal to do with how things happened in Tennessee's past too. Look for this sign to read about how the land in Tennessee changes people's lives—today and in the past.

Explore Tennessee!

Whenever you see this sign, you will read about an exciting, interesting, or mysterious place in Tennessee. These are places you can visit today, so you may want to take your family to see some of them.

Tennessee Portraits

The story of Tennessee's history is really the story of its people. Tennessee Portraits tell you about interesting people in Tennessee. Some of the people were very brave. Some of them became famous. Some Tennessee Portraits tell you about regular people who did great things. Maybe someday there will be a Tennessee Portrait about you!

Terrific Technology

Technology is a big word that means using tools and science together. Your computer is a good example of technology. When you see the Terrific Technology sign, you will read about the ways technology has changed people's lives and jobs in Tennessee.

Memory Masters

At the end of each lesson, you will find a few questions. These questions give you a chance to test your memory. They help you review the things you have learned.

What's the Point?

At the end of each chapter, you will find a short paragraph called "What's the Point?" This paragraph describes the chapter's main ideas. It also reminds you of the most important things that happened in the chapter.

Becoming Better Readers

These activities will help improve your reading skills. Do you like to read? Or do you think reading is hard? If something is hard, practicing it will make it easier. For example, have you ever learned a new sport? When you played the first time, you may have made a lot of mistakes. But the more you played, the more skilled you became, right? Reading is like that too. The more you read, the better reader you will become.

Climbing to Connections and Evaluation Station

Activities are a fun way to learn about history. They give you a chance to do more with what you learn. Sometimes you will pretend you lived in Tennessee long ago. Sometimes you will play a game, draw a picture, or make a map. Some activities will ask you to read, research, or write about an event.

Other Tools

There are other tools to help you on your journey through this book. At the beginning of the book, there is a **table of contents.** It tells you what pages the chapters start on. It also tells you where the maps and activities are.

At the end of the book, there is a glossary and an index. The **glossary** explains the meanings of all the Words to Understand. The **index** lists the page numbers where you'll find important subjects, people, and places. Can you find the glossary and index pages?

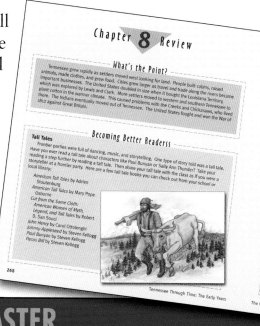

1 MEMORY MASTER

1. Name one sign or feature of this book.
2. What is a timeline?
3. What is technology? Give an example.

WORDS TO UNDERSTAND

artifact
document
evidence
historian
oral history
point of view
pottery
primary source
secondary source

Your Story and Tennessee's Story

We live in a place called Tennessee. That means we are Tennesseans. Like all places, Tennessee has a story. The story of the past is called history. Our state's history tells us the story of how Tennessee came to be. It is the story of how things changed over the years.

Before you begin reading about Tennessee's story, think about your own story. Your story is all about you, but it is connected to other stories. It is connected to the stories of your parents and grandparents. Your story (your history) is part of the larger story of Tennessee and American history.

Do your parents or grandparents tell you stories about when they were young? What do you think this man is telling his grandson?

Both your history and Tennessee's history are still being written. As you grow, you will make decisions that will change the story of your life. In the past, people made decisions that changed Tennessee's story too. If people had done things differently or made other choices, our state might be very different than it is today.

Learning from the Past

Can you imagine what it would have been like to live without electricity? Can you see yourself walking or riding in a wagon across Tennessee? All these things have to do with the past. The past is everything that happened up until this very moment.

When we learn about the past, we see that sometimes people in Tennessee tried to get along. Other times they didn't. History is not always peaceful and pleasant. People often had conflicts because they had different ideas about things. Today we can see some of the mistakes made by people in the past. We can also see the good things they did. By studying history, we can learn from the past and make better choices for our future.

Think Like a Historian!

People who study history are called *historians*. As you read *Tennessee Through Time*, you can think like a historian. To find out what really happened in the past, historians need *evidence* (proof). Some evidence may be hard to find. Historical evidence comes in two forms: primary sources and secondary sources.

Have you ever seen an old car in a museum? Can you imagine what it would be like to ride in a car like this one?

Primary Sources

Primary sources are actual records and objects that have survived from the past. Primary sources were made by people who were involved in an event or who saw it happen. Studying things people made, used, or wrote long ago tells us a lot about their lives.

Artifacts

One important kind of primary source is an *artifact*. Artifacts are things people made or used in the past. An Indian basket is an artifact. By looking at one, you will learn what materials people had. You might also be able to tell how they used the basket. This would tell you something about their lives.

What can you guess about the people who used this trunk or these baskets?

Photographs

Most photographs are primary sources. They record what happened at a certain moment in time. By looking at photographs from the past, you can often see what people wore, what their homes were like, or how they lived.

Newspapers and Magazines

Newspapers and magazines are primary sources if they were written at the time that an event took place. When you read the words of people who were actually there, you begin to understand what an event was really like.

Linking the Present to the Past

Some people have artifacts in their homes. You may know someone who has a collection of Indian arrowheads. You may also know someone who collects items from the Civil War or another war. Can you think of an artifact you would like to collect?

Activity

Comparing Photographs

What can you learn by comparing photographs from the past to photographs of today? You can see how things change over time. Look at these two pictures of Memphis. One was taken in 1920. The other was taken more than 80 years later. What is different?

What Is It?

This bottle, made of **_pottery,_** is almost 600 years old. What does it tell you about the person who made it? He or she must have known clay could be shaped and baked until it became hard. The bottle has a handle and a spout, so it probably held liquids.

Why do you think the bottle is shaped like an animal? What kind of animal do you think it is? Do you think it was a pet? Some ancient people were buried with their dogs. Do you think they loved their pets as much as we do?

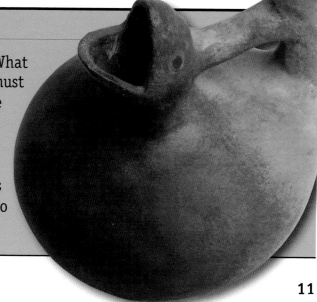

Journals and Letters

There are other types of primary sources. A letter from one person to another is a primary source called a *document.* Documents are papers, letters, or forms. Your birth certificate is a document. Journal pages are documents too.

Oral History

Have your grandparents ever told you what life was like when they were children? If so, they were giving you an *oral history.* Oral history is history that people speak or record but don't write down. Listening to oral histories is another way to learn about the past.

Long before email or text messaging, people wrote letters. Have you ever written or received a letter?

Activity

Your Travel Journal

Pretend you traveled to Tennessee in 1839. You came to the United States on a steamship that docked in New Orleans, Louisiana. Then you took a smaller boat up the Mississippi River to Memphis.

You wrote in a journal every day on your trip to Tennessee. Your journal describes what it was like to travel on a steamship and to move to a new place. It even tells about some of the things you saw and people you met.

Write about one day of your trip to Memphis. Were you excited about coming to a new place? Explain why you decided to travel to Memphis. Describe the foods you ate and the things you saw, smelled, and heard that day.

PASSPORT TO HISTORY

Oral History

If you could travel back in time, who would you want to meet? What would you ask him or her? Wouldn't it be amazing to hear the point of view of someone who lived 1,000 years ago? Even though we can't do that, we can record our oral histories today. Then someone living many years from now can hear our points of view.

With an adult's help, record a bit of oral history. You can tell a story about something that happened in the past or something that happened today. It can be a story that someone older than you told you. After you have made the recording, share it with the class to get a stamp in your passport. Save your oral history recording. Years from now you can travel back in time and watch or listen to the story again!

Secondary Sources

You can probably guess what a *secondary source* is. It is something written, said, or made by someone who was not present at an event. For example, a book written today about the first settlers in Tennessee is a secondary source. It is a secondhand account. Sometimes secondary sources add facts that were not available at the time of an event.

What Do You Think?

If you have a dress your great-grandmother wore in a parade in the 1940s, it is a primary source. But if your mother sews a dress that looks like the one your great-grandmother wore, it is a secondary source. Can you explain why?

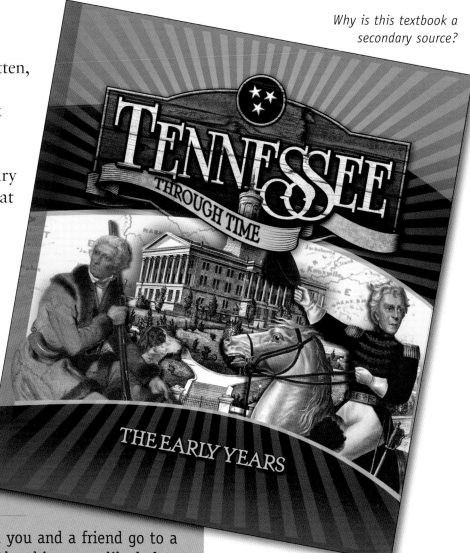

Why is this textbook a secondary source?

Point of View

To understand **point of view,** pretend you and a friend go to a movie. After the movie, you describe all the things you liked about it. You are sharing your point of view. Perhaps your friend did not like the movie and tells you why. You and your friend's opinions about the movie are different. That does not mean one of you is right and one of you is wrong. It simply means you see things differently. Point of view is seeing things differently. It can change due to a person's age, education, family life, or neighborhood.

There are different points of view in history. For example, a long time ago there were battles between settlers and Indians. If you could ask both a pioneer and an Indian about the battles, you would probably get two very different answers. That is because their points of view are different. Even today, many people have different points of view about historical events. As you read this book, watch for different points of view.

Places to Learn About Tennessee History

Our state has many places that teach us more about our history. You can visit these places, or you can study about them at home. As you learn about new places and events, you should ask: What? Who? When? Where? Why? How? What was the result? As you answer these questions, Tennessee's story will begin to unfold.

Libraries

Your school library and your public library have books and other materials that can teach you about Tennessee. Every county in Tennessee has a public library. Many of our public libraries also have local history rooms or sections. There you can find books about your city or county.

Museums

Museums across our state have many interesting artifacts and documents that teach us about Tennessee history. These items help us understand the story of our state. Museums usually have both primary and secondary sources. Some counties and cities have museums that tell us about local history. Which museums have you visited?

EXPLORE TENNESSEE!

The Tennessee State Library and Archives

The State Library and Archives is across the street from the Tennessee State Capitol Building in Nashville. It holds more information about the history of Tennessee than any other place in the world. It is a wonderful place to learn about our state.

Do you like to go to the library? What is your favorite book?

Historic Sites

Tennesseans are proud of their history and have worked to preserve the places where historic events took place. Old houses and buildings help us understand what life was like when people lived in them or used them.

In Memphis, Graceland tells us about the life of Elvis Presley. The Ryman Auditorium in Nashville tells us about the history of country music. The Rhea County Courthouse in Dayton was the site of the Scopes Trial. That is one of the most famous court trials in our nation's history.

A popular place to visit is the James K. Polk home in Columbia. Have you ever been there?

The Internet

Vast amounts of information about Tennessee history are available on the Internet. If you use the Internet, you must learn how to know if the information is accurate. One of the best Internet sites about our state's history is the Tennessee Encyclopedia of History and Culture at tennesseeencyclopedia.net. Another great website, www.tnhistoryforkids.org, has lots of kid-friendly information about the history of Tennessee.

What Do You Think ?

At some historic sites, you can take a tour. A guide might show you around the site and tell you all about it. Should you consider point of view while listening to the guide? Why or why not?

Cemeteries

Did you know a great deal of history can be learned in a cemetery? Cemeteries hold information that often cannot be found in any other place. Gravestones usually have the full name of a person along with his or her birth and death dates. Some gravestones even say the person was a good mother, a brave soldier, a loving child, or something else. You can learn much about a community by walking through its oldest cemetery.

Have you ever visited a cemetery? What did you see while you were there?

2 MEMORY MASTER

1. What is history?
2. What two forms of evidence do historians study?
3. What is oral history?

WORDS TO UNDERSTAND

agriculture
commerce
motto
represent
slogan
symbol
volunteer

Introducing Tennessee

Our state has **symbols** that represent things that are important to Tennesseans. A symbol is something that **represents** (stands for) something else. Some of Tennessee's symbols are our state flag and state seal. Others are beautiful plants that grow and unique animals that live in Tennessee. The symbols remind us of special things about our state. They also tell us something about who we are.

The Tennessee State Motto

The Tennessee **motto** describes how we think about our state. It is a saying that reflects the spirit of Tennessee. Our state motto is "Agriculture and Commerce." **Agriculture** is farming, and **commerce** is business. These words appear on our state seal. We also have a state **slogan.** It is often used on letters, signs, and brochures that invite people to visit our state. Our state slogan is "Tennessee—America at Its Best."

The Tennessee State Flag

Our state flag is our most important symbol. It represents all Tennesseans. It shows that no matter how different we are, we are united by love for our state. Our flag is beautiful and colorful. You can see it flying over the state capitol in Nashville. It flies over other government buildings in Tennessee too. The state flag always flies below the U.S. flag.

The flag's background is crimson (red). The three stars are white and stand for the three Grand Divisions of the state: East Tennessee, Middle Tennessee, and West Tennessee. The stars are together on an endless circle of blue to show that the three parts of Tennessee are tied together as one state. The blue bar on the end of the flag has no special meaning. It was put there so the flag wouldn't show too much red when it is not waving.

The Tennessee state flag was adopted in 1905. It is red, white, and blue. What other important flag is red, white, and blue?

The Tennessee State Seal

Our state seal is used to mark important government papers. Sometimes it appears on state buildings. In the center of the seal are our state motto and symbols that represent agriculture and commerce. As symbols for agriculture, the seal shows a plow, a sheaf of wheat, and a cotton plant. A boat is the symbol for commerce.

Tennessee's first constitution said the state's official seal was to be called the "Great Seal of the State of Tennessee." The seal is kept by the governor and stamped on all official papers. It has the Roman numeral XVI at the top and the year 1796 on the bottom. The Roman numeral shows that Tennessee was the 16th state to join the United States. The year 1796 shows the year Tennessee became a state.

What Do You Think ❓

Do you think the plow, sheaf of wheat, cotton plant, and boat represent our state today? Do you think "Agriculture and Commerce" describes Tennessee today?

Do you think Tennessee should change its seal? Why or why not?

Linking the Present to the Past

The first Tennessee state seal had a boatman in the boat. In the seal used today, the boat looks different, and the boatman is gone. Our first state seal was designed in 1802. How many years ago was that?

State tree: tulip poplar

State wildflower:
passion flower

State butterfly:
Zebra Swallowtail

State flower: iris

**State agriculture
insect:** honeybee

State insects:
firefly, ladybug

State wild animal:
raccoon

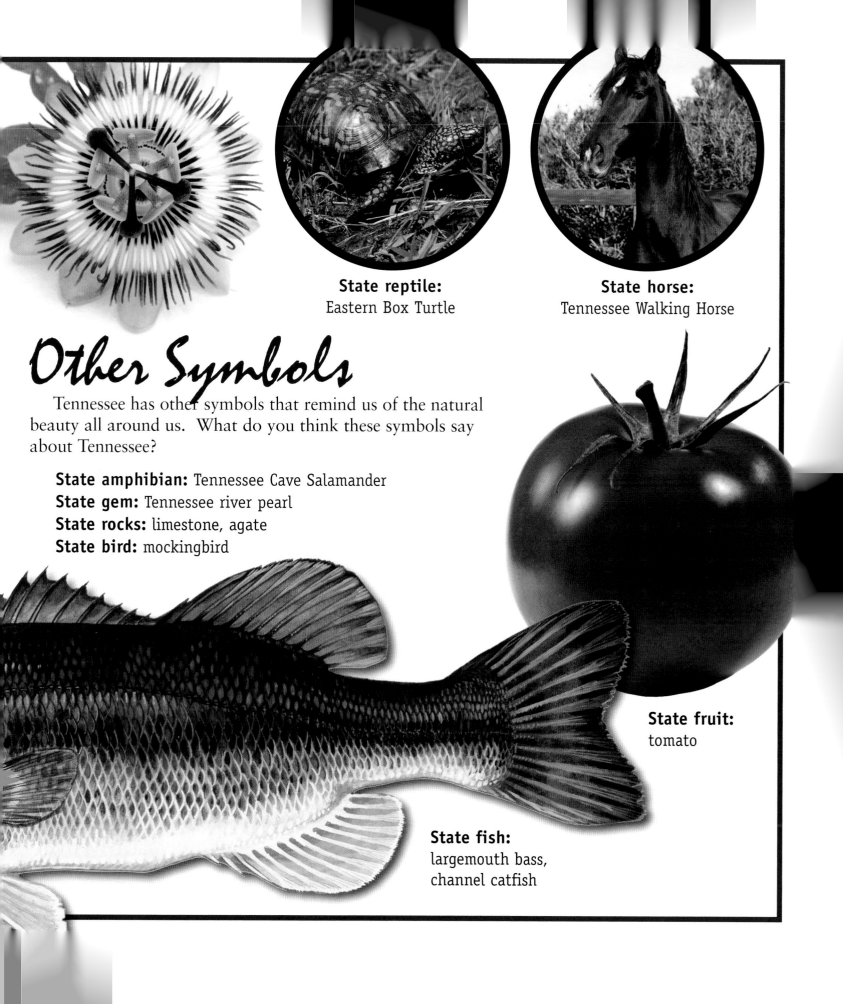

State reptile:
Eastern Box Turtle

State horse:
Tennessee Walking Horse

Other Symbols

Tennessee has other symbols that remind us of the natural beauty all around us. What do you think these symbols say about Tennessee?

State amphibian: Tennessee Cave Salamander
State gem: Tennessee river pearl
State rocks: limestone, agate
State bird: mockingbird

State fruit:
tomato

State fish:
largemouth bass,
channel catfish

Tennessee's State Songs

Several types of American music were born in Tennessee, so we have more than one state song. In fact, Tennessee has seven official state songs. The two songs that are best known are "Tennessee Waltz" and "Rocky Top."

State Nickname

A nickname is a name for a person or place that is used instead of a real or official name. The most popular nickname for Tennessee is the "Volunteer State." Do you know what *volunteer* means? To volunteer is to offer to do something. Tennessee is called the "Volunteer State" because so many Tennesseans have volunteered to fight in America's wars.

Rocky Top

Rocky Top, you'll always be
home sweet home to me;
Good ol' Rocky Top;
Rocky Top, Tennessee;
Rocky Top, Tennessee

Activity

Discovering Our State Songs

Go to the website listed below and look up the rest of the words to "Rocky Top." Look up the words to "Tennessee Waltz" too. Can you find Tennessee's other official songs? Which of these songs do you think best describes our state? Why?

www.tennesseeanytime.org/
homework/songs.html

The Brave Volunteer

The earliest mention of Tennesseans as volunteers is found in a poem written by Jacob Hartsell. In 1812, the United States was at war with Great Britain. Hartsell was a soldier, and the army needed more men. Hartsell's poem is a call to Tennesseans to join the army. Here are a few lines from "The Brave Volunteer":

Our Counties Invaded ohare the alarme
Turn out Sons of Tennessee and gird on your armes
We air Sons of columbia and Straingers to fear
Sure heaven will Smile on the brave Volunteer

The blood of our fathers has bought Liberty
And raised up a nation proud hearted and free
Their Sons will maintain its freedom so dear
And to meet their invaders turn out Volunteer

Hartsell had little education, so some words in the poem are spelled strangely. Can you tell what the words are? How do you feel when you read this poem? How does Hartsell feel about this country? How does he feel about Tennessee?

Your Tennessee Adventure Is About to Begin

Now that you know what history is, you are ready for your Tennessee adventure. The adventure begins thousands of years ago when the earth was much colder than it is today. On your journey, you will learn about the people who lived here before you did. You will learn about their ideas, their families, and the experiences they had. Some of their stories will seem very different from yours.

During this adventure, you will study many important events. You will ask questions, and you will find answers. When our adventure ends, you will understand how your story is a part of our state's story. You will understand how this land became the great state of Tennessee.

③ MEMORY MASTER

1. What is a symbol?
2. What is our state motto?
3. How did Tennessee become known as the "Volunteer State"?

Chapter 1 Review

What's the Point?

History is the story of the people of the past. By studying Tennessee's history, we can see how the choices people made shaped our state. We can learn about ourselves. There are many tools, such as primary and secondary sources, to help us study Tennessee history. When we see our state symbols or hear our state song, we feel proud of our state and its history.

Becoming Better Readers

Looking for Sources

Is this book a primary or secondary source? If you think it's a secondary source, you're right! Inside this book are many examples of both primary and secondary sources. On a piece of paper, draw a chart like the one below. Then look through this book. Choose five pictures, and write the page number on the chart and write what the picture is of. Then put an X in one of the boxes next to the picture to show whether it is a primary or secondary source.

Page Number	Picture	Primary	Secondary

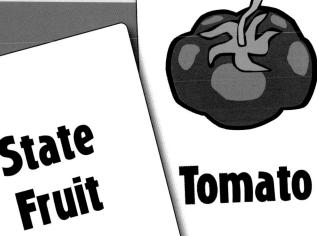

Tennessee Flash Cards

This chapter has many facts about Tennessee's state symbols. Do you remember the state fish or the state flower? Make your own set of Tennessee flash cards. You will need index cards and crayons, markers, or colored pencils.

Use the symbols listed in the first section of Lesson 3. On one side of the index cards, write the words for the symbols. On the other side, draw pictures of the symbols. Be sure to include the state motto, song, and nickname. When you have finished, you will have colorful flash cards that will help you study Tennessee state facts!

── Climbing to Connections ──

Being a Historian

1. Identify the things a historian does.
2. Describe the things historians use as clues.
3. Give an example of a primary source and a secondary source.
4. Select two places where you can learn about history from pages 14 and 15, and compare what you could learn in each place.
5. Design a list of primary and secondary sources you would use to learn about the history of your town.
6. Explain why preserving documents is an important part of history.

── Evaluation Station ──

Making Good Choices

In this chapter, you learned that history is not always peaceful or pleasant. You learned that sometimes people cooperated and made good choices, but other times they didn't. Who do you know who makes good choices for Tennessee? It could be your parent, family member, teacher, friend, or neighbor. On your own paper, write the person's name. Then list three ways this person helps Tennessee. What choices will you make to help Tennessee's future?

Beautiful Tennessee, Beautiful America

Chapter

When you hear the word "Tennessee," what do you picture in your mind? Take a moment to look out the window. Do you see grass, hills, trees, or birds? Do you see cars, houses, or businesses? All these things are parts of our home. No matter where you live in the state, you can be proud to be a Tennessean.

This is the view from Morton Overlook in the Great Smoky Mountains National Park.

Have you ever visited a farm?
Tennessee has some of the richest
farmland in the United States.

The Place We Call Home

Tennessee is our home, so it is important to us. In this chapter, we will learn more about our state by studying its *geography*. Geography is the land, water, plants, animals, and people of a place. It is also the study of where places are located on the earth.

Geography affects where and how we live. In some parts of the state, we have tall mountains. In other parts, we have rolling hills where the leaves turn bright colors in the fall. We also have flat, *fertile* farmland with very few trees. We have thousands of miles of rivers, lakes, and streams. If you travel to different parts of Tennessee, you will see how the land changes from place to place.

As we study our geography, we will learn about our state's location in the United States. We will see how people in Tennessee are connected to people and places all over the world. We will also learn about our state's economy. We will read about the many products that come from Tennessee.

Locating Places on the Earth

Pretend you meet some people from a different country. They want to visit Tennessee. Could you tell them how to find it? There are two ways you can describe a location.

Relative location describes where a place is in relation to other places or things. For example, Tennessee is between Kentucky and Alabama. It is next to North Carolina and Arkansas. You could tell someone you live near the Clinch River or next to the school. You could tell them you live down the hall from your friend's apartment or in the neighborhood east of town. These are all relative locations.

Absolute location is the exact position of a place. Every place on the earth has an absolute location. An address is an absolute location. What is your address?

PLACES TO LOCATE

Appalachian Mountains
Mississippi River

WORDS TO UNDERSTAND

absolute location
accent
cardinal directions
elevation
equator
fertile
geography
grid
hemisphere
intermediate directions
latitude
longitude
prime meridian
relative location

Do You Have a Tennessee Accent?

Have you lived in Tennessee all your life? If you have, has anyone from another state ever told you that you talk funny? People from other places say many Tennesseans have accents. An **accent** is a special way of saying words. People who live in the same area often have accents that are alike. Some people study accents. They can guess where a person is from just by listening to his or her accent!

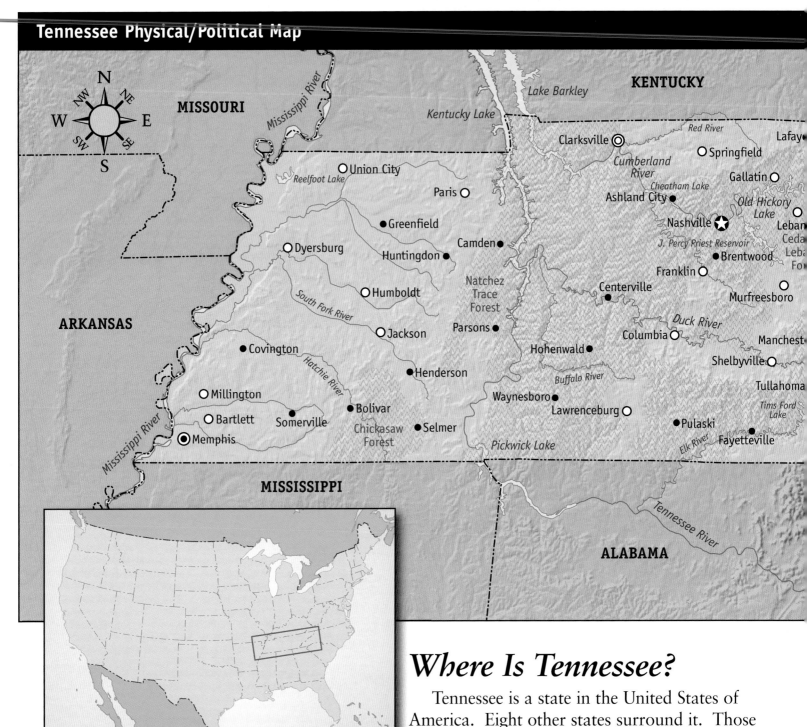

Where Is Tennessee?

Tennessee is a state in the United States of America. Eight other states surround it. Those states are Kentucky, Virginia, North Carolina, Georgia, Alabama, Mississippi, Arkansas, and Missouri.

Look at Tennessee's borders. Our eastern border is the highest point of the Appalachian Mountains between Tennessee and North Carolina. Our western border is the Mississippi River. Look carefully at our northern and southern borders. At first glance, they appear to be straight lines. But if you look very closely, you can see the borders are not perfectly straight.

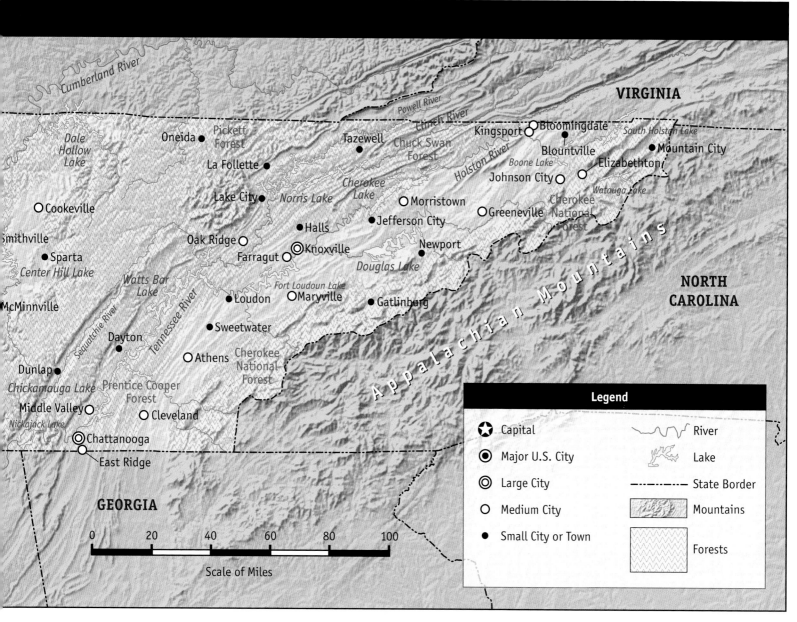

Activity

Geographic Map Features

1. Which mountains are in the eastern part of our state?
2. Which river forms Tennessee's western border?
3. Which river is farther east, the Tennessee River or the Mississippi River?
4. Locate and name three forests in Tennessee.
5. Locate and name three major rivers in Tennessee.
6. Locate and name three cities on plains and three cities in valleys of Tennessee.

Beautiful Tennessee, Beautiful America

Latitude and Longitude

Another way to describe absolute location is by using lines of *latitude* and *longitude*. These are the lines you see on a globe or a map. They are not real lines on the ground. If you were to walk across the border between Tennessee and Kentucky, you would not see a line there.

Look at the globe to the left of this paragraph. Find the *equator*. It is the latitude line that runs around the middle of the earth.

Now find the *prime meridian*. It is the longitude line that runs from the North Pole to the South Pole.

Other latitude and longitude lines go north, south, east, and west of the equator and prime meridian. On a map, the lines cross each other to make a *grid*. If you know the latitude and longitude of a place, you can find an exact location anywhere on the earth.

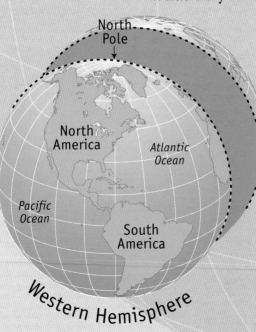

Hemispheres

There is another way to divide the earth. We can pretend that it is cut into two equal pieces. Each half is called a *hemisphere*.

Look at the drawing to the left again. Find the equator. Then find the hemisphere north of the equator. Since north is usually at the top of a map, the hemisphere north of the equator is the Northern Hemisphere. Find the hemisphere south of the equator. What do you think it is called?

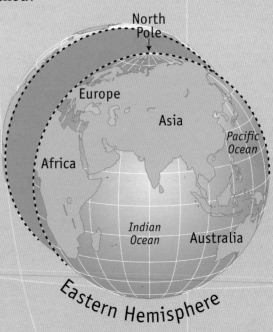

Mapmakers sometimes divide the earth into eastern and western parts too. Can you find the drawings that show the Western and Eastern Hemispheres? Is Tennessee in the Northern or Southern Hemisphere? Is Tennessee in the Eastern or Western Hemisphere?

Activity

Drawing Lines Around the World

Look at this map of Tennessee. Most maps have lines that run side to side and up and down. They are lines of latitude and longitude. Here's a way to remember which lines are which:

- **Latitude lines** run east and west (side to side) in the same direction as the equator.
- **Longitude lines** run north and south (up and down) in the same direction as the prime meridian.

Latitude and longitude lines are numbered. Each number has a tiny circle by it. This is the symbol for a degree. A degree is a way to measure a circle or a globe. The equator is 0° latitude, and the prime meridian is 0° longitude.

Study the map to see what Tennessee's latitude and longitude lines are. You can trace these lines all the way around the world!

1. Tennessee's border with Mississippi, Alabama, and Georgia is at about what degree latitude?
2. Nashville is nearest what degree of latitude?
3. Chattanooga is nearest what degree of longitude?
4. What Tennessee city is at about 84° longitude and 36° longitude?
5. Memphis is nearest what degree of longitude?

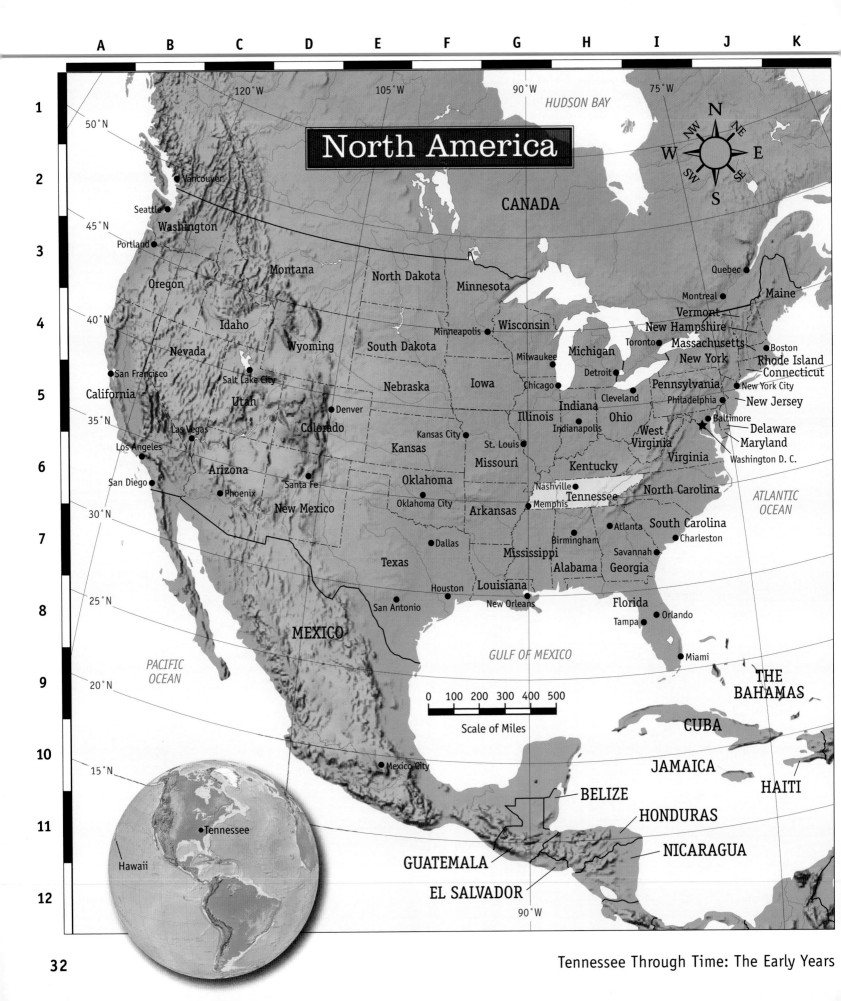

North America

A B C D E F G H I J K

1 2 3 4 5 6 7 8 9 10 11 12

HUDSON BAY

N NW NE W E SW SE S

50°N
120°W   105°W   90°W   75°W

CANADA

Vancouver
Seattle
Washington
45°N
Portland
Oregon
Montana
North Dakota
Minnesota
Quebec
Montreal
Maine
Vermont
New Hampshire
40°N
Idaho
Wyoming
Minneapolis
Wisconsin
Michigan
Toronto
Massachusetts
Boston
Nevada
South Dakota
Milwaukee
New York
Rhode Island
Connecticut
San Francisco
Salt Lake City
Nebraska
Iowa
Chicago
Detroit
Cleveland
Pennsylvania
New York City
California
Utah
Denver
Illinois
Indiana
Ohio
Philadelphia
New Jersey
35°N
Las Vegas
Colorado
Kansas City
St. Louis
Indianapolis
West Virginia
Baltimore
Delaware
Maryland
Los Angeles
Kansas
Missouri
Kentucky
Virginia
Washington D. C.
San Diego
Arizona
Santa Fe
Oklahoma
Nashville
Tennessee
North Carolina
ATLANTIC OCEAN
30°N
Phoenix
New Mexico
Oklahoma City
Arkansas
Memphis
Atlanta
South Carolina
Dallas
Birmingham
Charleston
Mississippi
Savannah
Texas
Alabama
Georgia
25°N
Houston
Louisiana
Florida
San Antonio
New Orleans
Orlando
MEXICO
Tampa
Miami
PACIFIC OCEAN
GULF OF MEXICO
20°N
THE BAHAMAS

0 100 200 300 400 500
Scale of Miles

CUBA

JAMAICA
15°N
Mexico City
HAITI
BELIZE
HONDURAS
Tennessee
NICARAGUA
Hawaii
GUATEMALA
EL SALVADOR
90°W

Reading a Map

Maps help us understand where we are. They help us find our way from one place to another. There are many kinds of maps. There are maps that show towns and cities and maps that show mountains and rivers. Some maps show the number of people living in a place. Here are some things to look for when you read a map.

Compass Rose

Most maps and globes have a compass rose. The four longer pointers show the four main directions: north, south, east, and west. These directions are called **cardinal directions.**

Halfway between north and east is northeast (NE). Southeast (SE) is between south and east. These are called **intermediate directions.**

Legend or Key

Mapmakers use symbols. The symbols stand for cities, airports, parks, campgrounds, and other things. A legend or key on the map tells what each symbol means. Most maps use the color blue for rivers and lakes. Some maps use colors to show **elevation.** Elevation means how high a place is above the level of the ocean. How can you see on the map that western Nebraska is higher than eastern Nebraska?

Scale of Miles

Maps show us how far apart things are. Some maps have a scale of miles. The scale helps us measure the distance between places.

Map Grid

Longitude and latitude lines are one type of map grid. Sometimes maps have grids that use letters and numbers. On this map, letters run across the top of the grid and numbers run down the side. The location of a place can be described by where it is on the grid. For example, Nashville is in H-6.

Now that you know how to read a map, you can answer these questions:

1. Which direction would you travel to get from Washington, D.C., to Nashville?
2. Which latitude line is closest to Los Angeles, California?
3. What is the grid location of Mexico City, Mexico?
4. Which direction would you go to travel from Tennessee to Hawaii?
5. Is Toronto north or south of Tennessee?

Only one other state besides Tennessee touches eight states. Can you find it on the map of the United States?

1 MEMORY MASTER

1. What is geography?
2. What is the difference between absolute and relative location?
3. Which latitude line runs around the middle of the earth?

PLACES TO LOCATE

Indian Ocean
Mount St. Helens
New Madrid Fault Line
Reel Foot Lake
Rocky Mountains
Pacific Ring of Fire

WORDS TO UNDERSTAND

boulder
dormant
earthquake
erosion
fault
glacier
lava
physical feature
plate tectonics
tsunami

OUR LAND OUR LIVES

Thousands of glaciers exist in the United States today. You can see massive glaciers in Alaska. Hundreds of smaller ones lie high in the mountains of Washington, California, Montana, Wyoming, Oregon, Colorado, Idaho, Nevada, and Utah.

Physical Features

All places have things that make them different from other places. These things are called features. Features that are part of nature are *physical features*. They are things like mountains, valleys, rivers, and lakes.

The physical features we see today have not always been here. The earth is millions of years old. Let's look at some of the forces that have changed and shaped the land over time.

Warm Seas and Frozen Glaciers

Long ago, the entire state of Tennessee was covered by a warm, shallow sea. There were hundreds of swamps with thick patches of plants and trees. Many creatures lived in the warm waters that covered the land.

Time passed, and the earth entered the Ice Age. Some parts of the United States were covered by huge sheets of ice called *glaciers*.

Did you know glaciers move? They are frozen rivers of ice.

Over time, gravity pulled on the heavy glaciers, causing them to slide. The sliding glaciers smoothed and polished the land. In some areas, they carved deep valleys. They also carried gravel, soil, and even giant *boulders.*

When the earth became warmer, the ice melted. The water from the melting ice created huge lakes that covered miles and miles of land. Most glaciers disappeared, but the gravel, soil, and enormous boulders they carried were left behind.

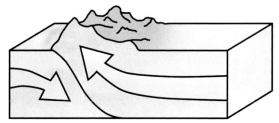

As one plate slides under another, it lifts and wrinkles the top plate, creating mountains.

Plate Tectonics

Beneath the earth's crust, there are giant layers of rock called plates. Sometimes these plates move. This is called *plate tectonics.* People who study plate tectonics try to predict where and when *earthquakes* will happen.

Some plates are the size of entire continents. Others are much smaller. The plates are always moving, but the movement is so slow that we can't see it. As the plates move, they slowly change the size and shape of the land. Over millions of years, this forms great mountains and deep valleys are formed.

Forces deep within the earth also create pressure in the earth's crust. This pressure causes cracks or weak spots in the crust called *faults.* The movement of the plates sometimes causes the two sides of a fault to hit, slip, or push against each other. When that happens, there is an earthquake. The ground rumbles, the land slides, and sometimes new landforms are created.

Earthquakes that occur beneath the ocean can cause great tidal waves. That is what happened on December 26, 2004. An earthquake under the Indian Ocean created a giant tidal wave called a *tsunami.* Walls of water up to 100 feet high slammed the coasts of Asia and Africa. Nearly 230,000 people were killed in the disaster.

Linking the Present to the Past

The New Madrid Fault is a crack in the earth's crust that runs through Missouri and West Tennessee. Nearly 200 years ago, one of the most powerful earthquakes in history occurred along the New Madrid Fault. This earthquake caused the Mississippi River to actually flow north for a while! After the ground stopped shaking, Tennessee had a new lake. It is Reelfoot Lake in the northwest part of our state.

● Reelfoot Lake

Erosion

Erosion is the natural process of wearing away. It changes the earth's surface. Do you remember how glaciers eroded the earth in the past? Wind, water, ice, and gravity continue to erode the land today.

When a section of land has few plants, rain can wash away much of the dirt. Wind and rain together cause even greater changes. Wind drives water into cracks on the earth's surface. When the water freezes, it expands (gets bigger) and widens the cracks. Over time, the pieces of earth or rock along the crack get looser. Then the wind blows them away. Millions of years of water, ice, and wind can wear away an entire mountain.

Moving water also erodes the land. As a river flows, twists, and turns, it carries soil away from both banks (sides) of the river. As time passes, the river grows wider and deeper. Sometimes the river even carves a new path. Have you ever seen a canyon created by a river?

Gravity is another natural force that erodes the land. Gravity tugs at soil and plants. Cliffs, hillsides, and other sloped landforms slowly sink. Sometimes gravity even causes landslides. All of the natural processes of erosion are still changing the shape of the land today.

AFRICA

ATLANTIC OCEAN

The Appalachian Mountains are very old. Scientists believe they formed when the earth's plates smashed together and lifted the land. The Appalachians contain rock from the land, from volcanoes, and even from the ocean! Long ago, these mountains were much taller, steeper, and rockier than they are today. Years of erosion have worn away much of them. The Rocky Mountains in the western part of the United States are taller and more jagged than the Appalachians. That is because they are much younger.

Rocky Mountains

Appalachian Mountains

Atlantic Ocean

Pacific Ocean

Gulf of Mexico

The Snake River Canyon in Idaho and Wyoming is wide and deep. It was carved by the movement of the powerful Snake River.

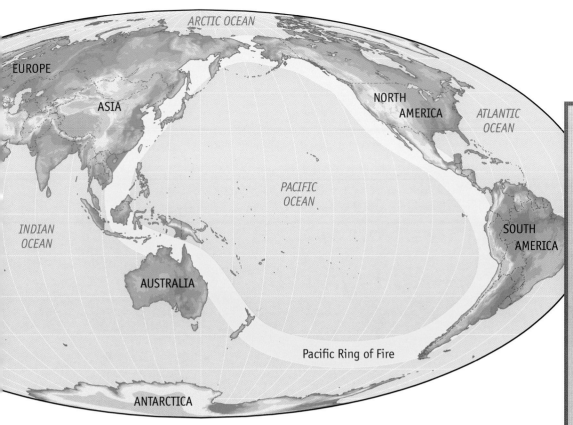

EUROPE
ARCTIC OCEAN
ASIA
NORTH AMERICA
ATLANTIC OCEAN
INDIAN OCEAN
PACIFIC OCEAN
SOUTH AMERICA
AUSTRALIA
Pacific Ring of Fire
ANTARCTICA

Volcanoes

Some mountains in the western United States were formed by volcanoes. Here's how: Steam and gases deep inside the earth create pressure. Sometimes this pressure grows greater than the earth can stand. Then the steam, gases, and melted rock, called *lava,* explode through the earth's surface. As the lava cools, it piles up and creates a mound. The mound grows higher and higher with each explosion.

Some volcanoes are active, and some are ***dormant.*** Dormant means asleep or inactive. The United States has several active volcanoes. They are in Hawaii, Alaska, Washington, Oregon, and California. These states form part of the Pacific Ring of Fire. The Ring of Fire is a circle of active volcanoes that lie around the edges of the Pacific Ocean.

In 1980, Mount St. Helens, a large volcano in Washington, erupted. A week before the blast, a churning brown landslide pulled tall trees and giant rocks down the mountainside. During the eruption, 26 lakes filled with mud and debris.

Then a towering cloud of ash and gas erupted from the volcano. It rose 12 miles into the air! Wind carried ash across the entire continent of North America. People as far away as Ohio, Kentucky, and Tennessee felt the earthquake caused by the blast.

Logs float on the surface of Spirit Lake. They were blown down by the volcano blast.

2 MEMORY MASTER

1. Name two kinds of physical features.
2. What is plate tectonics?
3. Name two things that cause erosion.

PLACES TO LOCATE

East Tennessee
Middle Tennessee
Nashville
West Tennessee

WORDS TO UNDERSTAND

boundary
generator
human feature
irrigation
landfill
pollutant
pollution
recycle
reservoir
solid waste material
turbine

One of the best ways to learn about history is to study how people have changed the land—and how the land has changed people.

Living on the Land

In Lesson 2, you learned about physical features of the land. In this lesson, you will read about the ways people use the water and the land. You also will read about *human features*. Human features are things made by people. Houses, dams, bridges, and roads are all human features.

Water—An Important Resource

Long ago, people ate wild animals, fish, nuts, roots, berries, and grasses. They wore animal skins for clothing. They cut trees and moved earth and rocks to build shelters.

As time passed, people began living in more modern ways. But there was one thing they still needed. Do you know what it was? If you guessed water, you were right! People have always built villages

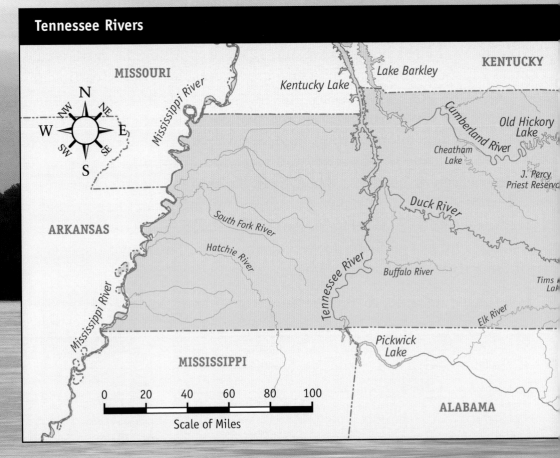

Tennessee Rivers

MISSOURI

KENTUCKY

Lake Barkley

Kentucky Lake

Mississippi River

Cumberland River

Old Hickory Lake

Cheatham Lake

J. Percy Priest Reservo

ARKANSAS

South Fork River

Duck River

Hatchie River

Tennessee River

Buffalo River

Tims Lak

Mississippi River

Elk River

Pickwick Lake

MISSISSIPPI

0   20   40   60   80   100

Scale of Miles

ALABAMA

or towns near rivers and lakes. Even today, people, plants, and animals cannot live without water.

Boundaries

Water is not just for drinking. People often use bodies of water for *boundaries.* The Tennessee River separates West Tennessee from Middle Tennessee. Which river separates Tennessee from Arkansas and Missouri?

Recreation

Tennessee's rivers and streams can also be used for fun. You can go swimming, boating, rafting, water skiing, fishing, and more! What fun things have you done on the lakes, rivers, or streams of our state?

Have you ever gone rafting? Does it look like fun?

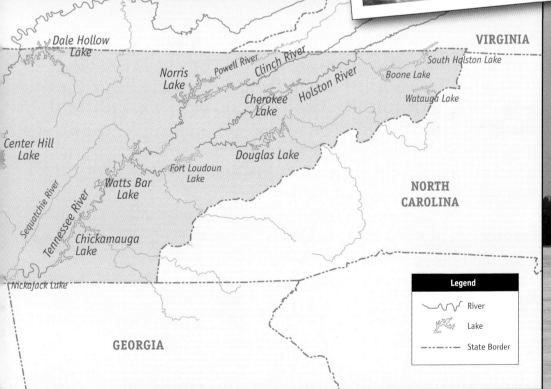

Dale Hollow Lake

VIRGINIA

Powell River Clinch River

Norris Lake

South Holston Lake

Boone Lake

Holston River

Cherokee Lake

Watauga Lake

Center Hill Lake

Douglas Lake

Fort Loudoun Lake

Sequatchie River

Watts Bar Lake

Tennessee River

NORTH CAROLINA

Chickamauga Lake

Nickajack Lake

GEORGIA

Legend

River
Lake
State Border

OUR LAND OUR LIVES

Water is one of Tennessee's most important resources. In fact, our state has over 50,000 miles of streams! We use water at home, at work, at school, and for play.

Food

Tennessee's lakes and rivers are home to many animals that people use for food. Fish and mussels live in the water, but hundreds of other animals live near it. Rivers attract ducks, deer, raccoons, beavers, otters, rabbits, and other kinds of wildlife. For thousands of years, rivers have been good places for people to hunt for food.

The soil near rivers is very rich and fertile. Some of our state's most fruitful farms are along rivers. These farms grow corn, wheat, tobacco, cotton, fruit, vegetables, and other crops. If farms are far from rivers, farmers use pipes to move water to their crops. Farmers also use ditches and canals to move water. This is called *irrigation*. Farms, ditches, and canals have changed the land. They are all human features.

Crops are planted in rows so water can get to them more easily.

Transportation

People use rivers, streams, lakes, and oceans to send goods around the state, the country, and the world. Many of the goods that arrive from other places travel by water too. The rivers of Tennessee are like highways. For thousands of years, it was faster, safer, and easier to travel on water than on land.

Business and Energy

Water power is also used in making goods to sell. In the past, mill owners built mills on rushing rivers. The movement of the water turned a huge wheel outside the mill. That wheel was connected to large grinding stones inside the mill. When the water turned the wheel, the stones turned and ground whatever was placed between them. Millers ground wheat into flour and corn into meal. Have you ever eaten bread made of stone-ground wheat? It is yummy—and good for you!

Today, the dams on Tennessee's rivers use water power to make electricity. They also create *reservoirs* when a river backs up behind a dam and fills in a valley. A reservoir is a natural or man-made lake used to store water. Mills, dams, and reservoirs are human features.

A paddle wheeler floats down the Mississippi River.

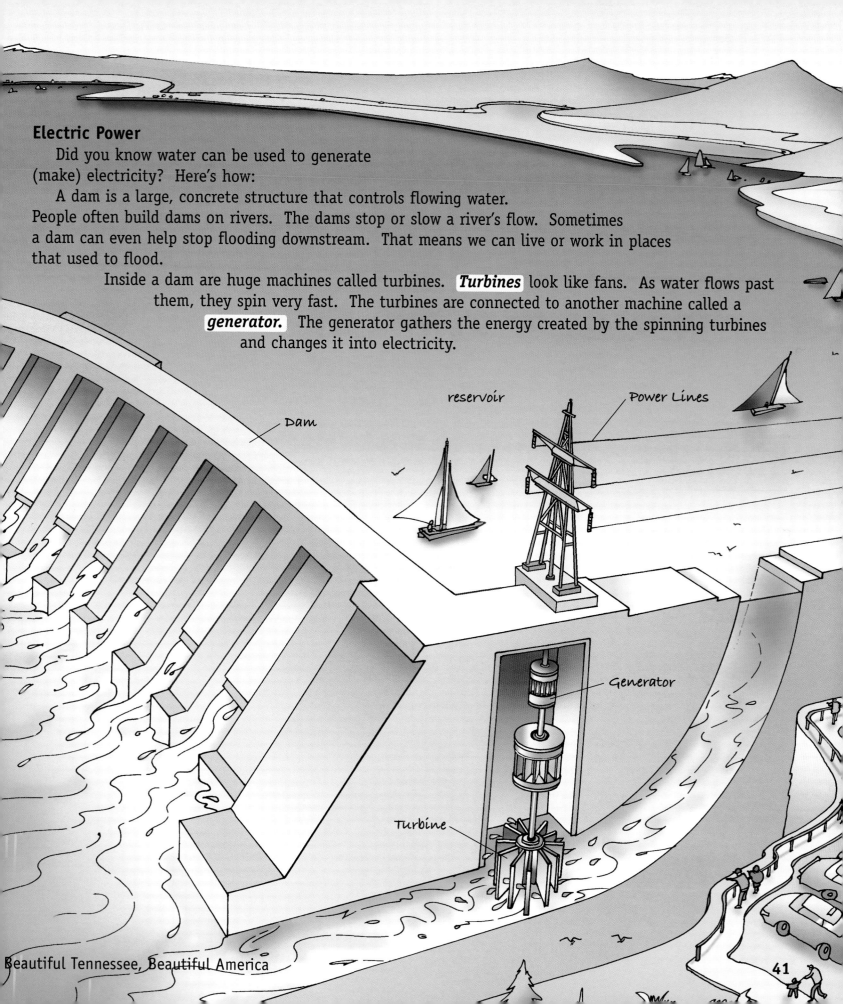

Electric Power

Did you know water can be used to generate (make) electricity? Here's how:

A dam is a large, concrete structure that controls flowing water. People often build dams on rivers. The dams stop or slow a river's flow. Sometimes a dam can even help stop flooding downstream. That means we can live or work in places that used to flood.

Inside a dam are huge machines called turbines. **Turbines** look like fans. As water flows past them, they spin very fast. The turbines are connected to another machine called a **generator.** The generator gathers the energy created by the spinning turbines and changes it into electricity.

reservoir

Power Lines

Dam

Generator

Turbine

Can you see the many ways people have changed the land in this picture?

Tennessee Through Time: The Early Years

The Effects of Human Features

Long ago, there were few people in Tennessee. As time passed, more people moved here, and some places became crowded. Landowners began changing the land so it could support the growing population.

Workers cut down trees for wood to build houses and make other products. They made bricks out of clay taken from the earth. They dug coal from the ground to use for fuel. They blasted through mountains to build roads. They dammed rivers, creating reservoirs and new lakes. They even changed the path of some rivers and streams. By doing these things, people changed the land, air, and water. Some of these changes damaged our natural world.

Linking the Present to the Past

Did you know air **pollution** was a problem in the world over 1,000 years ago? In Europe, people burned coal and wood to heat their homes. This filled the air in cities with thick, black smoke and ash. The king of England passed a law that said people could not burn sea coal because the smoke it created had a bad odor.

Do you think people have the right to use the land any way they want? Why or why not?

Automobiles are one of Tennessee's major sources of pollution.

The Air We Breathe

In large American towns and cities, people drive thousands of cars and trucks, and huge factories operate day and night. These things fill the air with *pollutants.* Pollutants are things like dirt and chemicals. By the 1960s, the air in many large American cities became so dirty that it made some people sick. Citizens grew concerned and began working for change.

Since that time, our country and our state have made great progress. The air has grown a little cleaner each year for the past 35 years. Cars used to be one of the worst sources of pollution, but that is changing. Today, it takes 20 cars to create the same amount of pollution as one car from the mid-1960s!

Our Water Supply

Water supports all forms of life. We use it every day. Most of the earth's surface is made up of water, but less than 3 percent of it is safe for our use. The rest is too salty, too dirty, or frozen. We see water flow from our faucets each day, so we don't realize how precious it is. As the world's population increases, we use more and more water.

How Much Water Does It Take?

Have you ever thought about how much water you use? The average American uses 140–160 gallons of water every day. That seems like a lot, doesn't it? Here's how much water it takes to complete everyday tasks:

To flush a toilet. . . . . 5–7 gallons
To run a dishwasher . . . . 15–25 gallons
To wash dishes by hand . . . . 20 gallons
To take a shower . . . . 25–50 gallons
To take a bath. . . . . 50 gallons
To wash a small load of clothes. . . . . 35 gallons
To brush teeth (with the water running) . . . . 2–5 gallons

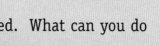

The water in Tennessee's rivers and lakes is used for drinking, swimming, and fishing. But a special report in 2000 showed that almost 8 percent of our rivers are too polluted for at least one of those uses. Our lakes are even worse. Seventeen percent of them are polluted. What can you do to make a difference?

One important problem with our water supply is pollution. Pollutants come from factories, farms, parking lots, driveways, sidewalks, roads, and many other places. They even come from our houses. When pollutants enter our water system, they can harm people, plants, and animals. We should all work to protect our state's water systems.

What do you think happened to these fish? What can you do to help keep Tennessee's rivers and streams clean and safe?

You Can Make a Difference

Do you believe one person can make a difference? You can! Here's how:

- You can turn off the water while brushing your teeth.
- You can turn off the water while washing the dishes.
- You can place paper products and other waste in a garbage can instead of washing it down the drain.

These may seem like small things. But if everyone would do them, our water would become much cleaner and safer.

Garbage

Solid waste materials (garbage) are things we don't need anymore. We want to get rid of them, so we throw them away. Garbage comes from homes, schools, restaurants, businesses, hospitals, and many other places.

Americans create nearly 420 billion pounds of garbage every year! That is hard to imagine, isn't it? As the number of people who live in a place grows, so does the garbage. We know about plastic wrappers, cans, paper, and other trash, but there is a lot of garbage we never see. It comes from factories and large companies. Where do you think all our garbage goes?

There are four ways to take care of garbage. We can bury it, burn it, reuse it, or recycle it. But we never really get rid of it. It just goes somewhere else, and someone else has to deal with it. That person might be a garbage collector. It might be a worker at a burn plant. It might be a sorter at a *recycling* center. What would your family do if your trash wasn't picked up every week?

At a *landfill,* workers bury tons of garbage under layers of dirt. If we make less garbage, then our landfills will last longer.

Linking the Present to the Past

Did you know that hogs used to take care of garbage? Long ago, there were no garbage trucks or landfills. People threw their garbage into the streets, and hogs roamed about eating it. But the hogs left behind their own smelly waste. Today, most cities have landfills. Can you imagine what your town would look like—and smell like—if hogs were wandering around eating all the garbage? Gross!

Everyone has to do his or her part to keep Tennessee clean and beautiful.

Taking Care of the Land

For many years, only a few people understood that it was important to take care of our environment. There weren't as many people, and it seemed as if there were enough natural resources to last forever.

Today we know that if resources are to be available in the future, we must use them wisely. We must take care of the air, land, and water. Many people are working to protect our environment. They have helped pass laws to keep our natural world clean and safe. What can you do to help?

Protecting Our Environment

Did you know that our state is very concerned about pollution? An entire department of the state government is dedicated to protecting our environment. It is called the Tennessee Department of Environment and Conservation. Its mission statement is:

To safeguard human health and the environment for all Tennesseans by protecting and improving the quality of our land, air, and water for present and future generations.

③ MEMORY MASTER

1. What are human features?
2. Give three examples of how humans change the land.
3. What are pollutants?

PLACES TO LOCATE

Kingsport
La Vergne
Nashville
Smyrna
Union City
Warren County

WORDS TO UNDERSTAND

barter
consumer
economics
employee
goods
manufacturing
market economy
producer
professional management
profit
retail
salary
services
supply and demand
wage

Meeting Our Needs

You have read all about the land. You have learned how people have used it and changed it to meet their wants and needs. All people have needs. They need food, clothing, and shelter. People also have wants. They want things like cars, books, toys, and video games. These things are called **goods.**

Sometimes people need help from other people. They need medical care from doctors and dentists. They need education from teachers. Some people might need help fixing a leaky washing machine or a broken window. Bankers, painters, delivery people, repair workers, firefighters, and garbage collectors all provide **services.**

Most goods and services have something in common—they all cost money. **Economics** is the study of how people make and transport goods and buy and sell goods and services. It is also the study of how people earn and use money.

Adults usually work to meet children's needs. As you grow older, you will work to meet your own needs. You will have to learn how to earn a living. In this lesson, we will see how people in Tennessee and the United States earn money to meet their needs.

Does a doctor provide a good or a service?

If you had no money, which of your belongings would you be willing to trade away?

Money

Today, we use money to pay for the goods and services we need, but that was not always so. Before money was invented, people **bartered** goods they had for goods they wanted. Bartering is another word for trading.

In Tennessee's early days, people traded things like quilts, food, and deerskins. If a man needed to buy salt, he might have to carry a heavy load of skins with him to pay for it. That would be hard to do, wouldn't it?

Money made it easier to get the things people needed. Money created problems too. At first, banks in towns and cities printed paper money. Some places accepted it, but others didn't. Then state governments printed money, but other states sometimes thought it was worthless. Finally the federal government printed paper money and made coins that were valuable in every town, city, and state.

Economic Systems

An economic system is a way of producing and selling the goods and services people need and want. Different countries use different systems, but all economic systems answer three basic questions:

- What goods and services should be produced?
- How will the goods and services be produced?
- Who will buy the goods and services?

A Market Economy

The United States has a *market economy.* A market is any place where goods and services are bought and sold. In a market economy, economic choices are made by buyers and sellers, not by the government. People are free to make, sell, and buy goods and services.

How a Business Makes a Profit

How do business owners make money? Making money seems easy, but it isn't. When you go to a restaurant, you pay for your food. The restaurant has to pay its employees, pay for the building, and buy the food it serves you. After paying all of those expenses, the amount left over is called a *profit.* A business cannot survive if it does not earn a profit. Let's look at an example.

Expenses: $6
A pizza store pays for flour, tomatoes, cheese, toppings, and a box for a pizza. It also pays the employee to make the pizza. These are expenses.

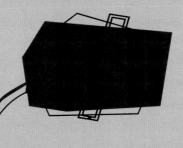

Price: $9
The pizza store sells the pizza for more than it costs to make it.

Price – Expenses = Profit
$9 – $6 = $3
Profit is the money the business has left after all expenses are paid.

Buyers are sometimes called *consumers*. Sellers are sometimes called *producers*. Sellers are people who own the factories and companies that produce goods and services. They decide how much to produce and what prices to charge. They decide where to do business. They decide who they want to help them.

Business owners hire *employees* to work for them. Employees earn a *wage* or a *salary*. Many adults in the United States are employees. They use their wages or salaries to buy the goods and services they need.

Look at all the goods in this photo. Do you think this store has a problem with supply?

Supply and Demand

Have you ever wondered how business owners decide what prices to charge for goods and services? The selling price often depends on the cost of the materials used to make it. For example, the price of a pair of shoes might depend on the cost of leather, plastic, or rubber. The price can also depend on the number of shoes the company makes.

Still another thing that affects price is how much people want the product. If the shoes are popular, the shoe company can charge more for them. What happens if a company makes a lot of shoes and no one buys them? Stores that sell them may drop the price so more people will want to buy them.

Sometimes only one company makes a certain product. If buyers want that product or service, they have to pay whatever price the company charges. All these things are parts of the rule of *supply and demand.*

When there is a large supply of something, the cost is lower. When there is a small supply of something, the cost is higher. For example, if a store has too many basketballs, the balls might go on sale.

FedEx employs almost 34,000 people in Tennessee. It is the second largest employer in our state.

Tennessee's Changing Jobs

Not long ago, almost everyone in our state worked in farming. Today, people in Tennessee do many different kinds of jobs. They build homes. They teach school. They work in factories, department stores, and office buildings. They work in hundreds of jobs that did not exist in the past.

Activity

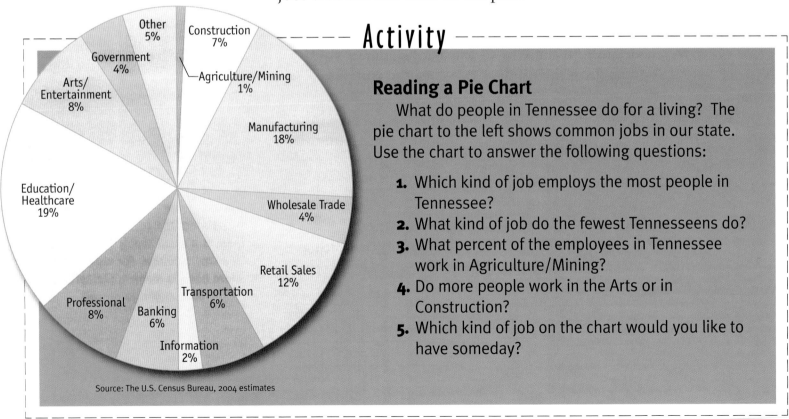

Source: The U.S. Census Bureau, 2004 estimates

Other 5%
Construction 7%
Government 4%
Agriculture/Mining 1%
Arts/Entertainment 8%
Manufacturing 18%
Education/Healthcare 19%
Wholesale Trade 4%
Professional 8%
Banking 6%
Transportation 6%
Retail Sales 12%
Information 2%

Reading a Pie Chart

What do people in Tennessee do for a living? The pie chart to the left shows common jobs in our state. Use the chart to answer the following questions:

1. Which kind of job employs the most people in Tennessee?
2. What kind of job do the fewest Tennesseens do?
3. What percent of the employees in Tennessee work in Agriculture/Mining?
4. Do more people work in the Arts or in Construction?
5. Which kind of job on the chart would you like to have someday?

Service Industries

In Tennessee, more people work in service jobs than in any other kind of job. Five of Tennessee's ten largest employers are service industries. They are FedEx, Vanderbilt University and Hospital, Le Bonheur Children's Medical Center, UPS, and U.S. Xpress.

Service workers do not make products. They are paid to perform services for other people. Have you ever been paid to mow a lawn? If you have, you have been a service worker. The money you were paid was for your time and effort. Babysitters and daycare workers provide services too.

Manufacturing

Companies that make goods are called *manufacturing* companies. Manufacturing is the second largest industry in our state. Workers in Smyrna make cars, and workers in Kingsport make books. Did you know the Eastman Chemical Company, also in Kingsport, makes plastic? Over 7,500 employees work there!

Have you ever been to a tire store? The Bridgestone/Firestone Company in Nashville, LaVergne, and Warren County makes thousands of tires every year. The tires on your family car might have been made right here in our state. Another major tire producer in Tennessee is Goodyear. That factory is in Union City.

Your teacher has a service job. So do the lunchroom workers, the office staff, and the custodians at your school.

Thousands of rubber tires are made each year in Tennessee.

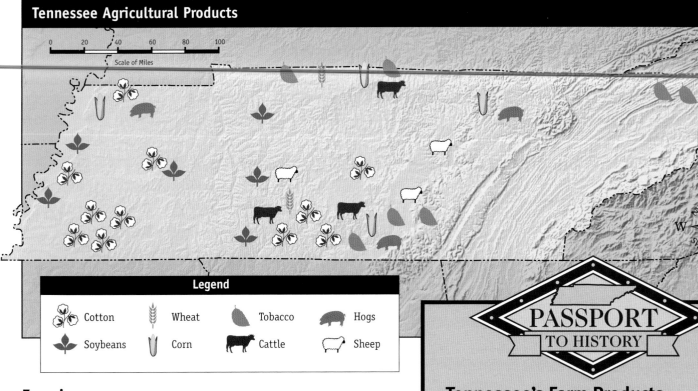

0   20   40   60   80   100
Scale of Miles

Legend			
Cotton	Wheat	Tobacco	Hogs
Soybeans	Corn	Cattle	Sheep

N
NW NE
W   E
SW SE
S

Farming

Even though fewer people today work as farmers, farming is still important in our state. Take a look at the map to see all the important goods our farmers produce.

PASSPORT TO HISTORY

Tennessee's Farm Products

Pretend you work for our state government. Your job is to tell the governor all about Tennessee's farm products. The governor will ask you many questions. Answer the following to help you prepare for your first meeting.

1. Of the eight farm products on the map, how many are animal products?
2. Name three important crops grown in Tennessee.
3. Which kind of animal appears on the map most often?
4. Which crop is most important in the southwest?
5. Does Tennessee grow more tobacco or wheat?
6. Which animal is most important in the northeast?
7. Do Tennessee farmers grow corn?
8. Which crop appears on the map the fewest times?

Retail Sales

Retail sales is the business of selling goods in stores. It is the third largest industry in Tennessee. Think about all the things your family buys. Food from the grocery store is part of retail sales. So are things like clothing, toothpaste, and a garden hose. Every time you buy goods in a store, you are making a retail purchase.

The largest employer in Tennessee is a retail sales company. Can you guess what it is? It's Wal-Mart! Are you surprised? Wal-Mart is not only the largest employer in the state; it is the largest employer in the whole country.

Professional Management

Some businesses need help staying organized. Other businesses need help with certain problems. Still other businesses are so large that they need help just keeping track of everything. Companies that help these businesses are called *professional management* companies.

Professional management is the fourth largest industry in Tennessee. One reason it is so important in our state is because of hospitals and healthcare. HCA (Hospital Corporation of America) is a professional management company based in Nashville. It manages 191 hospitals and 82 surgical centers in the United States, England, and Switzerland. Many other large professional management companies are also based in Tennessee.

Have you ever shopped at a Gap store? The Gap is one of the largest retailers in Tennessee.

Elvis Presley's pink cadillac is parked in front of Graceland, his beautiful home in Memphis.

Does this look like a good place to keep watch for the enemy? It is on Lookout Mountain.

Do you like country music? This is the Country Music Hall of Fame and Museum in Nashville.

Arts, Entertainment, Recreation, and Tourism

For many Americans, Tennessee means great music and lively entertainment. It also means scenic parks, forests, and rivers. Our state is known throughout the world as a place for every kind of fun. Each year, tourists spend millions of dollars exploring our beautiful land and enjoying our talented artists and musicians.

It takes many workers to put on all the shows and concerts in our towns and cities. Some people play musical instruments, and others sing. Some people run cameras, and others make costumes. Some people sell tickets, and others look for new performers. All these jobs have made arts, entertainment, recreation, and tourism the fifth largest industry in Tennessee.

Activity

Touring Tennessee

The Tennessee Tourism Department has created a website to help people plan trips to our state. The state is divided into three travel regions and five areas of interest. Take a few minutes and go to www.tnvacation.com. Look around the site. What are the three travel regions? What are the five areas of interest?

Once you find the region map, find five places to visit in your own region. Then look at the other two regions. Find at least five fun things to do in each of the other two regions. When you are finished, you should have a list of 15 exciting places to visit right here in Tennessee!

What Do You Want to Do?

Adults often like to ask, "What do you want to be when you grow up?" You may already have an idea about this. But most people have more than one kind of job during their lifetime. Ask your teacher or parents what they wanted to be when they were your age. How many different kinds of jobs have they had?

④ MEMORY MASTER

1. What is the difference between goods and services?
2. What kind of economy does the United States have?
3. What is supply and demand?

Chapter 2 Review

What's the Point?

Studying Tennessee's geography is a good way to begin learning about our state's history. Many physical and human features have shaped the land. Some human features damaged the land, but people are working to repair the damage. The United States has a market economy. People work in many kinds of jobs to earn money to take care of their needs.

Becoming Better Readers

Main Ideas

This chapter is divided into four lessons. Each lesson has a main idea and text that supports the main idea. Pick your favorite lesson from this chapter. Write the main idea for that lesson at the top of a sheet of paper. Then make a list of five things that support the main idea. Compare your main idea and list with classmates who chose the same lesson you did. Did you list some of the same things?

Climbing to Connections

How Does It Happen?

How is our land shaped? Think about the physical processes that shape our land, and answer these questions. Refer to pages 34–37 of this book for help.

1. Define erosion.
2. Describe the different types of erosion.
3. Illustrate how a volcano creates a mountain. You may explain it in words or draw a picture.
4. Analyze the picture of the continental plates on page 35. What patterns in plate movement do the people who study plate tectonics look for?
5. What would life be like if you lived at the time the glaciers in Tennessee melted? Write one sentence and draw a picture of what the land looked like.
6. Think about the land of the United States. Do you think it stays the same? Or do you think it changes? Give two reasons for your answer.

Evaluation Station

Money or Barter System?

If you had to decide whether your state would keep the money system or change to a barter system, which would you choose? Evaluate both economic systems. On your own paper, make a T-chart. Label the left column "Money System." Label the right column "Barter System." Under each heading, list three reasons why the system is better. Then list three reasons why the system is worse. After you have evaluated each system, circle the one you would choose for Tennessee. Why did you choose that one?

Activity

Time Zones

Have you ever thought about time? Our world would be very confusing if we didn't have clocks. How would you know when to go to school? How would you know when your favorite television show began?

Long ago, people figured time by looking at the sun. When towns were built, the courthouse or church had a large clock. Townspeople set their watches according to the town clock. When the railroads were built, it became important for cities along the railroad lines to have the same time. If they didn't, people could miss the train.

The United States is a very wide country. It takes more than five hours for the sun to travel from coast to coast. That means setting every state to the same time would not work. Government leaders divided the country into five time zones. The line that separates two of the time zones goes right through Tennessee! East Tennessee is in the Eastern time zone. Middle Tennessee and West Tennessee are in the Central time zone.

Pretend you live in Jackson and your grandparents live in Dayton. Those cities are in different time zones. When you call your grandpa at 10:00 Jackson time, it is 11:00 in Dayton. Which time zone do you live in?

Time Zones of the United States

CANADA

| PACIFIC 10:00am | MOUNTAIN 11:00am | CENTRAL 12:00noon | EASTERN 1:00pm |

Jackson • Dayton

ALASKA 9:00am

MEXICO

HAWAII 8:00am

Use the map to answer the following questions:
1. Which time zone is California in?
2. Name two states in the Eastern time zone.
3. Name two states in the Central time zone.
4. How many states are in Hawaii's time zone?
5. Which time zone is Utah in?

"*Still majestic in decay stand the great [Indian] temple mounds. The temples that once crowned their heights, like the hands that built them, have long since crumbled to dust.*"

—*Thomas M.N. Lewis and Madeline Kneberg*

Mississippian leaders, dressed in their finest ceremonial clothing, stand on a mound and watch the Busk Festival activities. The people laugh and visit while the town's strongest athletes play a ball game. Beyond the game, Mississippian homes stretch on for miles.

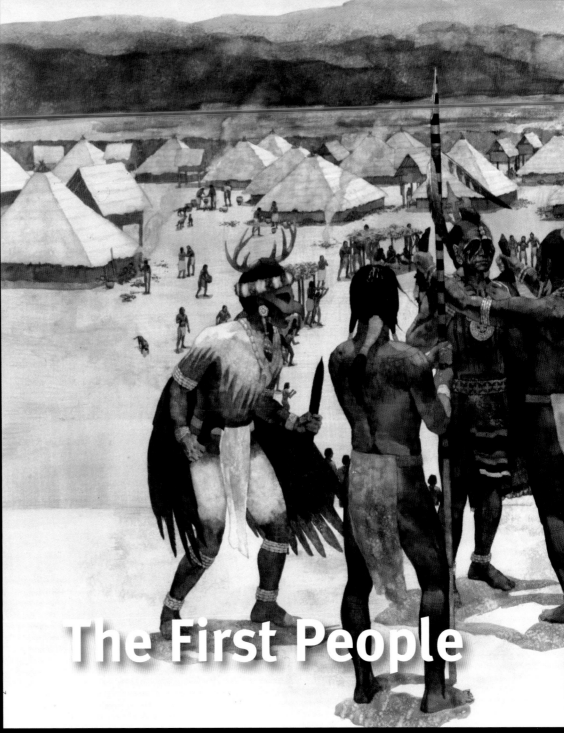

The First People

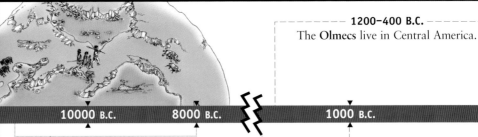

Timeline of Events

10000 B.C.   8000 B.C.   1000 B.C.   500 B.C.

1200–400 B.C.
The **Olmecs** live in Central America.

11000–8000 B.C.
Paleo Indians from Asia travel south into our region. They survive by hunting large animals and gathering wild plants.

8000–1000 B.C.
Archaic Indians live here. They shape simple tools and weapons. They add fruit to their diet. The Eva People settle in West Tennessee.

No one can tell us exactly how long people have lived here. Long before the first Europeans arrived, Native Americans lived and hunted on the land we call Tennessee. They walked on trails through the forests and mountains. They built temples and burial mounds and traveled here to trade. Thousands of Native Americans live in Tennessee today. They are proud of their rich history.

300 B.C.–A.D. 850
The Mayas build complex societies in Mexico and Central America.

A.D. 1300–A.D. 1500
The **Aztecs** live in Mexico. They build the giant city of Tenochtitlán.

0 A.D. **500** A.D. **1000** A.D. **1500**

1000 B.C.–A.D. 900
Woodland Indians live here. They are the first to grow crops and live in villages. They build the first earthen mounds. They learn to make pottery and store food. They build the Old Stone Fort settlement and the Pinson Mounds.

The **Mississippian Culture** live here. They clear large sections of land and build great villages. They become good farmers. They learn to make better tools, weapons, clothing, jewelry, and pottery. They form governments and choose leaders. They hold feasts and ceremonies, and they play games. They build the Chucalissa Village.

A.D.900–1400

A.D. 1400–present
Historic Indians live here. The four main groups are the Cherokee, Chickasaw, Creek, and Shawnee. They hunt, fish, and grow crops. They trade for their first horses and become great warriors. They develop written language and complex societies.

61

PEOPLE TO KNOW

Archaic Indians
Eva People
Paleo Indians

PLACES TO LOCATE

Asia
Highland Rim
Mexico
North America

WORDS TO UNDERSTAND

archaeologist
archaic
atlatl
hunter-gatherer
native
Native Americans
paleo
prehistoric
spearhead

An ***ancient civilization*** is a very old culture or society.

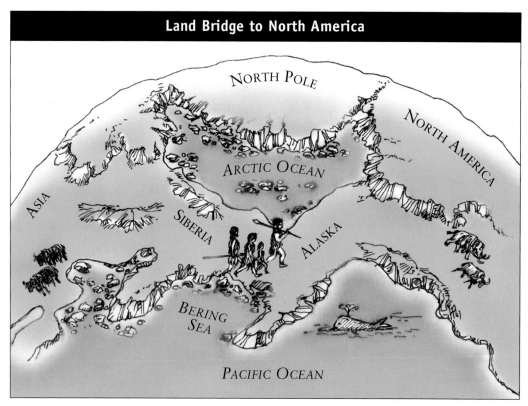

Land Bridge to North America

Scientists believe a land bridge once connected Asia and North America.

Paleo Indians

For many thousands of years, blankets of ice and snow covered most of North America. As time passed, the earth became warmer, and the ice melted. A strip of dry land appeared in the northern Pacific Ocean between Asia and North America. Historians often call this strip a land bridge, but it was several hundred miles wide. Hunters in small groups followed herds of animals across the land into North America. These first people are called Paleo Indians. ***Paleo*** means very, very old.

Hunter-Gatherers

Paleo Indians were *hunter-gatherers.* That means they gathered wild food from the land or hunted for all of their food. One of the animals they hunted was the mammoth. This large animal looked a lot like an elephant, but some mammoths had thick, woolly hair. They could be as tall as 11 feet high, and some had tusks that were 16 feet long. Mammoths spent most of their time eating because they required about 600 pounds of food a day!

The Paleo people used every part of the mammoth. They made tents and clothing out of skins. They made tools and weapons out of bones. The meat from one mammoth could feed a small band of hunters for two months. Whenever they could, the Paleo Indians also gathered foods from the earth, such as fruits, nuts, and roots.

A large mammoth provided the people with food for many meals. The people used the animals' hides for blankets and clothing.

Better Tools

At first, the Paleo people had only sharp sticks to use for hunting. Over time, they began chipping and sharpening stones and attaching them to the sticks. The sharpened stones, or *spearheads,* made it easier to kill large animals. Spearheads have been found in all parts of Tennessee.

Two kinds of spearheads have been found in Tennessee. They are Clovis points and Cumberland points. Clovis points get their name from Clovis, New Mexico, where the first ones were found. Cumberland points are found only in Tennessee.

OUR LAND OUR LIVES

Many Paleo artifacts have been found along the Highland Rim in Middle Tennessee. Like other parts of our state, this region has lots of water. All living things need water, so the Highland Rim was a good place to hunt or camp.

What Do You Think ?

You have just read about the food and weapons of the Paleo Indians. What do you think they used for shelter? What would you use for shelter if you lived in the wilderness?

Prehistoric People

The first Tennesseans left no writings about their lives. These people are called **prehistoric** because they lived before written records were kept. We learn about these people by studying the things they left behind. Today artifacts such as tools, cave drawings, clothes, and other things tell us much about early Indians' lives.

Archaeologists are scientists who study artifacts and other clues to learn how people lived in the past. Most artifacts are found in the earth because sand and dirt have covered them over the years. Archaeologists carefully remove one layer of dirt at a time. They keep notes about what they find. Even the smallest item may have a story to tell. It might offer clues about what people ate or what tools they used. Archaeologists have studied artifacts from over 100 Paleo Indian sites in North America.

Archaic People

Slowly the earth became warmer. The tall, lush grasses that were food for the woolly mammoths began to die. When the animals no longer had food, many of them died too. Others probably moved to places where there was more food. Smaller animals such as deer, antelope, and bears, replaced the large mammals.

During this time, Tennessee's climate, plants, and animals became a lot like they are today. The Paleo period ended, and the *Archaic* period began. Archaic means old or ancient. Archaic people still gathered fruits, nuts, and seeds. They also still hunted, but they used new tools they had invented. They made hooks, nets, and traps to help them capture animals.

Archaic Indians took everything they needed from the earth.

TERRIFIC TECHNOLOGY

The Atlatl

In both Mexico and North America, an important new tool appeared during the Archaic period, the *atlatl* (ATL-atl). It was a foot-long stick with a handle on one end and a hook on the other. The atlatl made a spear go farther and faster. Getting close to large animals was very dangerous, so an atlatl made hunting much safer.

Native means belonging to or coming from a place. The first people who lived here are called **Native Americans** because they are from North America. Some people call the first people Indians or American Indians. In the next chapter, you will learn why.

"I call myself an Indian."
—Rose Darnall, a Cherokee member of the Native American Indian Association

"We are not Indians, and we were here before America existed. I like the term Native People."
—Don Yahola, a Creek, president of the Alliance for North American Indian Rights

Tools and Baskets

Archaic Indians used tools to help them prepare foods from wild plants. For example, they used a grinding stone to grind seeds into meal or flour. They learned how to weave grasses into baskets that could hold seeds, roots, flour, or other things. Over the years, the people found better ways to weave. They made baskets that were beautiful as well as useful.

On the Move

Like Paleo Indians, Archaic Indians moved from place to place. Then they began camping in one place for longer periods of time. They returned to the same places year after year as the seasons changed. Archaic Indians camped along the rivers of North America, including those in Tennessee. Rivers provided many things the people needed. They drank and bathed in the water. They fished, gathered clams, and hunted the animals that came to drink. They built canoes and traveled swiftly on the water.

Native American women used stones like this one to grind seeds or grains into flour. How long do you think it would take to grind enough flour to make a loaf of bread?

The Eva People

One of the Archaic Indians' largest settlements was in West Tennessee on the Tennessee River near Camden. Today, this is known as the Eva site. Archaeologists named the people who lived there the Eva People.

From the artifacts found at the Eva site, we know the Eva People ate river clams. They also made jewelry. Archaeologists have found necklaces made from clam shells, bear and bobcat teeth, and even turtle bones! The Eva People traded with people from hundreds of miles away, buried their dead in graves, and had pet dogs.

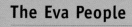

• Camden

1 MEMORY MASTER

1. Who were the first people in North America?
2. What does prehistoric mean?
3. What important tool did the Archaic people invent to help them throw their spears?

Woodland Indians

The land that later became Tennessee had hundreds of miles of forests. These forests were called the Eastern Woodlands. The people who lived here after the Archaic Indians are called Woodland Indians.

Crops

Woodland Indians hunted and gathered much of their food, but they also learned how to grow crops. Agriculture (growing crops) allowed the people to stay in one place because they did not have to search for food. Woodland people grew lots of corn. They also grew beans, squash, gourds, sunflowers, and other plants.

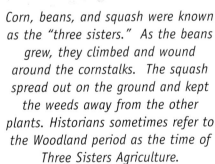

Corn, beans, and squash were known as the "three sisters." As the beans grew, they climbed and wound around the cornstalks. The squash spread out on the ground and kept the weeds away from the other plants. Historians sometimes refer to the Woodland period as the time of Three Sisters Agriculture.

New Inventions

The change from hunting and gathering food to growing crops took place over many years. Even after they began farming, Woodland people continued to hunt and to develop better tools and weapons.

The bow and arrow first appeared during this period. Bows were usually about three feet long and made of locust wood. The arrow shafts were made from cane that grew along the river. The points on the arrows were made from *chert,* a common rock.

Chert is a soft rock that chips easily. That is why Native Americans used it to make arrow and spear points.

Woodland Pottery

Pottery first appeared during the Woodland period. Woodland Indians shaped wet clay into bowls, pitchers, and other containers. After the clay dried, the people baked the items over hot coals. The heat made the clay grow hard and strong. Native Americans stored food for the harsh winter months in the pottery containers they made.

Leadership and Village Life

Woodland people began settling in small villages. They became better farmers and were soon growing more food than they could eat. They began forming larger communities and trading with one another. People became skilled at different tasks. Some people farmed, and others made tools. Soon people traded the things they made or crops they grew for the things they wanted. The first economic systems, which were based on farming, began.

The larger communities needed rules to maintain order. They also needed leaders or councils to help the people make good decisions. People became leaders by doing special things. If a person was generous or a good hunter, he might become a tribal leader. Some leaders had a lot of power and authority. They helped make decisions for the tribe and led rituals and ceremonies. Sometimes tribe members did not get along. When that happened, they often asked a leader to help them with their problems.

Native American leaders did not make decisions alone. They helped everyone come to an agreement.

Woodland Indians had shell necklaces like this one. They got them by trading with other groups who lived near the ocean.

Indian Mounds

Have you ever seen an Indian mound? It is a huge pile of dirt covered with grass and plants. It looks like a hill. Woodland Indians were the first people in Tennessee to build Indian mounds. Some are small, but others are very large.

Ancient people built the mounds by filling baskets with dirt and carrying them to the site. Wheels had not been invented yet, so Woodland Indians did not have carts or wagons to make their work easier. Archaeologists believe it took millions of baskets of earth to build large mounds.

Most mounds were used as burial sites. When village leaders died, the people buried them in mounds. All Woodland Indians believed the dead needed special things to survive in the next life, so they buried these items with the bodies. Archaeologists have found weapons, jewelry, baskets, clothing, and traces of food alongside the dead in some mounds.

This drawing shows how an Indian burial ground grew over time. How many people are buried in this mound?

Experts have spent many years studying the artifacts in the mounds. Some are made of things not found in Tennessee. That means Woodland Indians must have traded with people from far away. When trading, the people did not use money like we do. Instead they traded things they had, like animal skins, pottery, and food, for things they wanted, like beads and jewelry.

What Do You Think?

How do you think Woodland Indians traded with other Indians who lived hundreds of miles away? Do you think they walked? Do you think they met halfway?

EXPLORE TENNESSEE!

The Pinson Mounds

The second highest Indian mound in the United States is at the Pinson Mounds site, which is near Jackson. Archaeologists believe there were once at least 17 earthen mounds there. Indians used them for ceremonies and burials. Today you and your family can visit the Pinson Mounds. There are 15 mounds and a large museum in a building made to look like a mound. The museum has a theater, a library, and a "Discovery Room."

The Old Stone Fort

The Old Stone Fort, near Manchester, is another Woodland site in Tennessee. Like the Pinson Mounds, it was used for ceremonies and probably took centuries to build. Its name is misleading because it is not really a fort. It is a large, open area surrounded by stone. Archaeologists believe Woodland people built and used the Pinson Mounds and the Old Stone Fort but did not live in either place.

Pinson Mounds

Pinson Mounds   Old Stone Fort

Gulf of Mexico

Tres Zapotes

Laguna de los Cerros

La Venta

San Lorenzo

PACIFIC
OCEAN

● Olmec center

▨ Olmec heartland

0   50   100 Miles

0   50   100 Kilometers

The Olmecs

At the time Woodland Indians were living in North America, a people called the Olmecs lived in Central America. The Olmecs were another ancient civilization in the Americas. They built a few large cities and several smaller ones across the area that is now Mexico. They also built mounds shaped like pyramids. They were excellent farmers who grew corn, beans, squash, chili peppers, and avocados.

Religion and Art

The Olmecs built temples and carved statues of their gods. *Religion* was an important part of their lives. As part of their worship, they played a special ball game. Some experts believe games lasted for days.

Math and Science

The Olmecs studied the relationship between the sun, moon, and earth. With the knowledge they gained and their excellent math skills, they made accurate calendars. One of their calendars had 365 days in a year—just like ours! The Olmecs even developed a writing system. They used drawings of things to represent words. Over time, they shortened the drawings into symbols. The civilizations that followed the Olmecs used many of their ideas.

The Olmecs did not have cranes, electricity, or even carts with wheels. How long do you think it took them to build this huge temple?

The most famous pieces of Olmec art are giant stone heads. Some of them are almost 10 feet high. Some people believe the heads portray important Olmec rulers, but no one knows for sure.

THE MAYAS

The Mayas of Central America lived after the Olmecs. They used many Olmec ideas and built an even greater civilization. They lived in what is now southern Mexico, Guatemala, Belize, and El Salvador.

Pyramids and Temples

The Mayas built great pyramids of soil and gravel. On the tops of them were sacred temples used for religious ceremonies and worship. The king and noblemen lived in huge palaces around the pyramids. Others lived in large buildings with many housing units. These were a lot like apartment building today. In jungle villages, the city spread out in all directions, but temples, palaces, and ball courts were always in the middle.

Artists and Farmers

The ancient Mayas were skilled farmers. They planted crops in different areas each year so the ground would stay healthy. They also planted forest gardens and built canals to water the fields. They grew corn, sunflower seeds, cotton, and other crops, and they traded with one another.

The Mayas were also gifted artists. They carved figures on the outer walls of their temples and painted murals on the inside. They learned to mold and shape plaster to decorate buildings, and they made beautiful pottery and ceramics.

The Mayas even had a written language. Archaeologists have found writing on monuments, stone and wooden slabs, and pottery. They have even uncovered a few books made of tree bark.

This is the Temple of the Great Jaguar in Guatemala.

Mayan Cities of Central America

N W E S

Gulf of Mexico

Chichen Itza
Coba
Uxmal
Rio Bec
Calakmul
Caribbean Sea
Palenque
Tikal
Yaxchilán

PACIFIC OCEAN

Copan

0   100   200 Miles
0   100   200 Kilometers

● Major Mayan city
▨ Mayan lands 790 A.D.

Tennis Shoes for the Mayas?

Did you know that the Mayas had rubber? Even though it was very hard to do, the Mayas learned how to make rubber from a plant called *Castilla elástica*. They used the rubber to make all kinds of things, but one of their favorite inventions was balls for their ball games. Archaeologists have found a few balls at ancient Mayan sites. When the Spanish first arrived in Central America, they were amazed by the bouncing balls. Because they had never seen rubber before, the soldiers wondered if the balls were possessed by evil spirits.

The Mayas also used rubber to make shoes. They did this by dipping their feet into a liquid rubber mixture. When it dried, it left a springy, waterproof coating on their feet. Would you like to wear rubber shoes like that instead of your favorite tennis shoes?

The Mississippian Period

Far to the north of the Mayan empire, prehistoric Native Americans became more skilled at farming. They produced more food. They also learned ways to store and preserve food. More food meant more people survived, so the population grew quickly. The Mississippian people were the last prehistoric Indians to live in Tennessee. They built many *permanent* buildings and larger towns along rivers.

Farming

Because there were so many people, the Mississippians had to be organized. The towns had areas for living, areas for hunting, and areas for growing crops. Like the people who lived here before them, the Mississippians' most important crop was corn. They also grew potatoes, beans, squash, and pumpkins.

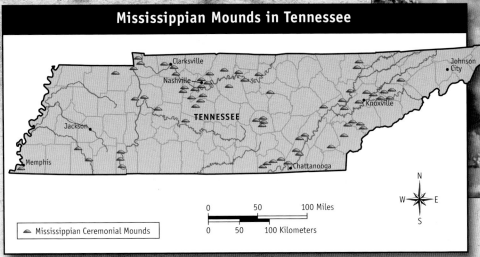

Mississippian Mounds in Tennessee

Mississippian Ceremonial Mounds

0 50 100 Miles
0 50 100 Kilometers

Chiefdoms

The larger villages needed leadership, so the Mississippians chose a *chief* to lead them. Chiefs were usually men, but there were a few female chiefs. When the chief died or became too old to lead, his son or daughter became the new chief.

The chief was responsible for helping all the people in the *chiefdom.* This was a large area that might have included several villages. Sometimes everyone in the chiefdom gathered in a council. The people talked about their plans or problems and voted on what to do. Meetings were not over until everyone agreed, so they sometimes lasted for weeks.

As the population grew, people began arguing about the most fertile sections of farmland. Sometimes villages attacked each other. To protect their homes and belongings, the Mississippians often built high walls or fences around the borders of their towns.

Mound Builders

Like the groups who lived here before them, the Mississippians were mound builders. They built temples or meeting houses on top of the mounds. When buildings grew old or needed to be replaced, the people tore them down. Then they added several feet of new dirt on top of the mound. This caused the mound to grow a little taller. After hundreds of years of this practice, the mounds became very tall.

In East Tennessee, Mississippians built a village at Hiawassee Island. Twenty miles downstream was another settlement at Dallas Island. The Mississippians built large mounds at both of these

Living in villages allowed the Mississippians to meet together often.

sites. They also settled in Middle Tennessee along the Harpeth and Duck Rivers.

After hundreds of years, almost all the Mississippian sites were abandoned. We do not know exactly why this happened, but much of Middle Tennessee was left empty.

The large, open area in the center of Mississippian villages is called the plaza. It was probably used for meetings, funerals, games, and celebrations.

EXPLORE TENNESSEE!

Chucalissa Archaeological Museum

The Mississippian Indians built a large village called Chucalissa (CHOO·kah·le·sa) on the Mississippi River near Memphis. The people who lived there were farmers, hunters, and fishermen. They were also artists and craftsmen. They built a large plaza complex and several large burial mounds.

Today, there is a museum, gift shop, nature trail, and picnic area at Chucalissa. You can take classes to learn about Mississippian food, medicine, arts, crafts, and hunting. You and your family can even camp or golf at Chucalissa! Each year, the Chucalissa Indian Heritage Festival is held there.

The Aztecs

As the great chiefdoms in North America began to die out, the Aztecs of Mexico became very powerful. They built a huge city called Tenochtitlán (tay·nohch·TEE·tlahn). It may have been the largest city in the world at the time. Tenochtitlán had many roads and canals, a palace for the emperor, and a huge temple complex. Experts believe it lies below modern-day Mexico City.

Temples and the Gods

Like the Mayas, the Aztecs built large pyramids and temples for religious ceremonies. Almost everything the Aztecs did had something to do with their beliefs. They believed a different god controlled each part of nature and blessed them with rain, good harvests, and other things. The Aztecs believed blood kept the gods strong, so they offered human *sacrifices.*

Quetzalcoatl was the Aztec god of plant life and growth. He also represented morning, brightness, the evening star, and other good things.

Farming

Even though the Aztecs did not have farming equipment or work animals, they were gifted farmers. Corn was the most important crop, but farmers also grew beans, squash, chili peppers, avocados, and tomatoes. Aztec "ranchers" raised turkeys, ducks, geese, and

OUR LAND
OUR LIVES

Floating Gardens

The land around Tenochtitlán was swampy and very wet. That made it hard to grow crops. The Aztecs needed more dry land, so they created **chinampas,** or artificial islands. Some people call them floating islands.

To make a chinampa, the Aztecs wove a huge reed mat. Then they drove posts into the swampy mud and tied the mats to the posts. At each corner of the mat, the Aztecs planted a tree. Next they piled mud on the mat. Over time, the trees, mud, and mat grew together and formed an island in the lake or swamp. Once an island was solid, the Aztecs planted crops and flowers on it.

quail. The Aztecs did not have metal or paper money, so they paid for things with cacao beans, cotton cloth, and salt.

Art and Tools

The Aztecs made tools and weapons, such as atlatls, out of wood, stone, bone, and volcanic glass. They spun thread on spools and then wove the thread into cloth. The people also learned to layer strips of clay and shape them into pottery. After the clay was fired, they decorated the pieces with sacred artwork. Drawing and painting the gods was another way of worshipping and showing respect for them. The Aztecs also made jewelry out of gold, silver, copper, emeralds, turquoise, and jade.

The Aztecs had written language. They used pictures to represent words.

The End of a Civilization

Europeans heard stories about Aztec cities of gold. Some Europeans wanted to find these cities and take the wealth for themselves. A Spaniard named Hernán Cortés set out to find the Aztecs. Cortés gathered more than 500 soldiers and sailed across the ocean to Cuba and then Mexico.

At first, the Aztecs welcomed the white-skinned strangers. But one of the Spanish soldiers had *smallpox,* and the disease spread quickly to the Aztecs. Their bodies could not fight the illness, and one-third of them died.

A few months later, fighting began. The Aztecs fought hard, but in the end, handmade weapons were no match for swords and gunpowder. Spain took control of the land, changed the language, and enslaved the few surviving Aztecs. In less than two years, Cortés and his men wiped out the entire Aztec civilization.

This is an Aztec calendar. It shows 20 weeks. Each week has 13 days. How many days is that altogether?

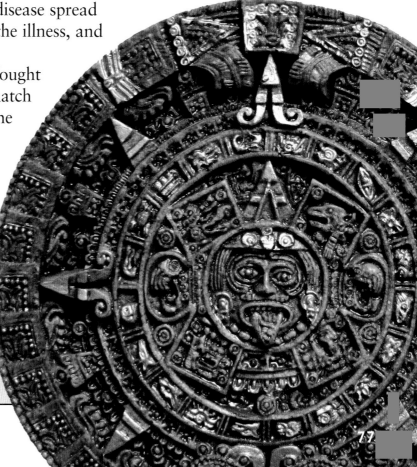

② MEMORY MASTER

1. What is an ancient civilization?
2. What common Tennessee rock did natives use to make arrows?
3. Name three important ancient civilizations that thrived in Central America.

PEOPLE TO KNOW

Cherokees
Chickasaws
Choctaws
Creeks
Europeans
Shawnees
Yuchis

PLACES TO LOCATE

Chickamauga and
   Chattanooga National
   Military Park
Cumberland River
Lookout Mountain
Nashville
Natchez, Mississippi
Rock City
Unaka Mountains

WORDS TO UNDERSTAND

chunkey
harmony
historic
nation
principal

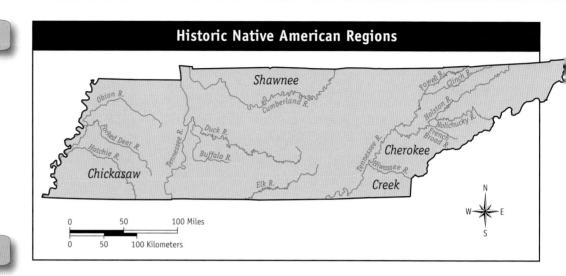

Historic Native American Regions

Tennessee's Historic Native Americans

When Europeans arrived in this region, there were several Native American tribes scattered across the Southeast. These tribes are called *historic* tribes because we have written records that describe how they lived.

The Cherokees

The Cherokee nation was the largest Indian *nation* in Tennessee and the Southeast. Within the nation, there were many smaller tribes. They lived in small villages in the Unaka Mountains along the Little Tennessee, the Hiawassee, and the Tellico Rivers. They also had settlements in North Carolina and Georgia. The Cherokees called themselves Ani-Yuniwiya, which means "principal people." *Principal* means first, highest, or most important.

The Chief and the Council House

The Cherokee nation had a principal chief, but each village had its own chief. The village chief helped the people make decisions about the community. Each village also had a council house for meetings. It looked like the other houses in the village, but it was much larger. In the center of the council house was a large pit where the sacred fire burned.

When the tribe had important things to discuss, the villagers gathered in the council house.

Explorers called the Native American settlements in Tennessee the Overhill settlements since they were on the western side of the Appalachian Mountains. The Cherokees here were known as the Overhill Cherokees.

The Cherokees believed in *harmony.* They wanted everyone to get along and make decisions together. Getting everyone to agree took a lot of time, so meetings sometimes lasted for days.

White Jobs and Red Jobs

The Cherokees and other tribes of the Southeast divided tasks into white jobs and red jobs. The white leader took care of day-to-day activities within his village. The red leader was a warrior who planned attacks and made decisions about war. Even though the Cherokees wanted harmony, they went to war with other tribes when they felt they had no choice.

Beloved Woman

The Cherokees had great respect for women. Women were allowed to help make decisions. The most powerful woman in the tribe was called Beloved Woman. The people believed the Great Spirit spoke to them through her.

Beloved Woman was sometimes called War Woman. This was because she was a member of the council that decided whether the tribe went to war. She also prepared the sacred Black Drink, which was a holy tea drunk by Indian warriors before a battle. Even though she had many duties related to war, she actually worked for peace. She even helped settle disagreements among members of the tribe. In a later chapter, you will read about Nancy Ward, the Cherokees' last Beloved Woman.

Nancy Ward

The First People

Home and Family

Cherokee society was (and still is) divided into seven clans. Each clan took its name from something in nature. They are the Deer Clan, Wolf Clan, Wild Potatoes Clan, Paint Clan, Blue Clan, Long Hair Clan, and Bird Clan.

Cherokees could not marry within their own clan. When two people got married, they lived with the wife's family. Their children became part of their mother's clan.

Summer and Winter Homes

Like other tribes in the Southeast, the Cherokees often had two homes. One was for warm weather, and the other was for cold weather. Summer houses were rectangular and made of poles that were placed close together in the ground. The people wove small branches around the poles and then covered the whole thing with a mixture of clay and grass. This kept the house cool and shady.

Inside the house, there was a dip in the center of the floor. This was the fireplace. A hole in the roof for the smoke to escape and the doorway were the only openings in these houses. There were no windows. Some summer homes were long and had two or three rooms. One room was for cooking, and the other was for sleeping. Some families had a third room for eating and visiting.

In the winter, the Cherokee built pit houses. First they dug a large, round hole in the ground. Then they built a round, pointed roof of wooden poles and covered it with a thick layer of clay. Because the house was mostly underground, it stayed warm inside when the weather was cold.

Pit houses were a lot of work to build. There were no trucks with giant shovels. The people had to dig the large holes for pit houses by hand.

Chunkey

The Cherokees enjoyed playing games. One of their oldest games was *chunkey.* In this game, one player rolled a flat, round stone across the ground. Other players then raced down the field and threw their poles after the stone. The winner of the game was the person whose pole landed closest to the place where the chunkey stone finally rolled to a stop.

TERRIFIC TECHNOLOGY

Dugout Canoes

Native Americans made dugout canoes so they could travel and fish on the rivers and streams. To make one, they first chose just the right tree. The tree had to be long enough, wide enough, and strong enough. They cut the tree down, removed all the branches, and cut it to the length they wanted. Next they burned and scraped out the center, making a hollow place where people could sit. The Cherokees also made wooden paddles so they could steer their canoes.

The First People

The Chickasaws

Linking the Present to the Past

The Chickasaw road into Tennessee was known as the Chickasaw Trace. It later became known as the Natchez Trace because it extended south to Natchez, Mississippi. Today, the Natchez Trace is a beautiful parkway that extends from Natchez to Nashville.

The Chickasaws were a small tribe that lived in Kentucky, Mississippi, and Alabama. They did not build permanent villages in Tennessee, but they shared hunting grounds and traded with other tribes. There were many animals in West Tennessee, so the Chickasaws claimed the entire area as their hunting grounds.

The Chickasaws lived much like the Cherokees. Instead of living in villages, however, the Chickasaws spread their homes for many miles along streams and rivers. The few villages they did build had high walls, so enemies could not get in. If another tribe attacked, the people gathered inside the village.

Each Chickasaw village had a chief and war leaders. These men had great power. Chickasaw boys began learning how to fight while they were very young. They learned that accepting pain without complaining was a way to show great bravery. Warriors shaved off all the hair on their bodies and had tattoos. The Chickasaws became the fiercest and bravest warriors in the Southeast.

How do you think these Chickasaw warriors felt when they found strangers setting up camp?

The Creeks

The Creeks lived mostly in Georgia, but they had a few settlements around what later became Chattanooga. The English named these people the "Creeks" because they lived along the Ocheese Creek.

The Creeks were much like the Cherokees and the Chickasaws. When the population of a Creek village got too large, part of the village split off and formed a new one. The new village was built just outside the older one. Each village was organized around a central plaza that was used for dancing, religious ceremonies, and games. There were many Creek villages across Georgia.

The Cherokees and Creeks were enemies. The Creeks came into the Tennessee region to hunt, but they often ended up fighting with the Cherokees. Finally the Cherokees and Chickasaws banded together and drove the Creeks out of the land.

The Shawnees

The Shawnees had several villages along the Cumberland River in the Tennessee region. One Shawnee village was near the present site of Nashville. Because the Shawnees lived between the Chickasaws in the West and the Cherokees in the East, there were many conflicts. Finally the Cherokees and the Chickasaws worked together and pushed the Shawnees out of the land that later became Tennessee.

Native American Culture

The Native American tribes in this area had many things in common, but they also had their own cultures. They spoke different languages, and their societies were organized in different ways. Sometimes the tribes fought about land and hunting rights. Other times, they got along well and worked together.

Some tribes grew or made things other tribes did not, so the people traveled on the rivers to trade. They did not use money to pay for goods. They simply traded what they had for what they wanted. After the trading was finished, the Indians often held celebrations. They played drums, sang, danced, and ate huge meals.

PASSPORT TO HISTORY

Compare Early Indian Trails to Today's Roads

Some of the early Indian trails became the roads we travel today. Do some research to see if there are any old Indian trails near your home. Find out if these trails are used as roads or highways today. If they are, draw a map that shows the trail. Label the trail with the name of the road it has become today. When you are finished, your teacher will give you a stamp in your Passport to History!

The Yuchi

The Yuchi were a small group of Native Americans who lived along the Tennessee River. Legend says "Yuchi" means "faraway people." They did not live in this area for long because other Tennessee tribes drove them out. They later joined with the Creeks.

Respect for the Land

One thing Native Americans did not trade was land. They did not believe land could be owned. It was for all to use and share. Native Americans had a deep respect for the earth and all living things. The sky, the water, the soil, and even the trees had spiritual meaning to them. They believed deer and other animals had spirits—just like people did.

Everything living on earth was part of a great web of life. The Indians of Tennessee saw themselves as part of that web. They protected and cared for the land because it protected and cared for them. It provided the Indians with everything they needed to survive, and they were very grateful for it. Native Americans believed the land was a gift from the Great Spirit, and it was sacred.

The Seasons

Changes in Native American life followed the changing of the seasons. The men went on hunts in the summer and winter. Women planted seeds in the spring and harvested the crops in the fall. The harvest was a time of great celebration. Spring, summer, fall, and winter were parts of the circle of life, and special ceremonies welcomed each new season.

Many tribes celebrated the Busk or Green Corn Ceremony. At the end of the summer, when the first corn became ripe enough to eat, the people of the village held a festival that lasted many days. They celebrated the good harvest.

Native American Names

As you travel across Tennessee, you will see many place names that came from Indian languages. The name "Chattanooga" is a Creek word for "rock coming to a big point." What large, pointed rock do you think Chattanooga is named for?

What Do You Think?

Do you think people should be able to own and change the land? Or should we try to live more like early Native Americans did? Why?

Green Corn Ceremony

It is a feast,
A ceremony of thanks,
For the corn that grows
Along the river banks.

This is the staple,
That keeps us in health,
Of sun-baked yellow gold,
A mountain of wealth.

We sing praises to Mother Earth
For blessings only you can give,
For without your guidance,
We could never live.

©TM by Buffalo Woman
Used by permission of Shadow
Wolf at www.shadowwolf.org

The Coming of the Europeans

Native Americans lived in this region for thousands of years. When the Europeans arrived, they thought they had discovered a new land. Actually the Indians had lived here all along. This was their home and hunting grounds.

Indians and settlers felt very differently about how the land should be used. They had different spiritual beliefs. They had different plans for living together. Soon there was trouble between the two groups. In the next chapter, you will read about how the settlers changed the lives of the Indian people.

Sometimes Native Americans and white settlers helped one another. Other times, they fought long, bloody battles.

Native Americans in Tennessee Today

Today, there are more than 10,000 Native Americans living in Tennessee. The Eastern Band of the Cherokee Indians owns land in East Tennessee and North Carolina.

The West Tennessee Choctaws still speak their native language. Many Cherokees in our state today also continue to read, write, and speak Cherokee.

EXPLORE TENNESSEE!

See Rock City!

High atop Lookout Mountain, overlooking Chattanooga, sit Rock City and the Chickamauga and Chattanooga National Military Park. Rock City has giant rocks and beautiful gardens. You can take a walk on a winding path through narrow passages, across high bridges, above and alongside a waterfall, and into a cave. From the military park, you can see far into the distance, while remembering the battles that took place there during the Civil War. You will read about this war in a later chapter. Some people believe you can see seven different states from this spot, but no one is really sure. You can drive to the top of Lookout Mountain by car or you can take the exciting Incline Railway.

Do you think you can see seven states from the top of Lookout Mountain?

3 MEMORY MASTER

1. Which tribe was the largest in Tennessee and the Southeast?
2. Which two tribes banded together to drive out the Creeks and the Shawnees?
3. How did Native Americans feel about owning the land?

Chapter 3 Review

What's the Point?

The first people in North America were hunter-gatherers called Paleo Indians. The climate warmed, and Archaic people invented the atlatl for hunting. Woodland people lived in small villages, built mounds, and planted crops. The last prehistoric group to live in our state was the Mississippians. Around this same time, the Olmecs, Mayas, and Aztecs were living in Central America. The Cherokees were the biggest Indian nation in Tennessee and the Southeast. The Chickasaws, Shawnee, Creeks, and Yuchi also lived here. Today, there are more than 10,000 Native Americans living in our state.

Becoming Better Readers

Do you like bedtime stories? Native American children used to sit by the fire and listen to stories about how the earth was created, why the owl stays up at night, and why the fox is sly. Each tribe had its own stories, or legends, which were always told from memory. Some of the old legends were passed down through families, and others have been written down. Here is one called "No 'Lost' Children":

So well taught and so much a part of the land and wilderness were the children of the Chickasaw that parents never worried about them going out into the woods and hills alone. Little Indian boys roamed at will from village to village or in the woods with their bows and arrows or blow-guns. They would be gone all day, and the mothers were not uneasy about them.

A Chickasaw boy went quietly through the wilderness taking note of every bush, tree, and rock, so he would always know his way back. His sense of direction was so good that he never became lost.

No "Lost" Children—A Chickasaw Legend from Ann Sheffield papers, Chickasaw Council House Museum

Find another Native American legend in the library or on the Internet. Copy it in your best writing on a blank sheet of paper. Now make a colorful border by drawing pictures from the story in the margins around it.

Activity

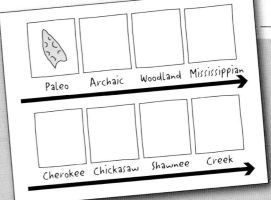

Tools Timeline

If there were no grocery stores, how would you get food? This chapter describes how native people hunted, gathered, fished, and planted crops so they could feed their families. Over the years, they invented new tools and found new ways to do things.

Draw a blank timeline on a piece of paper. Copy the names of the tribes in order as shown. Above each name, draw a picture of a tool that tribe used or invented. When you have finished, compare your tool timeline with other students' drawings. Can you see the pattern leading up to today? The better the tools were, the more food was grown and eaten. When a society has enough food, it grows larger and larger.

Climbing to Connections

Native American Groups Before 1700

1. Identify three Native American groups that lived in Tennessee before 1700. Which was the largest?
2. The Cherokees and the Chickasaws worked together to force other Native American groups off the land. Which two groups were forced out, and why was there conflict?
3. Native American groups had some similarities and some differences. How would you solve the problems between Native American groups?
4. During this time period, which groups lived in Mexico? How were they different from the Tennessee native groups?
5. If Tennessee Native Americans traded with Native Americans in Mexico, what would they trade? Hint: Look at pictures in the chapter, especially "The Eva People" section on page 67.
6. Which prehistoric group was the last to live in Tennessee? Draw conclusions about how farming changed this group's way of life.

Evaluation Station

Tribal Council

What do you know about how tribes resolved conflicts? Look at the image of a tribal council on page 69 of this book. What does it look like the people are doing? Imagine the tribal leader is trying to solve a disagreement between two people in his tribe. Answer these questions:

1. How do you think the leader will resolve the conflict?
2. Do you think this is a fair way to resolve conflicts?
3. If you were a tribal leader, how would you resolve conflicts among your people?

"*They were as much frightened as ourselves, and what we took for a signal of war was an invitation to come near that they might give us food.*"

—Father Jacques Marquette
on seeing the Chickasaw

How do you think Native Americans felt as they saw the first ships sailing toward them?

European Explorers in America

Timeline of Events

1000
Viking Leif Eriksson explores the islands and eastern coast of Canada.

1492
Christopher Columbus arrives off the coast of North America.

1513
Vasco Nuñez de Balboa crosses Central America and sees the Pacific Ocean.

1000 — 1490 — 1500 — 1510

1493
The Catholic pope divides the world between Spain and Portugal.

1499
Amerigo Vespucci arrives in South America.

1507
American continents first appear on a map.

1497
John Cabot claims all of North America for England.

152
Ferdinand Magellan enters an names the Pacific Ocea

Chapter 4

Many countries in Europe sent men to explore the Americas. These men made long voyages over the sea. They also made dangerous journeys over the land. Sometimes they found gold and silver. Other times they found great rivers, dense forests, deep canyons, or barren deserts. Always they found people who had been living here for thousands of years.

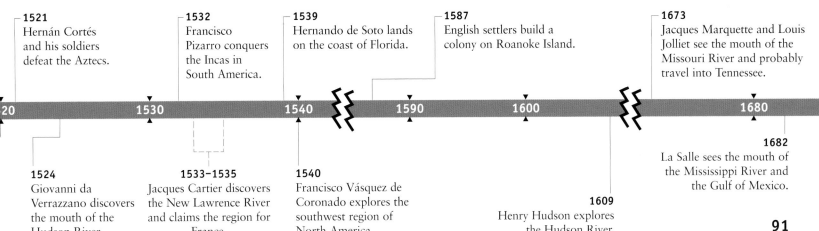

1521
Hernán Cortés and his soldiers defeat the Aztecs.

1532
Francisco Pizarro conquers the Incas in South America.

1539
Hernando de Soto lands on the coast of Florida.

1587
English settlers build a colony on Roanoke Island.

1673
Jacques Marquette and Louis Jolliet see the mouth of the Missouri River and probably travel into Tennessee.

20   1530   1540   1590   1600   1680

1524
Giovanni da Verrazzano discovers the mouth of the Hudson River.

1533–1535
Jacques Cartier discovers the New Lawrence River and claims the region for France.

1540
Francisco Vásquez de Coronado explores the southwest region of North America.

1609
Henry Hudson explores the Hudson River.

1682
La Salle sees the mouth of the Mississippi River and the Gulf of Mexico.

PEOPLE TO KNOW

John Cabot
Christopher Columbus
Leif Eriksson
King Ferdinand
Prince Henry
Queen Isabella
Amerigo Vespucci
Vikings

PLACES TO LOCATE

Asia
Cuba
Europe
Iceland
New World

WORDS TO UNDERSTAND

colonial
colony
exchange
explorer
immunity
navigate

A **colony** is a group of people who leave their homeland and build a settlement in a new country. **Colonial** means having to do with a colony.

The Vikings

Christopher Columbus was not the first European to visit North or South America. The Vikings, who lived in Iceland, sent **explorers** almost 500 years earlier. They built fast ships and explored the North Atlantic Ocean.

Leif Eriksson

Many experts believe Leif Eriksson was the first Viking to visit North America. He discovered Greenland and started two colonies there. As he continued his explorations, he sailed farther and farther west. Six hundred miles off the coast of Greenland, he came to a new land. It was probably Newfoundland.

Eriksson traveled farther south until he came to Nova Scotia. He named this place Vinland because it was covered with vines. Eriksson and his men built a small camp there. Newfoundland and Nova Scotia are part of Canada today.

The Vikings were great explorers. They visited many foreign lands.

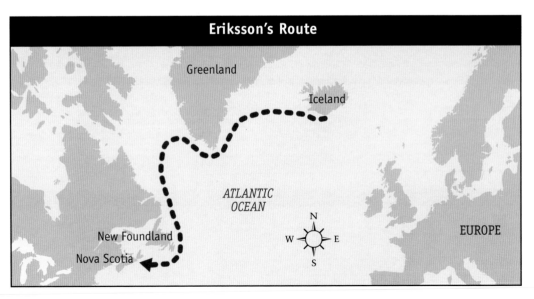

Eriksson's Route

Greenland
Iceland
ATLANTIC OCEAN
New Foundland
Nova Scotia
EUROPE

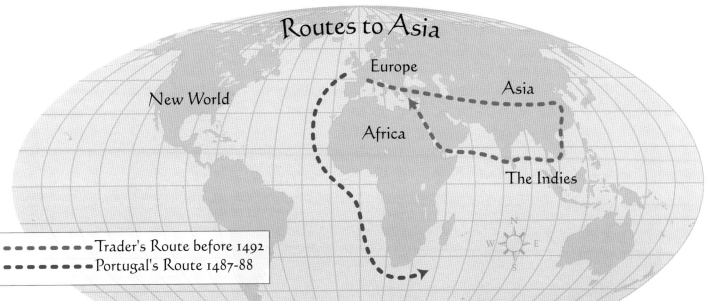

Routes to Asia

New World
Europe
Asia
Africa
The Indies

- - - - - Trader's Route before 1492
- - - - - Portugal's Route 1487-88

The Vikings did not stay in North America. We do not know why they abandoned their camps. Perhaps it is because there are icebergs in the cold North Atlantic Ocean. When a ship hit an iceberg, it usually sank. The icebergs may have kept people from trying to sail between North America and Iceland.

A Trade Route to Asia

Hundreds of years after the Vikings, other European explorers and traders began traveling far from home. They bought goods in foreign countries and sold them to people all across Europe. As traders searched for more goods, they made their way to China.

People in China and other parts of Asia made delicate glassware and beautiful fabrics. They also gathered rare spices. These goods became very popular in Europe, so traders became very rich.

The trip from Europe to Asia across the land was long and dangerous. Then a few government leaders in Asia closed the road to traders. They had to look for a new route. Some traders thought the fastest and safest way to get to China was to sail across the ocean. They sailed east around Africa, but it was a very, very long trip.

The land route to Asia was very difficult.

What Do You Think ?

Have you ever taken a long trip? What do you think it would be like to sail on a boat for weeks or months?

navigation.

The Portuguese

Prince Henry of Portugal was excited about sailing and exploration. He wanted to find a water route to China so Portugal could trade with the Chinese. He spent so much time and money on sailing that he became known as Prince Henry the Navigator.

Prince Henry started a school that trained young men to become sailors. Students learned to make maps and to *navigate* by looking at the stars. Before sailors learned to use the stars, boats had to stay close to the land so they wouldn't lose their way. With their new knowledge, sailors could sail far out into the ocean. This allowed explorers to find new lands.

Linking the Present to the Past

Many people today think people who lived long ago believed the world was flat. Even 500 years ago, people knew the world was round. What kept many sailors from traveling far away was their fear of getting lost if they could not see land.

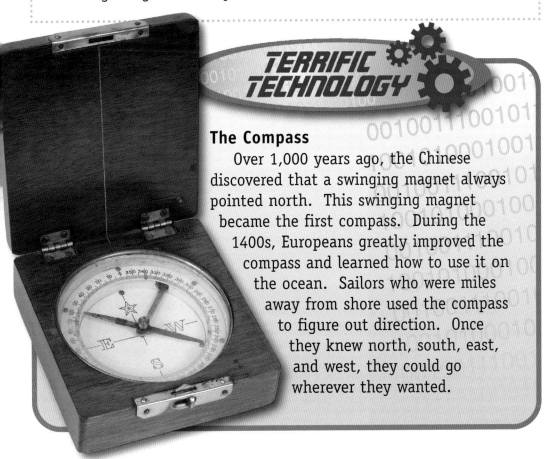

TERRIFIC TECHNOLOGY

The Compass

Over 1,000 years ago, the Chinese discovered that a swinging magnet always pointed north. This swinging magnet became the first compass. During the 1400s, Europeans greatly improved the compass and learned how to use it on the ocean. Sailors who were miles away from shore used the compass to figure out direction. Once they knew north, south, east, and west, they could go wherever they wanted.

Christopher Columbus

Christopher Columbus grew up in Italy and became a skilled sailor. He knew China was in the Far East, but he believed he could get there faster by sailing west. He wanted to find out, but the journey would be very expensive.

Columbus visited the king of Portugal and asked him to pay for his trip. The king thought it was a bad idea and refused. Columbus then went to the kings of England and France, but they also refused to give him any money. Finally Columbus met with King Ferdinand and Queen Isabella of Spain. They agreed to pay for his trip because they thought it was very important to teach their religious beliefs to the people of the Far East.

The First Voyage

In 1492, Christopher Columbus sailed west from Spain with three ships and 90 men. After traveling for weeks, the men grew tired and impatient. They begged Columbus to turn back toward Spain. On October 9, he told his men that if they did not reach land in three days, they would go home.

Christopher Columbus

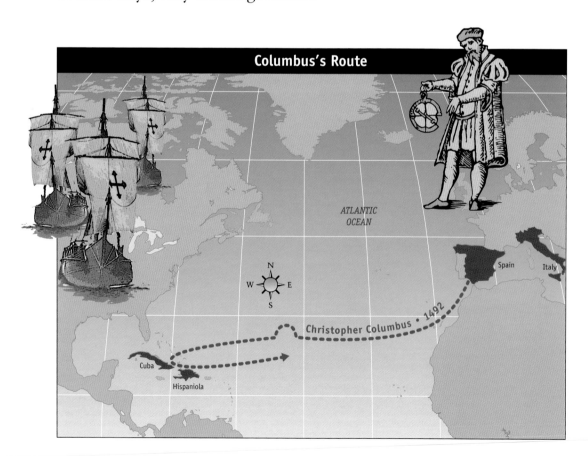

Columbus's Route

ATLANTIC OCEAN

N
W E
S

Christopher Columbus • 1492

Spain

Italy

Cuba

Hispaniola

This is Christopher Columbus landing at San Salvador. If you discovered an island, what would you call it?

On October 12, three days later, Columbus and his men saw land. They thought they were on an island off the coast of Asia, but they were really in the Caribbean. Columbus stepped off his ship and raised a Christian cross and the Spanish flag. He named the place San Salvador, which means "Holy Savior."

The Indians

Columbus called the people who lived on the island "Indians" because he thought he was near India. The native people he met were actually Tainos, a group of peaceful, friendly fishermen. The Tainos showed Columbus around the Caribbean and took him to an island called Colba. Today, this island is called Cuba. Columbus built a fort on Hispaniola, the island where Haiti and the Dominican Republic are today.

Linking the Present to the Past

The Tainos introduced Spanish soldiers to tobacco, a plant that grew on the islands. The native people burned the leaves in pipes and inhaled the smoke. The Spanish quickly learned to grow and smoke tobacco. Today, raising tobacco is an important business in the United States. But researchers have found that smoking causes cancer and other health problems.

The New World

After several weeks of exploring the islands, Columbus returned to Spain. He took seven Tainos with him and left 39 sailors on the island. He also took parrots and gold trinkets for King Ferdinand and Queen Isabella. The king and queen loved their gifts and gave Columbus the title Lord Admiral of the Ocean Seas. A priest who heard the report Columbus gave called his discovery the "New World."

Would you like to have been a sailor on Columbus's ship? Why or why not?

Columbus's Other Voyages

The next year, Christopher Columbus returned with 17 ships and more than 1,200 men. He also brought farmers, horses, and sugarcane plants. Columbus planned to establish a sugar plantation. He hoped to become wealthy by selling sugar to Europeans.

PASSPORT TO HISTORY

Party with the Royals

When Columbus returned to Spain, he told people about the place he had found. His stories encouraged others to explore the New World. Pretend you are Columbus and you are attending a party given by King Ferdinand and Queen Isabella. At the party, many people ask about your voyage to the New World.

Write a short story about the things Columbus might have described. Start by describing what the land looked like. Here is a sentence to help you start your tale: "The sight of land was glorious, as I had promised my men we would reach land or turn around." Share your story with the class to get a stamp in your passport.

When Columbus reached the islands, he learned all of the men he had left there were dead. The Spanish had tried to force the Tainos to work for them, but the Tainos had rebelled and killed them. In response, Columbus and his men went from island to island, abusing and killing the Tainos.

The Columbian Exchange

Each time Columbus came to the New World, he brought things from Europe. He brought oranges, cattle, sheep, horses, and pigs. When he returned to Europe, he took potatoes, corn, and tomatoes from the Americas. This became known as the Columbian Exchange. Things that grew in the New World were *exchanged,* or traded, for things that grew in Europe.

How would you feel if someone in your family was very sick?

Invisible Threats

A few things the Spanish took to the New World could not be seen. They were the germs of diseases such as smallpox and measles. These germs traveled in the bodies of Columbus and his men. Rats on board the ships also carried diseases.

From the moment Columbus first arrived in the New World, germs began passing to the native peoples. Native Americans had never had these diseases before. They had no natural *immunity* to them. Indians on both American continents became sick and died. Scientists think that 90 percent of the Indians in some regions died from European diseases. The Native American culture never recovered.

Did you know that Native Americans taught the Europeans how to grow potatoes?

Changes in Europe

The Columbian Exchange also caused changes in Europe. When new kinds of crops were taken back to Europe, farmers learned to grow them. Potatoes became a major food source for many poor people in Europe. Europeans also grew corn to feed the animals. People began to live longer because they had more food, and the population in Europe grew rapidly. At the same time, the population of the Americas became smaller and smaller.

Columbus made four trips to the Americas. He explored the coast of South America, but he never found gold. He died still believing the land he discovered was China.

European Explorers in America

Do you think it would be exciting to discover new lands? Would you claim them as your own?

Other Nations Follow Spain

Stories about the voyages of Christopher Columbus spread very quickly across Europe. The kings of England, France, and the Netherlands soon sent ships across the ocean. Like the Spanish, they wanted to find a water route to China. They also wanted to claim land and build colonies in the New World.

John Cabot

The king of England hired Italian Giovanni Caboto to make a voyage to the New World. The English called him John Cabot. He

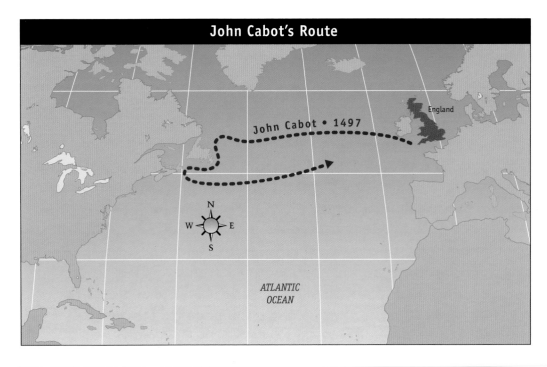

John Cabot's Route

John Cabot • 1497

England

ATLANTIC OCEAN

left England in 1497 with only one boat and 18 sailors. When he reached Newfoundland, he claimed all of North America for England.

Amerigo Vespucci

Amerigo Vespucci, another Italian, also made several trips to the New World. He did not believe Columbus had found islands off the coast of India. Vespucci believed Columbus had discovered a new continent.

In 1507, a German mapmaker drew a map of the world that showed a large continent between Europe and Asia. He called the continent America because Amerigo Vespucci was the first to believe the land was a new continent.

North and South America were not really new continents. Millions of people had been living there for thousands of years. To those people, it was home.

Amerigo Vespucci

Portuguese Brazil

After Christopher Columbus told people about his discovery, the Catholic pope divided the world between Spain and Portugal. At the time, South America had not been discovered by Europeans.

The Portuguese were not happy about the pope's dividing line. They met with the Spanish, who agreed to move the boundary much farther west. When explorers mapped South America several years later, Spain still had far more land than Portugal. As the years passed, the Portuguese took more and more Spanish land.

When the final boundary was drawn, Portugal controlled far more land in South America than Spain did. The Portuguese land was called Brazil. Today, the people who live in Brazil speak Portuguese. Throughout the rest of South America, people speak Spanish.

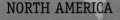

NORTH AMERICA

Brazil

SOUTH AMERICA

 MEMORY MASTER

1. Who were the first Europeans to visit the Americas?
2. What was a swinging magnet used for?
3. What invisible threats did the Europeans bring to the Americas?

PEOPLE TO KNOW

Vasco Nuñez de Balboa
Hernán Cortés
Incas
Ferdinand Magellan
Montezuma
Francisco Pizarro
Giovanni da Verrazzano

PLACES TO LOCATE

Central America
Pacific Ocean
Tenochtitlan

WORDS TO UNDERSTAND

conquistador
plantations
stowaway
strait

Vasco Nuñez de Balboa

Vasco Nuñez de Balboa was a young man who lived in Spain. Like many other Europeans, he hoped to find gold in the New World. He managed to get to the islands of the Caribbean, but he did not have enough money to go exploring. Instead he had to work as a farmer.

Balboa did not like farming. He believed he would become rich if he could get to Central America. One day, Balboa saw a large Spanish ship. The ship was leaving the next day for Central America.

Vasco Nuñez de Balboa

What Do You Think ?

A person who hides on a ship and travels without anyone knowing is called a *stowaway.* What do you think it would be like to be a stowaway? Remember that a journey by sea took days, weeks, or months. How do you think stowaways survived?

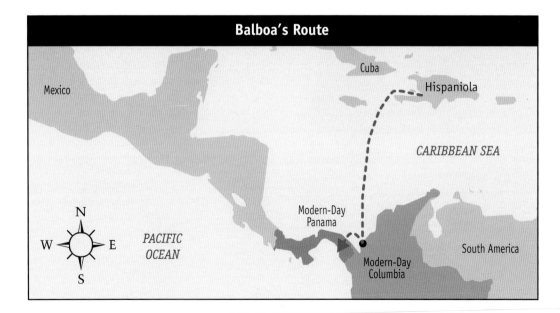

Balboa's Route

Mexico
Cuba
Hispaniola
CARIBBEAN SEA
Modern-Day Panama
PACIFIC OCEAN
South America
Modern-Day Columbia

N W E S

When no one was looking, Balboa and his dog crept aboard and hid in a flour barrel. They traveled all the way to modern-day Columbia without being discovered.

Balboa had a talent for getting people to do what he wanted. In South America, he convinced several people to go with him to a place he had seen on the coast of Central America. Once Balboa and his followers arrived, they built a colony. They named it Santa María de la Antigua del Darién, in honor of Mary, the mother of Jesus Christ. This was the first permanent European settlement in Central America.

The Ocean Sea

Balboa and his men continued to explore the thick jungles of Central America. They wore heavy armor. The heat and metal clothing made the journey very difficult. Balboa's group killed or wounded many native people as they searched for gold and riches.

In 1513, Balboa and his men climbed a high peak in what is now Panama. From the top of the mountain, they saw the Pacific Ocean. Geographers in Europe agreed there was a continent between Europe and Asia, but they thought there was only one ocean. They called it the Ocean Sea.

Experts believe Balboa was the first European to see the Pacific Ocean.

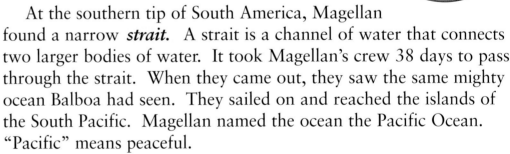

Magellan's Route Around the World

Europe
Asia
New World
Tenochtitlan •
Africa
The Indies
Straits of Magellan

GPS

Today, many navigators use electronic devices to help them find their way. One of these devices is a compass system that can find any place in the world. It is called a Global Positioning Satellite (GPS) system. One company named its GPS system Magellan. Can you guess why?

Ferdinand Magellan

Several years after Balboa's journey, a Portuguese sailor named Ferdinand Magellan sailed west from Spain. He took 5 ships and 250 men. Like Columbus, he was determined to find a water route to China.

Ferdinand Magellan

At the southern tip of South America, Magellan found a narrow **strait.** A strait is a channel of water that connects two larger bodies of water. It took Magellan's crew 38 days to pass through the strait. When they came out, they saw the same mighty ocean Balboa had seen. They sailed on and reached the islands of the South Pacific. Magellan named the ocean the Pacific Ocean. "Pacific" means peaceful.

Magellan was killed on the voyage, but his men were the first people to sail around the world. The journey took longer than three years, but they had gathered many valuable goods. The king and queen were impressed, but they decided it took too long to reach Asia by sailing west. They finally gave up looking for a western water route to China.

Linking the Present to the Past

The narrow strait Ferdinand Magellan and his crew sailed through has been named for him. It is called the Straits of Magellan.

Tenochtitlan had many canals and waterways, so people traveled around the city by boat.

New Spain

During their travels, Spanish explorers often heard stories about great cities of gold in Central America. Hernán Cortés was one of the Spanish who heard these stories. He organized a trip and sailed west to find riches.

Cortés arrived first in Cuba and then traveled to Central Mexico. He soon found the mighty Aztec city of Tenochtitlan, now the site of Mexico City. He later wrote that it was the most beautiful city he had ever seen.

The Aztec king, Montezuma, did not know Cortés had an army of soldiers, horses, and cannons waiting just outside the city. Cortés and his men captured Montezuma, conquered the Aztec people, and took control of the city. They renamed the region New Spain. Cortés became very rich, and the king of Spain made him the region's governor.

Verrazzano Discovers the Hudson River

Not to be outdone by the other European countries, the king of France sent Giovanni da Verrazzano to find a passage to China. Verrazzano traveled up the Atlantic Coast. He discovered the mouth of the Hudson River, but he did not find a way to China.

The Aztec king welcomes Cortés. He did not know Cortés planned to take control of the city.

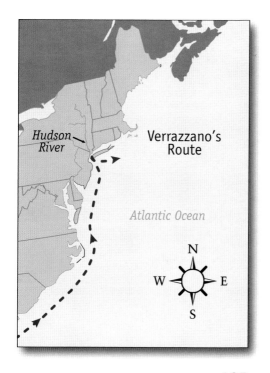

Hudson River

Verrazzano's Route

Atlantic Ocean

N W E S

Francisco Pizarro

Have you ever stayed in a hotel on a vacation? Machu Picchu was a vacation spot for the Incas.

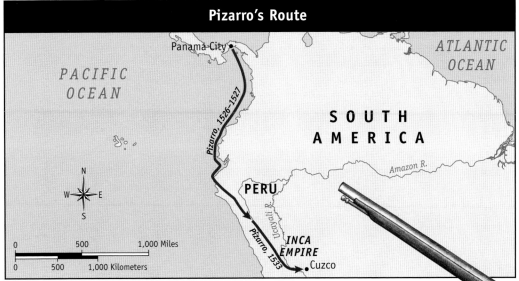

Pizarro's Route

PACIFIC OCEAN

ATLANTIC OCEAN

Panama City

Pizarro, 1526–1527

SOUTH AMERICA

Amazon R.

PERU

Ucayali R.

Pizarro, 1533

INCA EMPIRE

Cuzco

N W E S

0   500   1,000 Miles
0   500   1,000 Kilometers

Pizarro and the Incas

Another Spanish explorer in the New World was Francisco Pizarro. Pizarro had heard stories about a second wealthy settlement in South America. He traveled along the western coast of the continent in hope of finding it.

After three difficult journeys, Pizarro found Cuzco, the Inca capital in South America. The Incas were great architects and had built a recreation area called Machu Picchu, which still stands today. They also created many beautiful works of art from pure gold. Like Tenochtitlan, Cuzco was a large city with great wealth.

With 180 men, 67 horses, and 3 cannons, Pizarro captured the city. His men melted every piece of gold they found. Then they molded the gold into bars and took it back to Spain. By melting the precious art, the Spanish destroyed much of the Inca culture. As in other cities, European diseases killed more people than the soldiers did.

The Spanish Conquistadors

When the Spanish conquered Mexico, Peru, and other parts of the New World, they forced the people who lived there to work for them. The Spanish became known as *conquistadors,* which means conquerors.

Spanish soldiers received large blocks of land in the New World as payment for their work. By mining silver and gold, the soldiers became rich. Some conquistadors also grew wealthy by building sugar *plantations* (large farms) in the Caribbean islands.

How is this soldier's uniform different from a modern soldier's uniform?

The Spanish enslaved the native people and forced them to look for gold.

Why do you think the Spanish stamped crosses on their coins?

"For God, for Glory, and for Gold"

The Spanish were very religious. They said they were conquering the Americas "for God, for Glory, and for Gold." The Spanish believed the Indians needed to learn about the Christian God. The priests who traveled with the soldiers worked hard to convert the Indians to the Catholic Church. They believed the Indians' deaths from disease showed God wanted the native people to change.

With so many Indians dying from disease, there were fewer and fewer workers. The Spanish began buying slaves along the coast of Africa and forcing them to work on sugar plantations. The Spanish believed they were better than the Indians and Africans. They did not think it was wrong to treat the natives badly.

After gold and silver were discovered in Central and South America, Spain became the wealthiest nation in Europe. It was exactly what King Ferdinand and Queen Isabella had wanted. The other European nations became jealous. They wanted wealth and riches too. The Atlantic Ocean soon became busy with ships from all over the world.

2 MEMORY MASTER

1. Why did Magellan choose the name "Pacific" for the ocean he saw?
2. Where did Cortés establish New Spain?
3. Who were the conquistadors?

The Search for El Dorado Continues

The Spanish continued searching for wealth in the Americas. Many explorers had heard stories of seven cities of gold. They hoped to find El Dorado, which means "place of gold." The Spanish hoped the cities would make them rich.

Native people carved masks and other decorations out of pure gold. The Spanish knew these items were worth thousands of dollars.

Native Americans could do little to stop the Spanish invaders.

PEOPLE TO KNOW

Jacques Cartier
Francisco Vásquez
   de Coronado
Henry Hudson
Louis Jolliet
Lord La Salle
Jacques Marquette
Queen Elizabeth
Sir Walter Raleigh
Hernando de Soto

PLACES TO LOCATE

Hudson River
Mississippi River
North America
Roanoke Island
St. Lawrence River

WORDS TO UNDERSTAND

bluff
compete
expedition
missions
pueblo

European Explorers in America

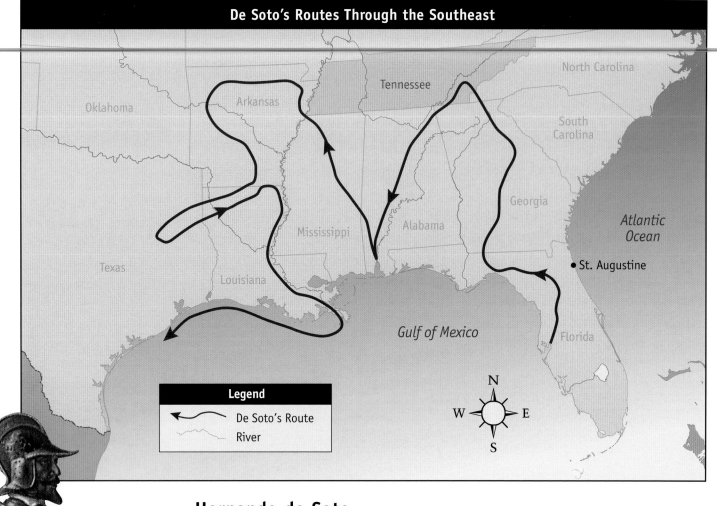

Hernando de Soto

Hernando de Soto was a Spanish soldier who had traveled with Pizarro. When he heard the stories of the golden cities, he decided to raise an army to search for them. In May 1539, de Soto and his men landed on the coast of Florida. They forced the Indians to give them food and to lead them to their cities. The Spanish were cruel to the Indians, often stealing their goods and burning their cities. As word of their arrival spread from place to place, the Indians tried to fight back.

De Soto and his soldiers crossed the Appalachian Mountains and followed the French Broad River to the Tennessee River. They traveled down the Tennessee River into the southeastern part of the land that later became our state.

De Soto and his soldiers never found gold. Many of them, including de Soto himself, got sick and died. Later, two more

Hernando de Soto was disappointed when he found no gold in Tennessee.

groups of Spanish explorers came into the region that is now Tennessee. Like de Soto, these groups found no gold or treasure among the Indians.

Francisco Vásquez de Coronado

Other Spanish explorers traveled north out of South America into what is now the southwestern United States. Francisco Vásquez de Coronado found small *pueblos,* but he did not find any golden cities. The Pueblo people tried to get rid of the Spanish by telling them stories about wealthy cities in the North. Coronado and his men marched all the way to what is now Kansas before they realized the Indians had tricked them.

The Great Spanish Empire

The Spanish built many successful colonies in the New World. This made Spain one of the largest empires in the world. Other European countries watched the Spanish grow in wealth and power. These countries wanted to establish colonies in the New World so they could become wealthy too.

Linking the Present to the Past

Some people thought of another way to get rich. They became pirates! Pirates robbed the Spanish ships that were loaded with riches. The Spanish finally built a fort to protect their ships. The fort, which is at St. Augustine, Florida, is the oldest permanent European settlement in North America.

Coronado and his men marched for weeks across the hot, dry deserts of the Southwest, but they did not find gold.

SPANISH MISSIONS

The priests who traveled with Spanish explorers built *missions* across the Southwest and along the coast of California. Some of the missions turned into settlements. At the missions, priests taught the Indians about the Christian God. The Spanish also taught them how to grow new crops and take care of farm animals. The Indians adopted many Spanish ways. They created a new culture that was a mixture of Indian tradition and Spanish culture.

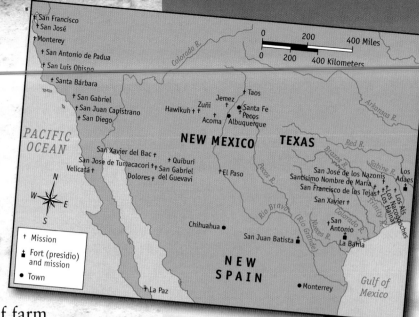

Date: August, 1615

The morning breeze awoke me early today. It blew right into my small adobe house, bringing with it the smell of the dry air and summer heat. The sunshine reminds me of the beautiful light that pours into our little church here.

There is much work for me today. I have been in California for but a few weeks, but this is my first chance to record my impressions.

My journey from Spain was long, but I had the companionship of my fellow priests. We prayed daily together with faith to convert the natives to God. Once in the new world, we each traveled to a different mission. We call this land Nueva España [Spanish for "New Spain].

Though I could travel to another mission by horse in a day, my mission is far away from ships or towns. It is a humble place. My orders from Spain are clear. We must have a fort here with enough supplies to last through the year. We will have very few visitors here, so we have to grow and save our own food. The huts are made from reeds and thatch, and we will need to build them of adobe and stone to make them last.

Father Garces, who was here before me, chose this site. There is a stream nearby, as well as much land for the livestock and the crops. Trees give us shade and wood. After Father Garces blessed this mission, he traveled north to start a new one. My job is to remain here and make this mission a strong house of God. Already we meet with the natives every day for prayer. I am learning to speak their language, and I have taught them to call me "Padre" [Spanish for "Father"].

This new land seems wild to me, but I am getting used to the new food and new people. The Indians are good hunters, and they share their meat with us at the mission. I am teaching them to plant gardens. We are working together to plant the seed of God in this new land.

Spanish priests and Indian workers built the San Xavier del Bac mission in Arizona more than 200 years ago. It was a place where priests taught about the Christian God.

Activity

Reading a Historical Passage

The passage on the opposite page is historical fiction. It is an example of what life at a Spanish mission in the old Southwest was like. Read the journal entry. Then answer the following questions.

1. How do you think this priest traveled from Spain to California?
2. What did the priests call the new land?
3. How was the site for the mission chosen?
4. What is the job of the priest who wrote this entry?
5. List three clues that show how the Spanish and the Indians combined cultures.
6. How do you think Spanish missions changed life in America?

England Comes to the New World

The queen of England decided to build colonies in the New World too. She asked Sir Walter Raleigh to start a colony along the eastern coast of North America. Raleigh convinced Queen Elizabeth to let him name the land after her. Since she was not married, she was known as the Virgin Queen. Raleigh named the land Virginia.

Roanoke Island

Raleigh's group of 117 people landed on Roanoke Island in the spring of 1587. The group was different from the groups that came from Spain and France. Raleigh sent families of men, women, and children instead of soldiers. But the people did not know how to survive in the wilderness. They did not know how to hunt or gather food.

Soon after the English arrived at Roanoke Island, one of the women had a baby. The baby's parents named her Virginia in honor of the new land. John White, the baby's grandfather, decided to return to England to get more people to come to the land of Virginia.

When John White arrived in England, Queen Elizabeth would not give him a ship to return to Roanoke. The queen needed all of her ships to fight a war against Spain. It was three years before anyone returned to Roanoke Island.

England's Queen Elizabeth wanted to build colonies in the New World.

Roanoke Island •

Who do you think carved the letters into the tree? Why do you think the person did it?

The Lost Colony

When the war between England and Spain ended, John White returned to Roanoke. All of the settlers were gone. White could not find his daughter or his baby granddaughter. The only things he saw were the letters "CRO" carved on a tree and the word "Croatan" carved into a fence post. Croatan was the name of a nearby island. Was this a clue that had been left for him?

White found a captain of a ship who agreed to take him to Croatan. The boat headed toward the island, but a huge storm arose. The captain turned the boat around and headed back to England. White never learned what happened to his family.

Sir Walter Raleigh's group became known as the "Lost Colony" because no one ever found out what happened to them. Had they gone to Croatan? Had they gone to live with the Indians? Had they been killed by the Indians? Had they starved to death? No one knew. The only thing people knew was that the English had failed to start a colony in the New World.

The Dutch and the Hudson River

Like the other nations of Europe, Holland wanted to have colonies in North America. Holland is also known as the Netherlands, and its people are the Dutch. A Dutch company hired Henry Hudson to explore the North American coast. Hudson sailed up a river that was later named for him—the Hudson River. He claimed the area for Holland and called it New Netherland.

What Do You Think

What do you think happened to the colonists at Roanoke?

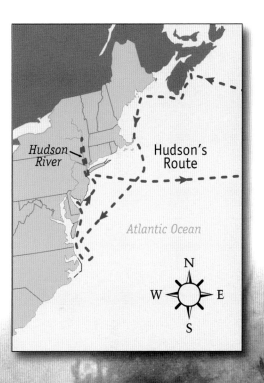

Native Americans heard stories about the cruel things some explorers had done. As time passed, Indians grew more fearful of strangers. Can you understand why?

The French in North America

A French explorer named Jacques Cartier sailed to the New World. He discovered the St. Lawrence River, which led to the Great Lakes. Cartier claimed the region for France and called it New France. The French explorers and settlers who came to North America settled in New France. New France later became Canada.

When French explorers met Indians, they were friendly and began trading with them. The Indians were good hunters and had many furs to trade. The French wanted the furs because they were worth a lot of money.

The Fur Trade Leads to Change

Before the Indians began trading with the French, they killed animals only to feed and clothe themselves. They soon began killing more animals than they needed for food because they wanted more furs to trade.

The fur trade also caused the Indian tribes to *compete* with one other. The tribes fought over hunting grounds. They also stole furs from one another. This led to many more battles between the tribes.

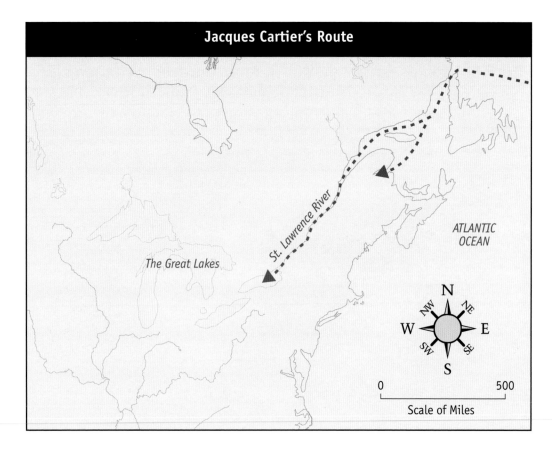

Jacques Cartier's Route

St. Lawrence River

ATLANTIC OCEAN

The Great Lakes

N
NW NE
W E
SW SE
S

0   500
Scale of Miles

Native Americans loved European goods. They killed many more animals than they needed so they would have more furs to trade.

117

Exploring the Mississippi River Region

In 1673, Jacques Marquette, a missionary, and Louis Jolliet, a mapmaker and fur trader, organized a canoe trip to explore and map the Mississippi River. They took five Frenchmen and two Indian guides and traveled down the river.

Along the journey, the group saw land Europeans had never seen before. Marquette and Jolliet saw the mouths of the Missouri River, the Ohio River, and the Arkansas River. Historians believe they stopped at the *bluffs* (high, steep banks) where Memphis sits today.

Fort Prud'homme

Nine years later, the king of France sent René Robert Cavelier, Lord La Salle, to explore the land south of New France (Canada). La Salle led an *expedition* of 40 men in canoes down the Mississippi River.

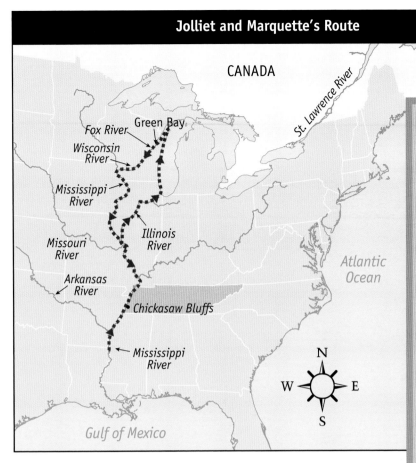

Jolliet and Marquette's Route

CANADA

Fox River
Green Bay
Wisconsin River
Mississippi River
Missouri River
Illinois River
Arkansas River
Chickasaw Bluffs
Mississippi River
St. Lawrence River
Atlantic Ocean
Gulf of Mexico

N W E S

TENNESSEE PORTRAIT

Jacques Marquette
(1637–1675)

Jacques Marquette was born in France and became a priest when he was 17. Several years later, he went to Canada to work as a missionary. Marquette learned the native languages and quickly made friends with the Indians. The native people loved and trusted him. They called him Black Robes because he wore the long black robes of a priest.

Marquette was sent to explore the regions around the Great Lakes. There he met another tribe of Indians. They told him about the mighty Mississippi River. A few years later, Marquette and Louis Jolliet set out to map the great river. All along the journey, friendly Indians helped them find their way.

One month after they left the Great Lakes region, Marquette and Jolliet entered the Mississippi River. They traveled down the river for many miles. They finally turned back when they realized they might get captured by Spanish soldiers. Once they arrived back at the Great Lakes, Jolliet continued on to Canada to tell people about the river. Marquette stayed in the Illinois region for a while longer. While he was there, he became sick and died. He was only 38 years old.

When the group arrived at the Chickasaw Bluffs, one of the men wandered away and got lost. La Salle built a temporary fort on the bluffs and named it Fort Prud'homme after the man who was lost. The group searched for Prud'homme and finally found him. Then they sailed down the river until they reached the Gulf of Mexico.

La Salle claimed all the land around the Mississippi River for France. He named the land Louisiane in honor of King Louis XIV. After these early journeys down the Mississippi River, French traders began traveling to the land that later became Tennessee.

3 MEMORY MASTER

1. What is El Dorado?
2. What were Spanish missions?
3. How did the French treat the Indians?

Chapter 4 Review

What's the Point?

Many countries and explorers came to North and South America. Experts believe the Vikings were the first. Christopher Columbus sailed to North America, met native people, and opened trade routes. Europeans brought diseases that killed many natives. Spain conquered many nations, built a great empire, and set up missions. England tried to set up a colony. The French built a colony in Canada and began trading with Native Americans.

Becoming Better Readers

Can you solve the mystery of what happened at Roanoke, the Lost Colony? Based on your reading in this chapter, consider what life was like on the island. Then write what you think happened to the colonists. Include details of how and why they disappeared. Why have they never been found? As a class, share your stories.

Climbing to Connections

Many Cultures Meet

How did Native American culture change as a result of contact with European cultures? Answer the following questions to help you reach conclusions.

1. Who did Columbus meet and take with him to Spain?
2. Name three things Columbus and his men introduced to the native people.
3. How were Native Americans affected by the Columbian Exchange and the French fur trade?
4. Analyze the conflict between Native Americans and Columbus's men. Compare it to the conflict between Native Americans and de Soto's men.
5. How did the combination of disease and loss of territory forever change Native American culture?
6. Of all the European cultures that encountered the Native Americans, which European culture was the least damaging to the Indians? Why? Support your choice.

Evaluation Station

Supply and Demand

After Columbus returned to Spain, many waves of Europeans traveled to the New World. Why did Europeans want land, gold, silver, spices, and other goods? Do you think demand for these things was good for worldwide trade? Why or why not?

Activity

People, Places, and Things

How did the world change because of exploration? Write down one change for each category below. Then share your answers with the class. Were any of the answers the same? How many different answers did your class think of?

People	Places	Things

Activity

Explorer Geography

You have read about many famous explorers. Each explorer sailed for a different country. Some explorers sailed for the countries where they were born. Other explorers sailed for any country that would pay for the trip. Match each explorer in the list below to the country for which he sailed. Write the country's abbreviation by explorer's name. Which country had the most explorers?

_____ Leif Eriksson
_____ Prince Henry the Navigator
_____ Christopher Columbus
_____ John Cabot
_____ Francisco Pizarro
_____ Amerigo Vespucci
_____ Vasco Nuñez de Balboa
_____ Henry Hudson
_____ René Robert Cavelier, Lord La Salle
_____ Ferdinand Magellan
_____ Sir Walter Raleigh
_____ Hernán Cortés
_____ Giovanni da Verrazzano
_____ Jacques Cartier

_____ Hernando de Soto
_____ Francisco Vasquez de Coronado
_____ Jacques Marquette
_____ Louis Jolliet

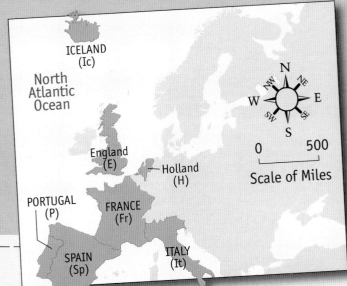

"The Great Being above is very good and provides for everybody. It is he that made fire, bread, and the rivers to run. He gave us this land, but the white people seem to want to drive us from it."

—Cherokee Chief
Attakullakulla
(Little Carpenter), 1769

Thirteen Colonies in North America

The first white settlers built forts like the one in this painting. Why do you think they surrounded the forts with high, pointed fences?

Timeline of Events

1607
Jamestown is founded in the colony of Virginia.

1620
The Pilgrims start Plymouth Colony.

1670
English settlers start the colony of Carolina.

1610 1620 1630 1640 1650 1660 16

1614
The Dutch start New Amsterdam, a small colony that later becomes the colony of New York.

1630
The Puritans start the Massachusetts Bay Colony.

Chapter 5

After the nations of Europe learned North America was a continent, they raced to build colonies here. They fought against one another for control of the land. They also fought with the people who lived here. As towns and settlements grew, the people blended their native countries' traditions and started new ones. Many new cultures were born during the colonial years.

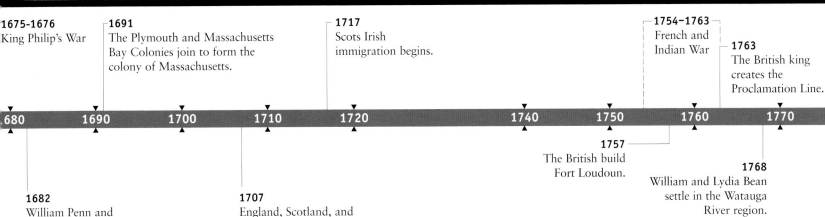

1675-1676
King Philip's War

1691
The Plymouth and Massachusetts Bay Colonies join to form the colony of Massachusetts.

1717
Scots Irish immigration begins.

1754–1763
French and Indian War

1763
The British king creates the Proclamation Line.

| 680 | 1690 | 1700 | 1710 | 1720 | 1740 | 1750 | 1760 | 1770 |

1757
The British build Fort Loudoun.

1682
William Penn and the Quakers settle in Pennsylvania.

1707
England, Scotland, and Wales unite and become Great Britain.

1768
William and Lydia Bean settle in the Watauga River region.

A New English Colony

The English colony at Roanoke failed, but England still wanted to build a settlement in the land called Virginia. After Queen Elizabeth died, King James gave another group a charter to begin a colony. A *charter* is a document that gives permission from the king to settle land. It allows people to set up local government.

Settling Jamestown

In December of 1606, nearly 150 men and boys left England on three ships headed for North America. In the spring, the ships arrived in the Chesapeake Bay, but only 105 sailors were left. Forty-five had died on the long journey across the ocean.

The men looked around for a good place to build their settlement. They finally chose a narrow strip of land next to a river. They named both the river and the settlement after England's King James. The river is the James River, and the settlement was Jamestown.

Can you imagine what it was like to stand on strange, new land and watch as the ships left for home?

These boats look like the first boats that arrived at Jamestown in 1607.

Jamestown was not a good place to live. The land was wet and full of mosquitoes, and the water made the settlers sick. The men who came to Virginia were not prepared for the work of building a colony. They did not know how to plant fields and build houses. They brought along servants to do the work for them. The men's goal was to make money and then return to England. Some hoped to find gold. Others still hoped to find an easier way to get to China.

John Smith Takes Charge

John Smith brought order to Virginia. He traveled to Jamestown with the first group of men. Most of the men refused to work, and they began to starve.

Smith organized the colony. He found some helpful Indians who gave the colonists food to eat. The men chose him to be their governor. When Smith was later hurt in an accident, he had to return to England.

John Smith told the men that they had to work. He said, "He that will not work, shall not eate."

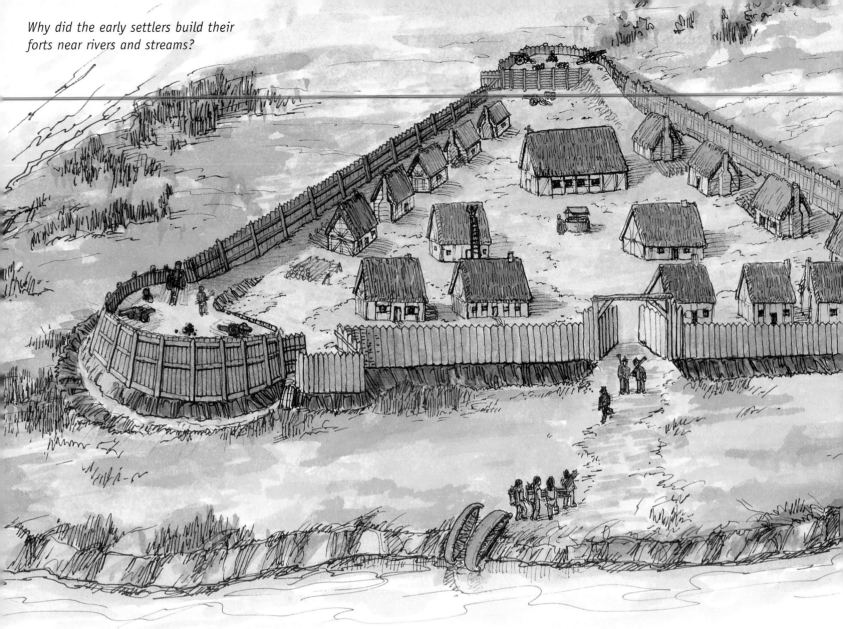

Why did the early settlers build their forts near rivers and streams?

The Starving Time

For a while, the settlers did not have a governor. More settlers came, and soon 500 people were living at Jamestown. During the early years of the colony, many people died. The settlers did not have enough food. By the end of the winter of 1609, only 65 of the 500 people at Jamestown were still alive. They called that winter the "Starving Time."

A New Governor

After the Starving Time, the remaining settlers wanted to go back to England. They boarded a ship and began traveling down the James River.

As they were sailing, they met another ship. Aboard this ship was Lord Thomas De La Warr, their new governor. The ship also carried food and more settlers. Lord De La Warr convinced the colonists to return to Jamestown.

Although there were still hard times, life in Virginia slowly improved. The settlers planted corn, fruit trees, and other crops. Once there was more food, the population began to grow. More settlers arrived, and the colony began to spread out. They moved up the rivers and farther away from the ocean. They took land from the Indians everywhere they went.

The First Colonial Government

Ten years after the first settlers arrived in Jamestown, the colony had grown. It needed leadership. The king allowed the colonists to choose *representatives* to make decisions for them. Known as the *House of Burgesses,* these representatives elected leaders and made laws for the colony. But the king of England still controlled the colonies.

The government in England was different from the other nations of Europe. In Spain and France, the kings had *absolute power.* No one could challenge their decisions. The English king, however, had to work with a group of leaders called *Parliament.* The king could not do whatever he wanted. His power was limited by Parliament.

Linking the Present to the Past

The state of Delaware was named for Lord De La Warr.

This is a model of a settler house in Jamestown. Why do you think there were so few windows?

Thirteen Colonies in North America

Tobacco, Servants, and Slaves

The colonists in Virginia began looking for a way to earn more money. A man named John Rolfe bought some tobacco seeds from a trader in the Caribbean. Rolfe planted the seeds in Virginia and shipped his first harvest to England. The tobacco brought a lot of money to the colony.

Indentured Servants

Farming tobacco required a lot of workers. The colony needed more people, but the trip from England was expensive. Some people who did not have money to pay for their trip became *indentured servants.* A colonist paid for an indentured servant's journey across the ocean to the colonies. Then the indentured servant worked for the colonist until the price of the journey was paid off.

After working for the agreed time, the indentured servant was free. He received a piece of land, some clothing, and a few tools. Some of the indentured servants who came to Virginia were from England. Others were from Africa.

For a long time, indentured servants worked in the tobacco fields. But using indentured servants created a problem for landowners. They had to keep looking for workers to replace the ones who repaid their debt.

Slaves

Landowners decided they needed workers who could not leave. They passed laws that allowed **slavery** in Virginia. Slavery was a cruel practice. Slaves had no rights. They were bought and sold like property and forced to work without pay. Some slave owners were harsh and mistreated their slaves. Many slave families had a hard time staying together because children and parents were sold to different owners. They might never see each other again. Parents could do little to protect their children from slave owners.

How would you feel if you were taken from your homeland and sold as a slave?

New Netherland

New Netherland

Hudson River

● New Amsterdam
(New York City)

People from Holland,
or the Netherlands,
are called Dutch.

Linking the Present to the Past

The island at the mouth of the Hudson is known today as Manhattan. It is part of New York City.

In the last chapter, you read about Henry Hudson. He explored and named the Hudson River. He also claimed the area around it for the Dutch and named the region New Netherland. It included part of what is now New Jersey and New York.

Hudson described the land in letters he wrote to people in Europe. He wrote about lands filled with animals that could be trapped for their beautiful furs. He said the rivers and ocean were filled with fish and the native people were friendly. Many Dutch people were interested in beaver fur and gold. They wanted to move to the new land.

New Amsterdam and New York

In 1614, a few Dutch settlers traveled to New Netherland. They built a small trading post on an island at the mouth of the Hudson River. They called the settlement New Amsterdam. People from many different countries settled there, so it became very *diverse*. Diverse means varied or different from one another.

Many years later, the English king gave New Netherland to his brother, the duke of York. The king had no right to do this because the Dutch still controlled the area. The governor of New Netherland did not want to fight the English, however, so he allowed the duke to take control of the land. The duke of York changed the name of the region to New York.

The Pilgrims

Thirteen years after the first English settlers arrived in Jamestown, another group left England for North America. They called themselves Pilgrims.

The Pilgrims were unhappy with England's laws about religion. All Englishmen had to belong to the Church of England. There was no freedom of religion. The Pilgrims wanted their own church.

New England

More than 100 Pilgrims boarded a ship called the *Mayflower* and sailed to the New World. They wanted to go to Virginia. After a difficult journey, they finally reached land in 1620. But they were not in Virginia. The Pilgrims were north of Virginia in a place they called Plymouth. Their charter stated the region would be called New England. It included much of Virginia.

The Mayflower Compact

Before the Pilgrims left the ship, they signed an agreement called the *Mayflower Compact.* The agreement said the government's power came from the people. It also said the people would obey the laws of the government. That meant the people governed themselves in a *democracy.* Democracy means government by the people. The Mayflower Compact was the first democratic government established by the colonists.

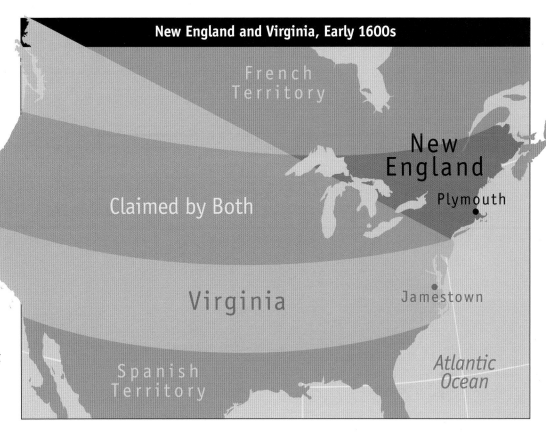

New England and Virginia, Early 1600s

French Territory

New England

Plymouth

Claimed by Both

Virginia

Jamestown

Spanish Territory

Atlantic Ocean

How did the Pilgrims make history when they signed the Mayflower Compact?

Inside the Mayflower

If you think the voyage on the *Mayflower* was fun, think again! Here is how one writer described it:

The ship is small, wet, and foul. The smells are horrid. There is no place to change or wash clothes. Each adult [has] a space below deck measuring seven by two and a half feet. Children get even less room. None of the passengers is allowed on deck; there is little fresh air below and many are sick. Fresh food soon runs out and then there is hard bread and dried meat that is wet and moldy. But the Pilgrims have onions, lemon juice, and beer to keep them from getting . . . **scurvy**.

—Joy Hakim

With a ruler or yardstick, measure seven feet long and two and a half feet wide on the floor. Mark the space with yarn. That is how much room each person had below deck of the Mayflower. *Can you see why the people wanted to go up on deck?*

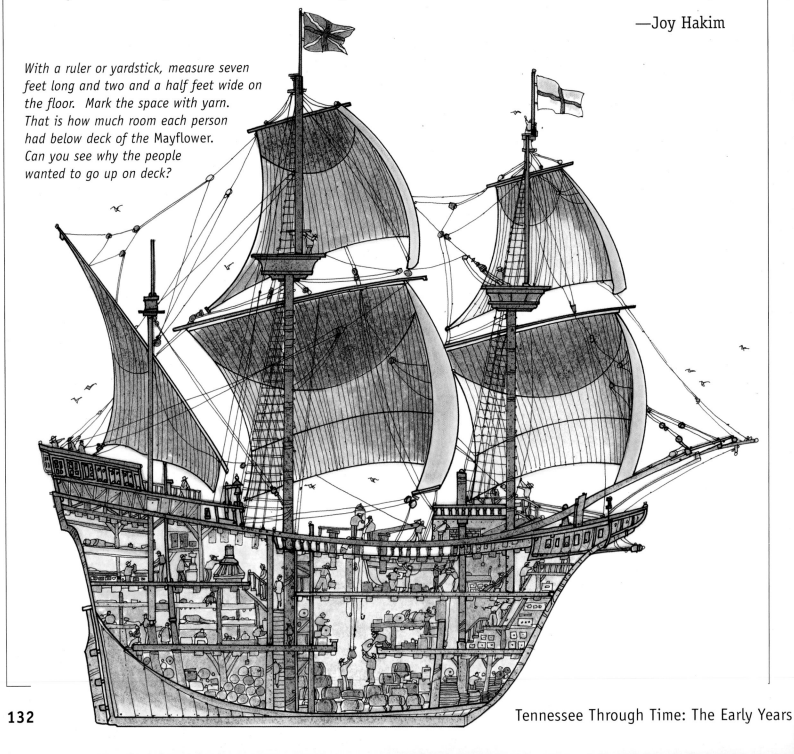

Tennessee Through Time: The Early Years

The Pilgrims were thankful they had finally reached land. Some people knelt and offered prayers right there on the shore.

Coming Ashore

The Pilgrims traveled as families. That meant men, women, and children all made the trip together. After going ashore, they thanked God for getting them safely across the ocean. They gazed at the miles and miles of empty sand dunes stretching along Cape Cod. William Bradford was there. He wrote:

> *They now had no friends to welcome them . . . nor houses or much less towns to [go] to . . . it was winter, and they that know the winters of that country know them to be sharp and violent . . . besides what could they see but a . . . wilderness before them . . . if they looked behind them, there was the mighty ocean which they had passed!*

Settling Plymouth

The Pilgrims struggled to start a colony. They spent most of the first winter on the boat, but there was no heat. About half the Pilgrims became sick and died. In the spring, Indians came to the little settlement the Pilgrims had built on the shore. The Indians taught them how to plant corn, beans, and squash. They showed them better ways to fish and hunt. They also taught the Pilgrims how to trade with other Indians and sailors.

What Do You Think

Can you imagine moving with your family to a wilderness? Everywhere you would look there would only be nature. What do you think you would do first?

New Hampshire

Three years after the Pilgrims arrived, a group of fishermen settled in the land north of the Pilgrims. The fishermen built a fort, and more settlers joined them. They wanted to build a successful fishing colony. About 60 years later, New Hampshire became a separate colony.

New Jersey

In 1623, a Dutch explorer named Cornelius Mey explored the Delaware Bay region. Mey started a trading post called Fort Nassau (later known as Camden). A year later, Mey returned with a few families and started a colony.

The Dutch had a hard time getting people to settle in the new colony. They began giving large pieces of land to Dutch men. Each of these men agreed to bring 50 people to settle on their piece of land. The new colonists were not all Dutch. Germans, Swedes, Finns, and English settlers also came. Slowly the colony began to grow.

New Sweden

Several years later, people from Sweden bought a very large piece of land south of the Dutch settlement. They called the region New Sweden and built a fort called Fort Christina in what is now the state of Delaware. The settlers who settled there were mostly from Finland. They traded with the Indians for land, furs, and other goods. The Swedes and Finns were honest and fair with the Indians. They set a good example for future settlers.

The End of New Netherland

Do you remember reading how the king of England later gave all of New Netherland to the duke of York? When that happened, it affected the Dutch and Swedish settlements in the region. The duke gave the land between the Hudson and Delaware Rivers to two of his English friends. It became the colony of New Jersey.

In 1683, the first Swedish settlers arrived and began a colony they called New Sweden.

New Settlements

New Hampshire

Hudson River

Delaware River

● New Amsterdam (New York City) Dutch

● Fort Nassau (Camden) Dutch

● Fort Christina (Wilmington, DE) Swedish

Thirteen Colonies in North America

ROBERT E. GOODIER

The Puritans

Ten years after the Pilgrims, another group of English settlers came ashore in New England. This group also came because they did not agree with the Church of England. They were called *Puritans.*

The Massachusetts Bay Colony

The 1,000 Puritans who came to North America were better prepared than the Pilgrims had been. They had a charter to build a settlement in the Massachusetts Bay area. Their leader, John Winthrop, had a dream of a "city on a hill." He made very strict rules that all the citizens had to follow. He wanted to show the world what a good community should be. The Puritans settled Salem and Boston. Boston became the city on a hill Winthrop had hoped for.

Even though the Puritans were prepared, they had a difficult time in the beginning. During the first winter, 200 people died. Many others returned to England.

Family and Education

In spite of the struggles, the Massachusetts Bay Colony grew. The people built towns and formed governments in each one. They held town meetings to make decisions. Families and education were very important to the Puritans. They wanted everyone to work hard and be able to read the Bible.

Map labels:
- Salem (Puritans)
- Massachusetts Bay Colony
- Boston (Puritans)
- Plymouth Colony
- Plymouth (Pilgrims)

Freedom for All?

Some of the Puritan laws were very strict. The Puritans came here for religious freedom, but they did not allow others to have the same freedom.

People who broke the law or disagreed with the Puritan teachings were hanged, whipped, or **branded** with a hot iron. Some were placed in the **pillory** (a wooden frame with holes in it for a person's head and hands) on the village green. A person's head, hands, or feet were locked into the pillary. Other people could pass by and look at the criminals.

An English visitor wrote about some of the punishments:

- *For being drunk, they either whip or . . . fine.*
- *For kissing a woman in the street, they either whip or . . . fine.*
- *For swearing or cursing, they bore through the tongue with a hot iron.*
- *For a gossiping woman, they gag her and tie her to a chair in front of her house.*

No Religious Freedom

The Puritans believed they were special people chosen by God. The leaders of the churches became the government leaders. These leaders did not accept *criticism* because they believed God directed them. They felt everyone should trust in God—and trust in them.

Roger Williams

Roger Williams was a popular Puritan minister in the Massachusetts Bay Colony. He had a gift for languages and spoke English, Latin, Greek, Dutch, French, and Hebrew. He treated the Indians kindly and fairly. Sometimes he stayed with them for days at a time. He learned their language, and they grew to respect him.

Williams disagreed with John Winthrop about many things. He did not think church leaders should be government leaders. Winthrop and other church leaders decided Roger Williams's ideas were wrong. They held a trial and forced him to leave the colony.

Starting the Colony of Rhode Island

Williams wandered in the wilderness until he found his Indian friends. They showed him beautiful land and told him he could settle there. He paid them seven beads for the land. Williams and 12 followers started the colony of Rhode Island.

Can you imagine wandering in the cold, like Roger Williams, with no place to go? Would you be scared?

The Swedish colonists traded with the Delaware Indians at New Sweden.

Delaware

In 1631, more Dutch settlers came to North America. They settled many miles south of the English colonies. The Dutch started a trading post, but within a year everyone in the colony had been killed by Indians. Seven years later, the king of Sweden sent people from Sweden, Finland, and Holland to start a colony in the same location on the Delaware River. Today, the region is known as Delaware. After the Swedish rebuilt the colony, the Dutch took control of it once again.

Connecticut

English settlers from the Massachusetts colonies settled the first three towns in the colony of Connecticut. The towns were Windsor, Wethersfield, and Hartford.

Windsor and Wethersfield

Edward Winslow left Plymouth Colony in 1633 to find land the Indians had told him about. The Indians said the land was full of fish and animals that could be hunted for furs. Winslow found the fertile land and bought it from the Indians. He wrote to his friends in Massachusetts and told them to follow him. More settlers arrived, and the town of Windsor began to grow. Settlers soon built a second town called Wethersfield.

Edward Winslow bought land from the Indians and started the town of Windsor.

Hartford

That same year, the Dutch built a trading post in the region that later became Hartford. In 1636, Thomas Hooker led 100 settlers from the Massachusetts Bay Colony to the same region. The settlers left Massachusetts because there was more land for farming and raising cattle. Another reason the settlers went was because they believed God wanted them to live there. Today, their settlement is the city of Hartford.

The Fundamental Orders

People in Windsor, Wethersfield, and Hartford followed rules and laws they brought with them from the Massachusetts colonies. After a few years, the townspeople wanted their own government. Thomas Hooker gave a powerful speech about the things he believed. The people listened to him and began writing a new set of laws. They called these laws the Fundamental Orders. This was the first written *constitution* in the colonies. A constitution is a set of rules and laws for government.

The Three River Towns

Men from the three river towns met at Hartford to write the Fundamental Orders.

The New England Colonies

After many years, the Plymouth and Massachusetts Bay Colonies joined together. They became one large colony called Massachusetts. Massachusetts, Rhode Island, Connecticut, and New Hampshire became known as the New England colonies.

Colonial Credit

The early colonists used little money. Instead they traded goods they had for goods they didn't have. For example, farmers traded eggs and vegetables for shoes. But sometimes trading didn't work. What if the shoemaker already had enough eggs and vegetables? Then the farmer had to offer something else the shoemaker wanted.

Sometimes colonists paid with tobacco, which was very valuable. Other times they used English, Spanish, or French coins. The colonists got the coins by selling things to people in faraway places. Sometimes the colonies printed slips of paper called bills of credit. **Credit** is a promise to pay for something in the future.

Farmers used bills of credit to do business with store owners. For example, a planter might get supplies from a store. He signed a bill of credit to pay for the supplies. The bill of credit said he owed the store owner the value of his next crop. After the planter sold his crop, he paid back the store.

Some people got into trouble with credit. They bought more than they could pay for. In England, people who could not pay their **debts** were sent to prison. Many of them went to North America as indentured servants.

Linking the Present to the Past

Many people today get into trouble with credit. They buy things thinking that they will be able to pay for them later. Sometimes people get sick or lose their jobs. Then they cannot pay for the things they bought on credit. How do you feel about buying things on credit? When is credit good? How can credit be abused?

1 MEMORY MASTER

1. What is a charter?
2. What is an indentured servant?
3. Name three colonies established during this period.

King Philip's War

As the New England colonies grew, people built more towns. The Indians watched as the colonists cut down more trees to make homes. The colonists cleared more fields to plant crops. They scared away many woodland animals. It became harder for the tribes to find unspoiled land. The Indians decided to fight for their land.

Metacom was the chief of the Wampanoag tribe of the Massachusetts region. The colonists called him King Philip. He brought all the tribes in the area together to fight the colonists. These tribes were called Algonquian Indians.

The war between the Algonquians and the colonists was called King Philip's War. It lasted for more than a year. Both sides fought hard, and many people were killed, but the Indians lost the war. The colonists killed King Philip and posted his head on a stake.

After the colonists had first arrived, they probably would not have survived without help. But before long, the colonists treated the Indians as though they were in the way. The people who had lived on the land for thousands of years were forced to move.

PEOPLE TO KNOW

Algonquian Indians
George Calvert, Lord
   Baltimore
King Philip
William Penn
Quakers
Scots Irish
Wampanoag Indians

PLACES TO LOCATE

Middle Colonies
New England Colonies
Southern Colonies

WORDS TO UNDERSTAND

treaty

Colonists attack an Indian village during King Philip's War, which was the bloodiest of the colonial wars.

The Southern Colonies

More groups from England traveled to North America and built colonies along the southeastern coast. These colonies included Maryland, North Carolina, South Carolina, and Georgia. Along with Virginia, they became known as the Southern colonies.

Most of the people in the Southern colonies were farmers. Many owned small farms and ran them themselves. But there were also wealthy plantations with many slaves.

Maryland

After Virginia, the next Southern colony established by England was Maryland. George Calvert, Lord Baltimore, a devout Catholic, had to give up his government job in England because of his religion. To make up for the lost job, the king of England gave Calvert land in North America. Calvert named the colony Maryland and decided there would not be one official church. All Christians could worship freely. Many Catholics came to live in Maryland.

Hundreds of Maryland's earliest settlers were indentured servants. In England, they had been in prison because they could not pay their debts. The colonies offered a way out of prison—and out of England. The English government allowed prisoners to move to Maryland as indentured servants.

The Carolinas

The next colony settled by the English was Carolina. In the beginning, North and South Carolina were one colony. Many Englishmen built large rice plantations in Carolina. Most of these men had been living in Barbados, an island in the Caribbean. When they came to Carolina, they brought hundreds of black slaves with them. Before these people became slaves, they had grown rice for generations in Africa. Their knowledge of rice farming and their hard work helped the colony become very successful.

The first city in Carolina, Charles Town, was very different from other colonial cities. The local culture in Charles Town seemed more like Barbados than England.

George Calvert

Yankee Traders

Because trade was so important in the North, southerners began calling northerners "Yankees Traders." No one is certain where the word "Yankee" came from, but there are at least two possibilities. One is that Yankee is a combination of two Dutch names, "Jan" and "Kees." Supposedly, the Dutch began calling the people who moved to New England Jan-Kees. The other possibility is that Yankee is a version of an Indian word for white man, "yancey."

Georgia plantations had many workers. It did not take them long to build large, roomy houses.

Georgia

The last Southern colony settled by the British was Georgia. James Oglethorpe wanted to build a colony that would protect the British colonies from Spanish Florida. The king of Great Britain feared the Spanish, so he quickly agreed to the charter for Georgia.

Oglethorpe wanted strong, hard-working farmers to guard the border. For this reason, slavery was not allowed in the Georgia colony. Oglethorpe knew if slavery were allowed, the slaves would become strong and healthy—not the landowners. As they had in the other colonies, many of Great Britain's poorest people moved to Georgia.

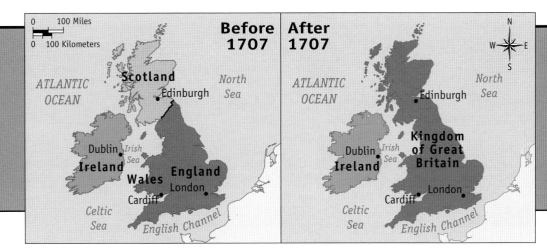

Before 1707, England was a separate country from Wales and Scotland. England's colonies in North America were English colonies.

After 1707, England joined with Wales and Scotland to form one large country called Great Britain. The English colonies were now British colonies.

English or British?

In 1707, England, Scotland, and Wales joined together and formed one country. The country was called Great Britain. After that, the English were called British.

Pennsylvania

New York, New Jersey, Delaware, and Pennsylvania became known as the Middle colonies. These were the most diverse of the colonies in North America. They proved that many different kinds of people could live together. The last of the Middle colonies to be settled was Pennsylvania.

Pennsylvania's founder, William Penn, was born to a wealthy family in London. His father was an officer in the king's royal navy. When Penn's father died, the king owed him money. Penn asked the king to give him a land grant in North America instead of money. Penn wanted the land so he could create a colony for members of his church, the **Quakers.**

People in England did not like the Quakers and often mistreated them. Penn wanted religious freedom in his colony. He called the colony his "holy experiment."

The king gave Penn a huge land grant. It was larger than all of England! Penn named the colony Pennsylvania, which means "Penn's woods." The name was Penn's way of honoring his father.

Philadelphia

Penn and a group of Quakers crossed the ocean and sailed up the Delaware River. Penn chose a spot on the river to build the capital of

Has anyone ever made fun of you? In England, people often made fun of the Quakers. They hoped to find peace by moving to the colonies.

his colony. He called the city Philadelphia, which means "the city of brotherly love." Penn planned and organized the city carefully.

The colony began to grow immediately. People from Germany, Scotland, France, and other countries moved there. They liked the freedom they had in Philadelphia. Some people said Pennsylvania was the "best poor man's country." Many indentured servants came to the colony. Philadelphia quickly became the largest city in the colonies.

William Penn felt the Indians owned their territory. He gave them money and goods in exchange for a large piece of the land.

Respect for the Indians

Pennsylvania was different from most of the other colonies because the colonists cooperated with the Indians. William Penn believed Indians should be treated with respect. When he arrived, he met with them and signed a *treaty*. The treaty said Penn would buy, not take, the land.

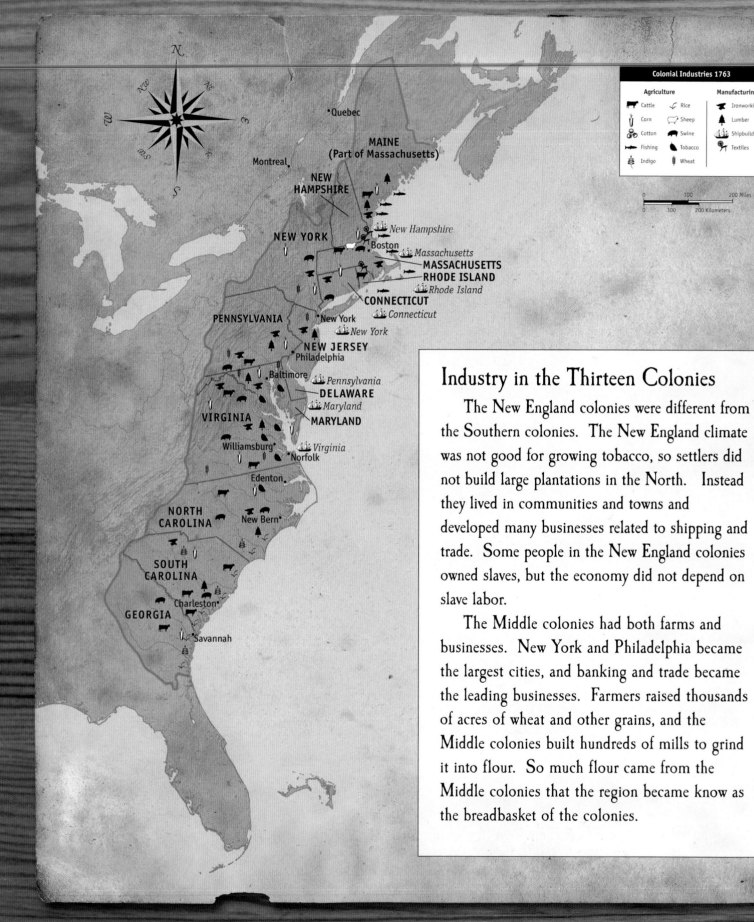

Colonial Industries 1763

Agriculture

- Cattle
- Corn
- Cotton
- Fishing
- Indigo
- Rice
- Sheep
- Swine
- Tobacco
- Wheat

Manufacturing

- Ironworking
- Lumber
- Shipbuilding
- Textiles

Quebec

Montreal

MAINE
(Part of Massachusetts)

NEW HAMPSHIRE

NEW YORK

New Hampshire

Boston

Massachusetts

MASSACHUSETTS

RHODE ISLAND

Rhode Island

CONNECTICUT

Connecticut

New York

New York

PENNSYLVANIA

NEW JERSEY

Philadelphia

Baltimore

Pennsylvania

DELAWARE

Maryland

MARYLAND

VIRGINIA

Williamsburg

Virginia

Norfolk

Edenton

NORTH CAROLINA

New Bern

SOUTH CAROLINA

Charleston

GEORGIA

Savannah

Industry in the Thirteen Colonies

The New England colonies were different from the Southern colonies. The New England climate was not good for growing tobacco, so settlers did not build large plantations in the North. Instead they lived in communities and towns and developed many businesses related to shipping and trade. Some people in the New England colonies owned slaves, but the economy did not depend on slave labor.

The Middle colonies had both farms and businesses. New York and Philadelphia became the largest cities, and banking and trade became the leading businesses. Farmers raised thousands of acres of wheat and other grains, and the Middle colonies built hundreds of mills to grind it into flour. So much flour came from the Middle colonies that the region became know as the breadbasket of the colonies.

The Scots Irish

After the first 13 colonies were established, another group of people wanted to leave England. They were the Scots Irish. They were called Scots Irish because the English had forced them to leave Scotland and move to Ireland. They did not like living in Ireland, however, because the Irish were Catholic. The Scots Irish were Presbyterians.

Like the Pilgrims and Puritans, the Scots Irish did not think church and government should be combined. Many decided to move to North America.

Which Colony?

When the first Scots Irish arrived in North America, they did not want to go to the Southern colonies. They did not feel comfortable around so many members of the Church of England. They also did not want to go to New England because they did not want to live near the Puritans. Many Scots Irish moved to Pennsylvania, where there was religious freedom. Since most of them were very poor, they came as indentured servants.

The Scots Irish were convinced they could have better lives in the colonies, but it was hard to leave home.

The Scots Irish were hard working and independent. They took care of themselves. The men knew how to cut down trees and quickly build cabins. The women knew how to milk cows and make butter. They also knew how to make cloth from wool and plant fibers.

The Scots Irish wanted land of their own and were willing to move onto Indian lands to get it. The Indian lands were like the land they had left at home, so the Scots Irish left the colonies. They moved across the mountains and down into the western river valleys. Some of the first settlers in Tennessee were Scots Irish.

Across the Mountains

The Scots Irish were not the only people to settle in the West. People from all the colonies began spreading out. They traveled into the mountains and farther beyond to trade with the Indians. It wasn't long before they began settling there too.

Englishmen James Needham and Gabriel Arthur traveled into the region that became Tennessee to trade with the Indians. They arrived in Cherokee territory in 1673. That was the same year Marquette and Jolliet traveled down the Mississippi River.

Trade Agreements

The English did not want the Cherokees to trade with anyone else. Seven Cherokee chiefs traveled to England to see the king. Among them was Attakullakulla, or the Little Carpenter. The king convinced the Cherokees to trade only with the English.

PASSPORT TO HISTORY

Do you think you would survive as a colonist? Pretend you have a chance to go to America as an indentured servant. Outline your plan for success and get a stamp in your passport by answering these questions:

1. Where will you live when you get to America? Why?
2. What will you do for a living?
3. What will you eat? How will you get it?
4. When your time as a servant is up, what will you do with the clothing, tools, and piece of land you have been given?

2 MEMORY MASTER

1. Why was King Philip's War fought?
2. Which country established the Maryland, Georgia, and Carolina colonies?
3. How were the New England colonies and the Southern colonies different?

These are the Cherokee chiefs who traveled to England. Why do you think they agreed to make the long journey to a foreign land?

Thirteen Colonies in North America

The British and the colonists worked together during the French and Indian War. They fought against the French and the Indians.

The French and Indian War

As more settlers from the colonies moved westward, the French moved south from Canada. The British and the French soon met in Ohio Territory. The wealth in the New World had made the European nations jealous of one another. This led to wars over control of the land.

The French built a fort at the fork of the Ohio River. The British colony of Virginia also claimed this land. British officials sent George Washington, a 21-year-old *surveyor,* to draw maps of the region. He and his men were also told to force the French to leave.

The Fighting Begins

In 1754, Washington traveled to the fort and told the French to leave. When they refused, fighting broke out. The Indians also did not want the British in Ohio Territory. They knew that wherever the British settled, the Indians were forced out. They knew the British settlers did not want to share the land.

The French were different from the British. The Indians enjoyed trading with the French. Many Frenchmen had married Indian women and lived peacefully on Indian lands.

The Creeks decided to help the French drive out the British. At the same time, the Cherokees decided to help the British. This caused great conflict between the Cherokees and the Creeks. They raided one another's villages and killed hundreds of people. The colonists called the war the French and Indian War because they fought both the French and the Indians.

Great Britain sent an army of soldiers to North America. Their general, Edward Braddock, did not know how to fight in this land. His men wore bright red coats that were easy to see. They marched in a straight line. The French and Indians fought differently. They did not march into battle. They hid behind rocks and trees when they attacked.

During the many years of the war, the British sent more soldiers and more generals. They soon learned the ways of their enemies. This helped them win many battles.

Nancy Ward
(1738–1822)

Nanye-hi, known throughout history as Nancy Ward, was Attakullakulla's niece. In her teens, she married Kingfisher, a Cherokee warrior. She had two young children by the time she was 17.

When the Cherokee raided a Creek village, Nanye-hi went with her husband into battle. As she fought, she sang a Cherokee war song. She also chewed sharp ridges into the lead bullets for her husband's rifle. The ridges made the bullets more deadly because they tore flesh. When Kingfisher was killed, Nanye-hi picked up his weapon and continued to fight. Her actions inspired other Cherokees to continue the fight as well.

After the battle, the Cherokees named Nanye-hi as a Beloved Woman of the tribe. As a Beloved Woman, tribe members listened to her. She settled disputes among the people, and they treated her with respect. She even attended the Cherokee Council of Chiefs and helped make decisions about war. Nanye-hi later took the name of her second husband, a white trader named Bryan Ward and became known as Nancy Ward.

In her later years, Nancy Ward was known as Granny Ward because she took care of so many children. Eventually she was forced to leave her homeland. She ran an inn for a few years and died at the age of 84. She is buried on a hill near Benton, Tennessee.

Fort Loudoun

During the French and Indian War, the Cherokees asked Great Britain to build a fort in the West. The Indians wanted British soldiers to help protect them from the French and the Creeks. In exchange for building the fort, the Cherokees agreed to go into Ohio Territory to fight the French. The British built Fort Loudoun on the Little Tennessee River in Cherokee territory. Troops from the South Carolina *militia* went to Fort Loudoun when it was finished.

At first, the Cherokees liked having the fort nearby. They went often to visit and trade with the British. But things soon changed. In South Carolina, the British killed 29 Cherokee warriors. The Indians decided that having Fort Loudoun on their land was a mistake.

The Cherokees surrounded the fort so the people inside could not get food. Soon the settlers were starving. Many were also dying from the heat. They surrendered the fort and asked the Cherokees to let them return to South Carolina. The Cherokees agreed, so the soldiers and their families packed up and headed out. They had been traveling only a day when more than 700 Cherokees suddenly attacked. They killed 29 British settlers—one for each Cherokee warrior who had died—and took the rest prisoner.

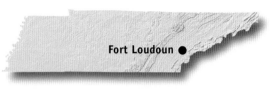

Fort Loudoun

Fort Loudoun was the first fort built on the land that later became Tennessee.

The Iroquois League

Benjamin Franklin believed the 13 colonies needed to work together since a war was being fought in North America. At a meeting in New York, Franklin suggested that the colonies come together like the Iroquois Indians had.

The Iroquois were a powerful group of first five and then six Indian nations that lived in the Northeast. They called themselves the Iroquois League of Nations. The Iroquois wrote a constitution and formed a central government. The constitution gave power to the government, not to individuals. It described how to choose leaders and how to conduct business. The Iroquois did not want anyone to be unhappy with the group's decisions. They held meetings until everyone agreed.

The league worked well for the Iroquois, but none of the colonies wanted to be a part of such a group. They did not want a central government. The colonists voted against Franklin's suggestion, but they remembered his ideas. They realized they could work together if they ever needed to.

In this picture, Iroquois leaders meet and recite the laws of the Iroquois League.

The Treaty of Paris of 1763

After nine years of fighting, the French finally surrendered. Leaders from Great Britain, France, and Spain met in Paris and signed a treaty to end the war. France gave Spain all the land it claimed in North America west of the Mississippi River. France gave Great Britain all the land east of the Mississippi River. Part of that land was the place we now call Tennessee. The British Empire became twice as big as it had been before the French and Indian War.

Many Indian tribes lived on the land between the Appalachian Mountains and the Mississippi River. They were not invited to Paris to attend the meetings between Great Britain and France. Because of the attack at Fort Loudoun, the Cherokees and British were now enemies. With the French gone, the British did not need help from the Indians anymore.

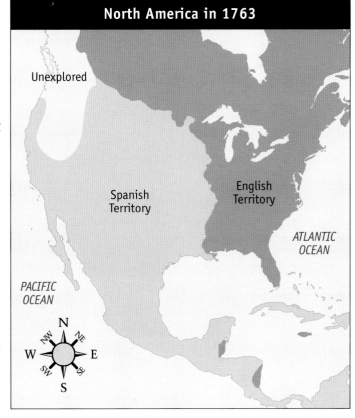

North America in 1763

Unexplored

Spanish Territory

English Territory

ATLANTIC OCEAN

PACIFIC OCEAN

N
NW NE
W E
SW SE
S

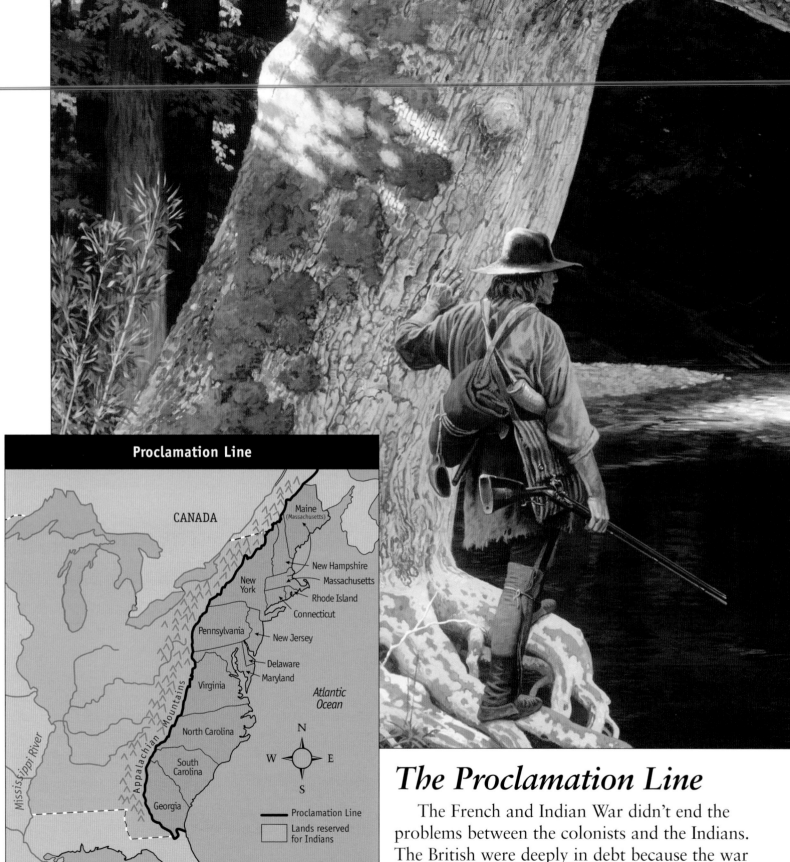

Proclamation Line

CANADA

Maine
(Massachusetts)

New Hampshire
Massachusetts
New York
Rhode Island
Connecticut
Pennsylvania
New Jersey
Delaware
Maryland
Virginia
North Carolina
South Carolina
Georgia

Appalachian Mountains

Mississippi River

Atlantic Ocean

N
W — E
S

— Proclamation Line
☐ Lands reserved for Indians

The Proclamation Line

The French and Indian War didn't end the problems between the colonists and the Indians. The British were deeply in debt because the war had cost a lot of money. The king could not afford to pay British troops to protect the colonists who settled on Indian land.

Some long hunters spent so much time in nature that they could predict what animals would do.

Dr. Thomas Walker traveled through the Cumberland Gap and into Tennessee. He canoed down the Cumberland River and named it in honor of the English Duke of Cumberland.

The Proclamation Line made many people angry. They ignored the new law and settled west of the Appalachians anyway.

The Long Hunters

Some of the first white men to cross the mountains were *long hunters.* They earned this name because they were gone for months at a time. The long hunters made friends with the Indians and traded with them. The long hunters also drew maps. They learned a great deal about the western lands.

Long hunters were able to cross the mountains safely because they discovered a mountain pass. The pass became known as the Cumberland Gap. Many long hunters explored the mountains and then went through the Cumberland Gap into Kentucky. Along the way, they hunted animals and gathered furs.

Down the Cumberland and Mississippi Rivers

Kasper Mansker was a long hunter who went south out of Kentucky to the French Lick. He and other long hunters used the Cumberland, Ohio, and Mississippi Rivers to travel to Natchez. There they sold the furs they had collected.

The king thought of a better way to keep the Indians and the settlers from fighting. On a map of North America, he drew a line along the tops of the Appalachian Mountains. The line became known as the Proclamation Line. The king said settlers could not move onto the land west of the line. That would be Indian Territory.

Land Speculators

A group of men called *land speculators* wanted to buy huge pieces of the land between the Appalachians and the Mississippi River. They hoped to divide it into smaller pieces and sell the pieces to other people. They planned to make a lot of money.

Daniel Boone and other long hunters explored the land and came to know the region well. Richard Henderson, a land speculator, hired Daniel Boone to look for land for him.

The Legends of Thomas Sharp Spencer

Thomas Sharp Spencer was a long hunter who went to Middle Tennessee and decided to stay. Spencer was a colorful character, and many legends were told about him. One of the legends was about a hunter who saw Spencer's footprints on the ground. Spencer had very large feet. The hunter who saw the footprints did not think a man could have made them. He told other hunters that giants lived in the Cumberland region. Another story about Spencer described how he lived for an entire winter in a hollow tree.

Daniel Boone
1734–1820

Daniel Boone was born in Pennsylvania and grew up in North Carolina. He married Rebecca Bryan, and they had 10 children. During the French and Indian War, Boone drove a wagon for the British army. He was very skilled with a gun. After the war, he began traveling across the mountains into the wilderness to hunt.

Daniel Boone built a settlement in Kentucky, but he also hunted in Tennessee. He was a great storyteller. When he returned home from his trips, he told wonderful stories about the things he had seen. He described the land across the mountains as being beautiful, with rich soil and many animals.

On one trip, Shawnee Indians stole Boone's furs and warned him never to return. The warning did not stop him. He opened the Wilderness Road and built Fort Boonesborough. Boone was once captured by the Shawnee. He lived with them for almost a year, and the Shawnee chief adopted him.

Boone finally escaped and lived the rest of his life with his wife and children.

The Watauga Settlements

Many people heard the long hunters' stories and decided to move across the mountains. Some wanted new land because they thought the soil in the colonies was getting worn out. Others did not like the rules and laws of the colonial government. They also believed they could get land across the mountains without having to pay for it.

William Bean, a Virginian, moved into the Watauga River region in what is now East Tennessee. Bean and his wife, Lydia, built a cabin on Boone's Creek where it flowed into the Watauga River. They were careful about deciding where to build their cabin. They wanted it to be hidden from Indians as they paddled down the river.

William and Lydia Bean cleared land and began to farm. Long hunters often stopped and visited at the Bean cabin. Settlers later moved across the mountains and joined the Beans. The region became known as the Watauga settlements. Some say the Beans were the first permanent white settlers in the land that became Tennessee.

3 MEMORY MASTER

1. Who fought in the French and Indian War?
2. What was the Iroquois League?
3. What was the Proclamation Line?

Chapter 5 Review

What's the Point?

Countries, such as Holland, England, and Sweden, established colonies in the New World. Several colonies were self-governed. New England colonies had towns, businesses, seaports, and small farms. Southern colonies had big farms, plantations, and slaves. With many groups living in the colonies, conflicts arose. In King Philip's War, Native Americans tried to drive European settlers out of the land. During the French and Indian War, the British tried to drive out the French. Many Indians fought alongside the French. Long hunters and surveyors explored the western lands. The king of England outlawed settlements west of the Appalachians. The Bean family settled along the Watauga River, establishing the first permanent settlement in the land that is now Tennessee.

Becoming Better Readers

Taking Notes

Do you know how good readers organize and remember what they read? They take notes. When taking notes, you shouldn't write down everything. You should just keep track of main ideas. In this chapter, you read about the 13 colonies. On a piece of paper, write the names of all the colonies or settlements you read about. Then next to each name, write a clue that helps you remember that colony. For example, next to "Georgia" you could write "Last Southern colony started by Great Britain." After you complete your notes, compare them with a neighbor's notes. Did you write any of the same clues?

Climbing to Connections

Colonial Settlement

1. Name three reasons for colonial settlement.
2. Distinguish between economic freedom and religious freedom.
3. Demonstrate your understanding of the ways colonists had more freedom in America than in their own countries.
4. Explain how colonists exercised religious freedom.
5. Make predictions about what will happen as more people settle in the colonies.
6. Measure the importance of basic needs against the idea of freedom. If colonists had no food or money, would other reasons for coming to America be important? Why or why not?

— Evaluation Station —

The Mayflower Compact

The Mayflower Compact gave the people power to govern themselves. What made the Mayflower Compact the first colonial government in the United States? To answer this question, your class should divide into two groups. One group should study the Mayflower Compact, and the other group should study the definition of government. Then the groups should come together and answer the original question in a class discussion.

— Activity —

The Meeting

Many different cultures lived together in the 13 colonies. Can you name all of them? Pick two of the cultures. In small groups, act out what you think happened when these two cultures first met.

— Activity —

Rivers and the 13 Colonies

1. What does this map show?
2. Why were the 13 colonies located along the Atlantic Ocean?
3. Why was location near water important to the settlers?
4. How did the early settlers use the rivers?
5. In which region of the colonies is Plymouth?
6. In which region of the colonies is Jamestown?

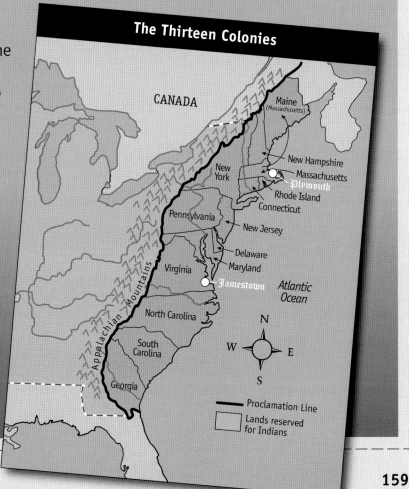

"*You have bought a fair land, but you will find its settlement dark and bloody.*"

—*Dragging Canoe at Sycamore Shoals, 1775*

The American Revolution

Delegates from every state had to approve the Declaration of Independence. Why do you think everyone needed to agree?

Timeline of Events

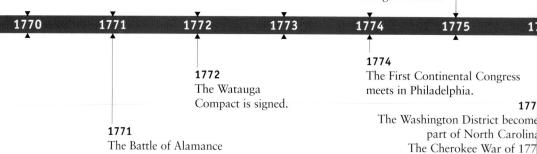

1775
Richard Henderson makes the Transylvania Purchase (Treaty of Sycamore Shoals).
The battles of Lexington and Concord begin the American Revolution.
The Cherokees lease land to settlers in the Watauga Purchase.

| 1770 | 1771 | 1772 | 1773 | 1774 | 1775 | 17 |

1774
The First Continental Congress meets in Philadelphia.

1772
The Watauga Compact is signed.

1771
The Battle of Alamance

177
The Washington District become part of North Carolina
The Cherokee War of 177

Chapter 6

The 13 colonies grew rapidly. British leaders did not want to lose control of them, so they passed new laws that tightened their hold on the colonists. Most of the new laws had to do with paying more taxes, and the colonists hated them. Each time Parliament and the king passed another new tax, the colonies protested.

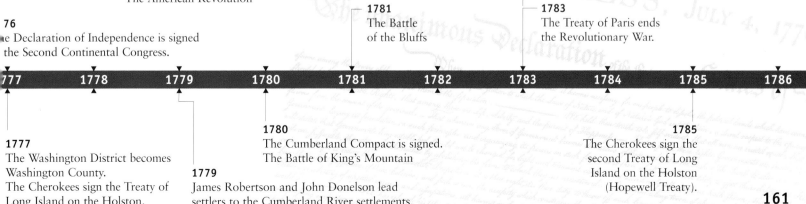

1775–1783
The American Revolution

76
e Declaration of Independence is signed
the Second Continental Congress.

1781
The Battle
of the Bluffs

1783
The Treaty of Paris ends
the Revolutionary War.

777 | 1778 | 1779 | 1780 | 1781 | 1782 | 1783 | 1784 | 1785 | 1786

1777
The Washington District becomes
Washington County.
The Cherokees sign the Treaty of
Long Island on the Holston.

1779
James Robertson and John Donelson lead
settlers to the Cumberland River settlements.

1780
The Cumberland Compact is signed.
The Battle of King's Mountain

1785
The Cherokees sign the
second Treaty of Long
Island on the Holston
(Hopewell Treaty).

LESSON ❶ Trouble with England

PEOPLE TO KNOW

William Bean
Dragging Canoe
Richard Henderson
Little Carpenter
Charlotte Robertson
James Robertson
William Tryon

PLACES TO LOCATE

Alamance Creek
Boston, Massachusetts
Watauga River

WORDS TO UNDERSTAND

boycott
intolerable
lease
quartering
Regulator
riot
shoal
tax

New Taxes

Before the French and Indian War, British Parliament allowed the colonies to grow without many rules. After the war, however, things needed to change. Thousands of miles of land had been added to the British Empire. Great Britain had to protect the land from being taken by another country. This required more soldiers, and the soldiers had to be paid.

Great Britain was already struggling to repay its war debts. There wasn't enough money to take care of everything. The British government decided to raise the colonists' taxes. A *tax* is money people pay to take care of expenses and provide the benefits of government.

The Sugar Act and the Tea Act

Parliament passed a tax on sugar and molasses. Every time the colonists bought sugar they had to pay a little money to the government. The colonists put sugar in their tea, which was a very popular drink. Most colonists drank it every day. The British also put a high tax on tea. The colonists were very unhappy that they had to pay more for these things.

The Stamp Act

Parliament then passed the Stamp Act. This law said certain papers and documents had to have stamps on them. The colonists had to pay for the stamps. Newspapers, books, letters, marriage licenses, and even playing cards had to have stamps. Buying so many stamps was expensive.

These are examples of colonial playing cards. Cards were very popular, so they were taxed by the Stamp Act. The British hoped to make money from the taxes on playing cards.

"No Taxation Without Representation"

When the British created even more new taxes, the colonists began protesting. They marched in the streets and held public meetings. They talked about how to solve the problems with England. The colonists felt they were being treated unfairly. They felt their rights were being ignored.

People in the colonies were not just angry about paying taxes. They were also angry that they did not have a say in the new laws that were passed in Great Britain. The colonists wanted to send representatives to speak for them in Parliament. Great Britain, however, did not allow the colonists to send anyone to speak for them.

The colonists felt this was unfair because Parliament made rules and laws the colonies had to obey. The rallying cry in the colonies became, "No taxation without representation!" That meant, "We won't pay taxes until we are allowed to help make the tax laws!"

The Colonists Protest

The colonists refused to pay the stamp tax. They wrote letters to Great Britain saying it was unfair. Colonial women organized **boycotts** and stopped buying items that were being taxed. Most colonists also stopped drinking tea. Sometimes they attacked British tax collectors. The colonists poured hot tar on them and covered the tar with feathers. The tar was very difficult and painful to remove.

Colonists were angry over the taxes. In this drawing, they are arguing with the British tax collectors.

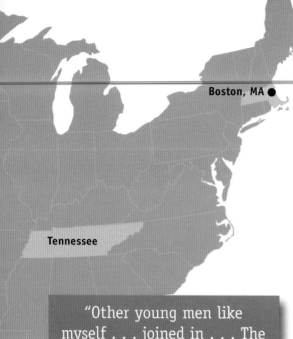

The Boston Tea Party

The protests finally worked, and the British stopped most of the taxes. There was only one left—the tax on tea. One night in Boston, Massachusetts, a group of men marched down to the wharf where the tea ships were docked. Some of the men were dressed up like Indians. They split into groups and boarded the ships.

First they took the captain and crew below deck. Then they cracked open the heavy chests of tea and dumped them into the water. They ruined thousands of dollars worth of tea that night. This event became known as the Boston Tea Party.

The British were angry. They wanted to punish the colonists. They closed the port of Boston until the people paid for the spoiled tea. No ships could move in or out of the harbor. Boston was a busy trading city, so closing the port hurt the colonists.

The Intolerable Acts

The British sent more soldiers to Massachusetts. New British laws said the colonists had to feed the soldiers and allow them to stay in their houses. This was called *quartering* of troops. Many colonists felt it was very wrong for soldiers to stay in their homes. They called the new laws the Intolerable Acts. *Intolerable* means unbearable.

"Other young men like myself . . . joined in . . . The chests were . . . opened, the tea emptied over the side, and the chests thrown overboard.

"Although there were many people on the wharf, [there was] no talking. Nothing was [touched] but the teas . . . the deck was swept clean and everything put in its proper place."

—Robert Sessions' diary

This painting shows groups of people gathering to throw tea into the harbor. The quote above is a first-hand description of this event from someone who was there. It is a primary source. The painting was created by someone who was not at the Boston Tea Party. It is a secondary source. In what way does it show a different view of what happened that night?

Governor William Tryon did not like the Regulators.
He believed they were unruly and dangerous.

The Regulators

While most colonists stayed in the colonies and protested, a few crossed the mountains and settled in western North Carolina. They wanted land of their own, but they did not want to pay more taxes. Several Scots Irish who lived in the western mountains organized a group known as the *Regulators.* These people wanted to decide, or regulate, their own taxes. They held protests, which sometimes turned into *riots.*

Some people thought the Regulators were an angry mob. The governor of North Carolina, William Tryon, ordered the group to break up. The Regulators refused, however, because they believed they had a right to protest. Governor Tryon sent the militia to take care of the problem.

The Battle of Alamance

Tryon's army of 1,000 men met 2,000 Regulators on a field near Hillsborough, North Carolina. Although the Regulators had more men, they were not trained soldiers. They did not have military weapons and lost after a short battle. It was called the Battle of Alamance because it was near Alamance Creek. Many frontiersmen fled to Tennessee after this battle.

North Carolina

Battle of
Alamance Creek

The Watauga Settlements

After the Battle of Alamance, Regulator James Robertson and his wife, Charlotte, traveled farther west and crossed the Proclamation Line. Several other Regulator families went with them. They wanted to get away from the colonies and the British laws. They were not wealthy farmers, but a few owned slaves and brought them along. The group settled at Watauga near William Bean's cabin. They built cabins on land that belonged to the Indians.

Watauga settlements ●

The Watauga Purchase

The Cherokees did not like the settlers taking their land. James Robertson and William Bean went to talk with Little Carpenter (Attakullakulla) and the other Cherokee chiefs about the problem. At the meeting, the Cherokees agreed to *lease* the land to the settlers for

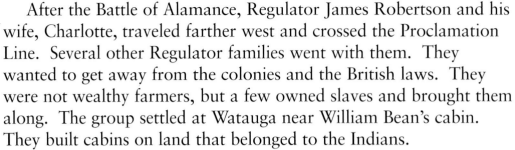

James Robertson
(1742–1814)

James Robertson was born in Virginia, but he is called the Father of Middle Tennessee. He married Charlotte Reeves, and the couple had 13 children. When Robertson was 27, he set out to explore the mountains west of the colonies. Like George Washington, he was a surveyor. Like Daniel Boone, he was a long hunter who worked for Richard Henderson.

Robertson came to know the land across the Appalachians well. He claimed some of it and planted corn. He also built a cabin to show the land belonged to him. Robertson became friendly with the Cherokees and learned to speak their language. They learned to trust him. He soon had the respect of both the settlers and the Indians, and he joined the Regulators.

Several years later, Robertson helped settle and build Fort Nashborough. The settlement was often attacked by Indians. Robertson lost two brothers and two sons in these attacks. Another son was wounded, but he survived. One day, Indians shot Robertson in the foot. Another time, he was shot in both wrists.

In Robertson's later years, the government hired him to help with Indian relations. He traveled across the country, meeting and visiting with different tribes. Robertson died when he was 72. He is buried in Nashville.

ten years. The settlers had to pay the Cherokees with trade goods. This agreement became known as the Watauga Purchase.

The Watauga Compact

A year after the Watauga Purchase, the settlers held a meeting to discuss problems in the settlement. They wrote a document called the Articles of the Watauga Association, or the Watauga Compact. It provided a basic government, rules, and a simple process for settling arguments. It also created a court of five judges, who made decisions for the settlement.

EXPLORE TENNESSEE!

Liberty: The Saga of Sycamore Shoals

On the last three weekends of July, reenactors in Elizabethton put on a two-act play called *Liberty: The Saga of Sycamore Shoals*. The play tells the story of the Watauga settlements. It shows what life was like in northeast Tennessee during these years. Some families travel to Sycamore Shoals every year to see this play.

Have you ever seen a play? The Wataugans gives people a chance to see how life was on the western frontier.

The Transylvania Purchase

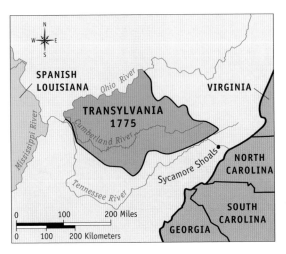

In the last chapter you read about a land speculator named Richard Henderson. Henderson wanted to buy a large piece of land and then sell it in smaller pieces. Since the region was not part of any colony, Henderson hoped to create a 14th colony. He wanted to call it Transylvania, which means "across the woods."

Henderson visited several Overhill Cherokee towns. He offered to buy thousands of acres of land and pay for it with valuable European trade goods. Little Carpenter and Nancy Ward traveled to North Carolina to look at the items the Cherokees would receive. When they returned, they reported that the offer was a good deal for the Indians.

"A Dark and Bloody Ground"

Henderson arranged a meeting with the Cherokees at the Sycamore Shoals of the Watauga River. More than 1,200 Cherokees attended the meeting.

Shoals are places in a river where sharp rocks lie just below the surface of the water. Traveling through shoals can be very dangerous.

A few of the Cherokees disagreed with Little Carpenter's decision to sign the treaty. They believed the treaty was taking away their homeland. One of those who disagreed was Dragging Canoe, Little Carpenter's son. Dragging Canoe tried to warn his father and the rest of the Cherokees of the danger of the agreement. He told them many tribes had already given away their land, and it had "melted away like balls of snow in the sun."

What do you think Dragging Canoe meant when he said the land pictured here was "dark and bloody"?

Dragging Canoe said he and the other young warriors would fight to defend their land. Dragging Canoe warned the settlers, "There is a dark cloud hanging over that country—it is a dark and bloody ground. You will pay a heavy price if you take it from us."

The Treaty of Sycamore Shoals

Little Carpenter and the other chiefs ignored Dragging Canoe. They wanted peace with the settlers, so they signed the treaty. The Cherokees gave Henderson's Transylvania Land Company more than 20 million acres between the Cumberland and Ohio Rivers. The agreement became known as the Transylvania Purchase, or the Treaty of Sycamore Shoals.

Linking the Present to the Past

The land Richard Henderson bought from the Cherokees is now much of central Kentucky and Middle Tennessee. Henderson did not have permission to make the treaty with the Indians. Most of the land he claimed actually belonged to Virginia and North Carolina.

① MEMORY MASTER

1. What is a tax?
2. Who were the Regulators?
3. What did the Cherokees lose in the Treaty of Sycamore Shoals?

Dragging Canoe was very angry when his father signed the treaty.

PEOPLE TO KNOW

John Adams
Benjamin Franklin
Thomas Jefferson
Robert R. Livingston
John Locke
Thomas Paine
Paul Revere
Jean-Jacques Rousseau
Roger Sherman
George Washington

PLACES TO LOCATE

Concord, Massachusetts
Lexington, Massachusetts

WORDS TO UNDERSTAND

American Revolution
betray
delegate
grievance
independent
Loyalist
minuteman
Patriot
revolution
traitor
tyranny

The First Continental Congress

While James Robertson was settling in the western lands, the problems in the colonies continued. People in every colony were unhappy, but they were not working together to find solutions. When British officials closed the port in Boston, the colonists finally realized they needed to work together.

In 1774, 12 of the 13 colonies sent *delegates* to a meeting in Philadelphia. That meeting was called the First Continental Congress. At this meeting, the delegates talked about all the problems they were having with the British government.

Some of the most important men in the colonies attended the First Continental Congress. George Washington was there. So were John Adams and Patrick Henry. The delegates prepared a list of *grievances* and sent it to Great Britain. They agreed to meet again the following year if things did not improve.

The delegates hoped things would get better, but they felt the colonies should prepare for war. The colonists began collecting guns and ammunition. The British also began preparing for war.

What Do You Think ?

By working together, the colonists were able to accomplish much more. Have you ever used teamwork to get something done? Did it make the job easier? How?

Delegates held the First Continental Congress at Independence Hall in Philadelphia.

British Injustice

In the years before the war, the British ignored laws that protected the colonists' legal rights. They also wrote new laws that affected the way the courts worked. Here are just a few of them:

- The British ignored the law that said soldiers could not search houses without an order from a judge. Soldiers searched colonists' homes whenever they wanted.
- The British created courts that did not require jury trials. One judge listened to cases, made decisions, and ordered punishments.
- The British passed a law that said colonists charged with crimes had to appear in court in Great Britain within 60 days. If people did not appear, they could lose all their property and be put to death. Most colonists had no means of traveling to Great Britain.

Many men in the colonies were lawyers. They had spent long years studying the law. When the British began changing laws, the colonial lawyers were outraged. One of the grievances later listed in the Declaration was "for depriving us in many cases, of the benefits of Trial by Jury."

The Fighting Begins

The British knew the colonists had begun working together. They sent more soldiers to Boston to try to maintain control of the Massachusetts colony. When the British soldiers learned guns were hidden in the nearby town of Lexington, they decided to try to take them.

Lexington

Paul Revere, a member of the colonial army, waited on horseback and watched the tower of Boston's Old North Church. A signal—one light if by land, two if by sea—would tell him how the British troops were traveling. When he saw two lanterns, Revere and two other men rode through the night to warn the colonists. By the time British soldiers arrived in Lexington, the colonists were waiting for them.

The British leader told the colonists to put down their guns and go home. The colonists stood their ground. There was shouting on both sides. No one is quite sure what happened next. A shot rang out. Soon more shots were fired. When the smoke cleared, eight colonists lay dead.

Paul Revere was working as an express rider for the Patriots. It was his job to carry news and messages from place to place.

Concord ● ● Lexington

The British were trained soldiers. The Patriots were farmers and ranchers. Some had never shot a gun before.

When the war began, colonial soldiers did not have uniforms. They wore the same shirts, pants, and hats they wore when working at home.

Concord

The British soldiers moved on to Concord. They wanted to take gunpowder and weapons from the colonists. But colonial **minutemen** were waiting there. The colonists called the soldiers "minutemen" because they had to be ready to fight in a minute.

When the British started firing, the colonists shot back. The colonists fired from behind trees, barns, and stone walls. The British were not used to this kind of fighting. They did not know which way to turn and shoot. They were worn out from their long march. Finally they stopped firing.

The Shot Heard Round the World

The battles at Lexington and Concord were the first battles of the **American Revolution.** A poet named Ralph Waldo Emerson later called the shot at Lexington "the shot heard round the world." Emerson's grandfather had watched part of the Battle of Concord. Here are a few lines from Emerson's famous poem:

By the rude bridge that arched the flood,
Their flag to April's breeze unfurled;
Here once the embattled farmers stood;
And fired the shot heard 'round the world.

Today, news travels fast! You can watch events on television as they happen. In the 1700s, news traveled slowly. It took several days for someone to ride from colony to colony, sharing the news. Once news arrived, it was printed in the newspaper. Almost every colony had a newspaper.

Patriots and Loyalists

The colonists did not agree about what to do when the war began. Friends and families argued about fighting with Great Britain. Some people believed the colonies should be *independent,* or free, from Great Britain. These people were called *Patriots.*

Other colonists were loyal to Great Britain and did not want to go to war. They were called *Loyalists.* A few colonists did not want to take sides in the conflict. They just wanted peace.

What Do You Think?

Have you ever heard a gunshot? You can't hear it from very far away. Why do you think Emerson called the shot that started the war "the shot heard round the world"?

A *revolution* is when people succeed in replacing one government with a different government.

Class Debate: Patriot or Loyalist?

If you were one of the colonists, do you think you would choose to be a Loyalist or a Patriot? Divide your class into two groups. One group will be Loyalists. The other group will be Patriots. Each side must give reasons for its decision to support the British or the colonists. You might want to think about these things:

- Were you born in Great Britain or in America?
- Do you still have relatives in Great Britain?
- How have Great Britain's rules and taxes affected you?
- What will happen if Great Britain wins the war?
- What will happen if America wins the war?
- Do you believe people should have the right to choose their own leaders?

To get a stamp in your passport, you must take part in the class discussion.

PASSPORT TO HISTORY

The Declaration of Independence

After the battles of Lexington and Concord, delegates met in Philadelphia again. Their second meeting was called the Second Continental Congress. Many of the delegates believed the 13 colonies should break away from England. They wanted to form an independent country.

The delegates decided to write another letter declaring the colonies' independence from Great Britain. They chose a committee to write it. The people on the committee were Benjamin Franklin, John Adams, Roger Sherman, Robert R. Livingston, and Thomas Jefferson. They quickly decided Thomas Jefferson should do the writing. At 33 years old, he was much younger than the other men. He was shy and did not like to speak in public, but he was an excellent writer.

Writing the Declaration

Thomas Jefferson spent 17 days writing a document called the Declaration of Independence. The words he wrote were clear and easy to understand. The document explained that because the colonists had been treated unfairly, they were cutting all ties with Great Britain.

Jefferson said there were laws higher than the laws of men. He wrote what many people living in the colonies had come to believe:

We hold these truths to be self-evident, that all men are created equal, that they are endowed by their Creator with certain unalienable Rights, that among them are Life, Liberty and the Pursuit of Happiness.

Jefferson listed all the unfair things the king had done to the colonists. He ended the document with this line: "These united colonies are, and of right ought to be, free and independent states."

174

Famous Writers, Circa 1776

Thomas Jefferson realized the Declaration of Independence was one of the most important documents that would ever be written. He knew people all over the world would read it for many years to come. If you had to write such an important document, how would you begin? Jefferson began by studying the writings of some very famous men.

John Locke
One of these men was Englishman John Locke. Locke wrote books and essays on government. He believed a government was only effective if the people supported it. He also believed government should protect "the natural rights of life, liberty, and estate."

Thomas Paine,
an English-born American, was another writer Thomas Jefferson studied. Paine wrote a best-selling pamphlet called *Common Sense*. In the pamphlet, Paine urged the United States to break away from England. He called government "a necessary evil" and said people should be allowed personal freedom.

This is the desk on which Thomas Jefferson wrote the Declaration of Independence.

Jean-Jacques Rousseau
Jefferson studied Jean Jacques Rousseau, a Swiss. Rousseau wrote that if men do not have laws, they become violent and greedy. He said this behavior leads to loss of freedom and death. Rousseau believed that if people worked together, they would remain healthy and free. He said working together helps people think about what is best for everyone, instead of what is best for one person. He also said people will obey laws if they help make them.

John Adams
The last person Jefferson studied was his close friend John Adams. Adams had a great political mind, but he had such strong opinions that many people did not like him. In 1765, he wrote about the evils of *tyranny* and people's power to overcome it. He described rights given to people from "the great Legislator of the universe." Who do you think that is?

Independence Day

What Do You Think?

Many weeks after it was approved, Great Britain's King George received the Declaration of Independence. What do you think he thought when he read it?

On July 4, 1776, the Declaration of Independence was finally adopted by Congress. Every delegate who signed it was now in great danger. By signing the document, they had **betrayed** Great Britain. The British government punished **traitors** with prison time or death.

The 13 colonies now called themselves 13 states. They were on their way to becoming a new country, but it was not going to be easy. The colonists still had to fight a long war.

An Uneven Match

When the war began, it appeared that the British had every advantage. Great Britain was the wealthiest nation in the world. Its

Linking the Present to the Past

Do you and your family watch fireworks on the Fourth of July? Most Americans do. They also celebrate with parades and picnics. They are celebrating the day the colonies declared independence from Great Britain.

Officers of the Continental army rode on horseback from camp to camp, checking on the troops. Soldiers remained outdoors in every kind of weather.

army was large and well trained. There were already thousands of British soldiers in the colonies when the war began.

The Continental Army

By contrast, the colonies did not have a real army. Each state had a militia, but these troops were not professional soldiers. They did not even have uniforms. General George Washington had the difficult job of training country farmers to become skilled soldiers.

The Continental army was not as well-trained as the British, but it had other strengths. One such strength was General George Washington. He was a fair-minded general, and his soldiers had great respect for him. Another strength was the Continental army's commitment to their cause. They were fighting for their freedom and for the future freedom of their children.

British Strategy

After the fighting began, the British developed a plan to quickly end the war. They cut off communication between New England and the rest of the colonies. They believed the other colonies would quickly surrender if they could not work together. But the British did not know George Washington was so skilled. In spite of many hardships, Washington's army kept the British from taking control of New England.

Support from France

When the colonists won an important battle in New York, the French decided to help the Continental army. France disliked Great Britain and sent thousands of soldiers to help the colonists fight. After the French troops arrived, the British changed their plan. They believed many people living in the South were Loyalists, who did not support independence. The British decided to send soldiers to the South to join the Loyalists.

John Adams, a signer of the Declaration of Independence, said the American Revolution was something most colonists wanted. He said, "The Revolution was in the minds and the hearts of the people."

As the war carried on, the Continental army became more organized. Colonial women sewed uniforms for the soldiers, which helped them feel like real soldiers.

2 MEMORY MASTER

1. Why did delegates go to the First Continental Congress?
2. Who were the minutemen?
3. What was the difference between a Patriot and a Loyalist?

Watauga Becomes the Washington District

The people in the Watauga settlements learned about the battles in Massachusetts and began preparing for war. They wondered if British soldiers would march into their homes. They also wondered if the Cherokees would help the British.

The Wataugans formed committees to protect the settlements. John Carter led one committee, and James Robertson led another. The Wataugans also renamed the region in honor of George Washington. It became the Washington District.

The Cherokee War of 1776

As the Wataugans had guessed, British leaders began meeting with Indian leaders. The British promised to drive out the settlers if the Indians agreed to help them fight the war. Dragging Canoe and other Cherokee warriors were eager to take back their land. They quickly agreed to help the British. Soon 30 British wagons filled with ammunition arrived in Cherokee territory.

Dragging Canoe told the British about his plans to take the land from the settlers. A British Indian agent, Henry Stuart, asked Dragging Canoe for time to move the settlers peacefully. Stuart sent a letter to the Wataugans. It said they had to leave within 20 days. The letter made the settlers angry, and they refused to leave.

Instead of leaving, the settlers in the Washington District built forts, or *stations*. While the forts were being built, chiefs from 14 northern tribes visited the Overhill Cherokees. They encouraged the Indians to attack the settlers. In July of 1776, the Cherokee chiefs held a meeting and planned to attack the settlements.

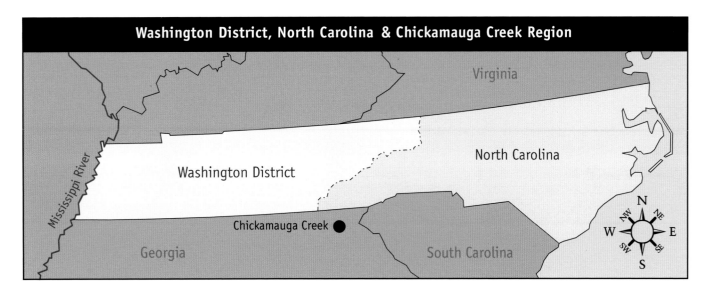

Nancy Ward Sends a Warning

Nancy Ward, the Cherokee Beloved Woman, learned of these plans and sent a message to warn the settlers. She wanted peace between her people and the settlers. Because of her warning, the settlers were ready when the attacks began.

The Indian attacks lasted three weeks. Finally the states of Virginia, North Carolina, and Georgia sent soldiers to help fight the Cherokees. The troops destroyed many Cherokee towns. Thomas Jefferson was governor of Virginia at the time. He said he hoped the Cherokees would be "driven beyond the Mississippi."

One story told after the attack is that during the fighting, the Cherokees captured William Bean's wife, Lydia. They carried her to a nearby village and tied her to a tall stake. Nancy Ward arrived in the village just as fire was being set to Lydia's feet. Nancy Ward saved Lydia's life and gave her a place to live for several months. During that time, the two women shared their secrets about preparing food and making medicines.

Another Treaty with the Cherokees

After a year of fighting, the Cherokees asked for peace. At a meeting in July of 1777, the Cherokees agreed to give the settlers more land. They signed the Treaty of Long Island on the Holston. This treaty brought two years of peace to the frontier.

Dragging Canoe refused to sign the treaty. He moved south from the Overhill towns to the Chickamauga Creek region near modern-day Chattanooga. The group that went with him became known as the Chickamaugan branch of the Cherokee tribe. Chickamauga means "River of Death."

Legend says that just before the first Indian attack began, John Sevier rescued a woman who had been working in the gardens outside the fort. He reached over the wall of the fort and pulled her to safety. After Sevier's wife died four years later, he married the woman he had saved, Catherine Sherill.

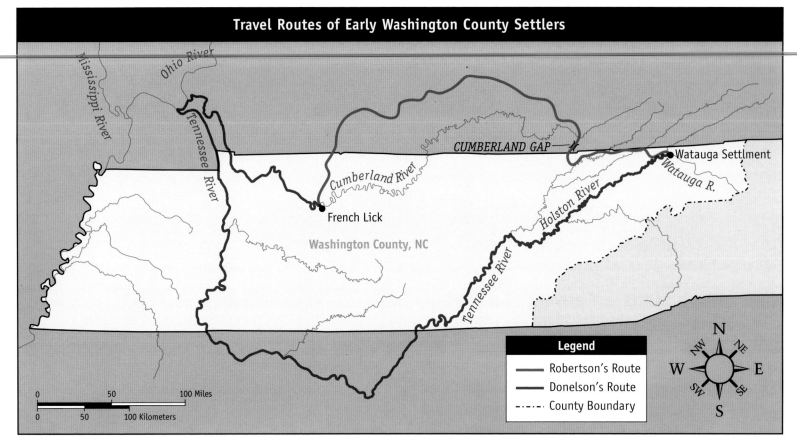

The Watauga Petitions

It soon became clear that the Revolutionary War was coming to the Washington District. The settlers decided they needed more protection. They sent letters to Virginia and North Carolina asking each new state to take control of the Washington District. The letters were called the Watauga Petitions.

Virginia did not respond to the letter. The North Carolina legislature, however, asked the settlers to send delegates to a state constitutional convention. The Wataugans elected five men, one of whom was John Sevier. Four of the five delegates attended the convention and signed North Carolina's first state constitution.

Washington County, North Carolina

The Washington District became part of North Carolina. Citizens in the district elected John Carter, John Sevier, and Jacob Womack to positions in North Carolina's state government. The following year, North Carolina changed the Washington District's name to Washington County. At that time, Washington County included almost all of present-day Tennessee. It was the first county in the United States named for George Washington.

The Cumberland Settlements

After the Cherokee War ended, Richard Henderson wanted to know more about the land he gained through the Treaty of Sycamore Shoals. Henderson hired James Robertson and a team of eight men to survey the region. Robertson returned home with glowing descriptions of the land at the French Lick. He said it was a good place for a settlement. The salt from the lick would help settlers cure meat. They planned to call it the Cumberland Settlements.

Robertson and another surveyor, John Donelson, worked out a plan to move settlers to the region. Robertson and a large group (mostly men) planned to walk or ride there on horseback. While they walked, their wives and children would travel on the Holston, Tennessee, Ohio, and Cumberland rivers. The problem with this plan was that the settlers had never traveled to the region by river. No one knew exactly how long the river journey would take.

Traveling by Land

In October, James Robertson's group left the Watauga settlements and began walking toward the French Lick. Some people rode horses while others walked. They took supplies and many animals with them. Robertson's 10-year-old son, Jonathan, was in charge of driving a flock of sheep.

The Robertson party went up through the Cumberland Gap and then over the Cumberland Road through Kentucky. Along the way, other people joined them. The group came into the Tennessee region near the present-day town of Clarksville. Then they headed south to the French Lick.

Linking the Present to the Past

Have you ever wondered why some of the place names in Tennessee have the word "lick" in them? Much of our soil has salt mixed into it. All living creatures (including people) need salt to live. Animals used to come here and lick the salt from the ground, so people called the places "licks." How many places can you think of that have "lick" in their name?

Christmas on the Cumberland

The journey overland took less than two months. The Robertson party arrived on the Cumberland River across from the French Lick on Christmas Eve. They wondered how they would get the livestock across the river. The next day the weather turned much colder. The river froze, and James Robertson walked across the Cumberland River to the French Lick. In a few days, the men walked the animals across the frozen river too. The travelers built log cabins and strong forts and waited for their families to arrive.

Traveling by Water

John Donelson was in charge of building the flatboats that would carry the women and children to the new settlement. When James Robertson's group left in October, they believed the flatboats were almost ready to leave.

But building the boats took much longer than anyone expected. Then winter came. The river froze for several weeks. The group did not begin its journey until the middle of February. It was another month before they reached the mouth of the Holston and headed down the Tennessee River.

What Do You Think

How would you like to cross a frozen river? Do you think it would be scary? Two-year-old William Rains and four-year-old Patsy Rains were members of the Robertson party. On Christmas Day, they slid across the ice on bearskins!

How do you think the men and animals would have crossed the Cumberland River if it hadn't frozen?

Danger on the River

To make matters worse, the journey by flatboat turned out to be very dangerous. The boats were big and hard to guide. They were also easy for Indians to see. After the group had been on the river for a few days, Mrs. Ephraim Peyton gave birth. Not long afterward, Indians attacked the boats. The Ephraim baby fell overboard and was drowned.

Then people on several boats became sick with smallpox. Smallpox killed many people every year, and the travelers were afraid. They put all the sick people on one boat. The boat with sick people fell behind. Indians attacked and killed everyone aboard. Some historians say that shortly after the attack, smallpox wiped out an entire Cherokee village.

The settlers had little information about the river, so they did not know what to expect. When the boats came to the Muscle Shoals, everyone feared they would break up on the rocks. The boat captains went slowly and carefully. They steered every boat safely through the shoals, and no one was hurt.

No one could have guessed the trip by water would take longer and be more dangerous than the trip by land.

ANNE ROBERTSON JOHNSON COCKRILL Sister of James Robertson. Conducted a small school on the "Adventure" the tiny boat which brought the early settlers from Fort Patrick Henry in the winter of 1779 and 1780.

School on the Water

Anne Robertson Johnson was James Robertson's sister. She was also the widowed mother of three little girls. Johnson taught her daughters and other school-aged children letters and numbers as the boats made their way down the river. She asked the children to draw letters in sand she collected from the riverbank. She also taught them many songs. Johnson continued teaching after she arrived at Fort Nashborough—even during terrible Creek and Cherokee battles. She is considered Nashville's first schoolteacher.

TENNESSEE PORTRAIT

John Donelson
(1718–1785)

John Donelson was the son of a Virginia planter and businessman. He worked as a surveyor and then joined the military. Donelson became a colonel and fought in battles against the Overhill Cherokees.

Richard Henderson asked Donelson to help move settlers to the French Lick. He took the assignment to lead several boats carrying many families. There were a few men, but most of the passengers were women and children. Along the way, another group of boats joined them. Donelson found himself leading 30 boats through 1,000 miles of dangerous, unknown waters.

The journey took more than four months. Donelson and his family claimed a piece of land and planted corn and cotton. Later that year, the river flooded his fields. Donelson grew frustrated that there wasn't enough food to feed his family. He moved his family to a safer spot.

Even though Donelson's crops had been flooded, they still grew. Donelson took one of his sons and some other men back to the region to harvest the corn and cotton. The men were floating down the river with the corn when Indians attacked. Donelson survived, but he decided living in the Cumberland settlements was too hard. He gathered his family and settled in Kentucky.

Donelson continued to travel between Virginia, Kentucky, and Tennessee. He was headed for Tennessee when he learned his family had moved back to the Cumberland settlements. Along the way to go meet them, Donelson was shot and killed. He is remembered as one of Tennessee's most important settlers.

There at Last!

The travelers finally reached the Ohio River. It took a great deal of strength and energy to get the boats up the Ohio and Cumberland Rivers. Everyone was exhausted. The men who were already at French Lick had become very worried about their families. The boats were two months late. They wondered what had happened to the people. Had there been an accident?

On April 24, a lookout on the bluffs saw a boat coming up the Cumberland. Soon everyone in the settlements was at the river to welcome the boats and their families. James Robertson had been saving food, so the group had a huge reunion dinner. The families shared laughter, tears, and exciting stories of their adventures. For a week, everyone in the new settlement celebrated.

Conflict with Indians

The arrival of the settlers in the Cumberland region upset local Indians. Although no tribes lived in the region, several groups used the land as hunting grounds. When the Indians saw the women, children, and farm animals, they grew concerned. These people were different from the trappers and traders who had come earlier. The people cleared the land, built cabins, and seemed to be there to stay. The Indians began to attack the settlements almost immediately.

The Cherokees had signed many treaties with white settlers, but the settlers continued to move onto Cherokee land. The Indians grew angry that the settlers did not honor the treaties.

The Cumberland Compact

Richard Henderson arrived in the Cumberland settlements at the same time as the flatboats. The settlers were 700 miles from the capital of North Carolina, and the people needed leadership. Henderson wrote a document called the Cumberland Compact. It provided a framework for government in the settlements.

The Cumberland Compact was similar to the Watauga Compact. It provided for a clerk to record property claims and for judges to settle arguments. It created eight stations to protect the settlers from attacks and said all men over the age of 16 had to serve in the militia.

Nashborough

Henderson wanted one of the stations on the French Lick to be named in honor of General Francis Nash of North Carolina. Nash had been the clerk of the court where Henderson served as judge. He had also served with James Robertson at the Battle of Alamance. Nash was killed in battle during the American Revolution.

Soon the name of the Cumberland settlements changed to Nashborough. A few years later, the name changed again to Nashville. The second change was to thank the French for helping to win the Revolutionary War. The French often used "ville" in place names.

An Educated Group

The Cumberland Compact was signed by 256 men. Almost everyone who came to the Cumberland settlements could read and write. Only one man was unable to write his name, so he signed with an X.

OUR LAND OUR LIVES

Isn't it strange to think that one of the reasons the site of the second largest city in Tennessee was chosen was because of salt? Of course that is not the only reason. The region also had rivers, streams, and fertile land. All these things made the French Lick a perfect place for new settlers.

The dogs at the fort had been trained to attack Indians.

Battle of the Bluffs

In the spring of 1781, the dogs inside Fort Nashborough began to bark. Charlotte Robertson knew what that meant. Indians were about to attack! All of the men were outside the fort. Charlotte and Caesar, a slave, left the settlement to try to warn the men, but they were not able to reach them. Charlotte and Caesar rushed back inside the fort just as the attack began.

The Cherokees quickly surrounded the fort. Charlotte realized the men would not be able to get inside. She had to act fast. She opened the gates and let the dogs out. They chased the Indians and created so much confusion that the men were able to slip safely inside. Charlotte Robertson became known as the Heroine of the Battle of the Bluffs.

The Second Treaty of Long Island on the Holston

After this battle, the Cherokee chiefs and the settlers signed a second Treaty of Long Island on the Holston. In the treaty, the Cherokees gave the settlers more land. This treaty did not end the conflict, however. It continued for another ten years.

Charlotte Robertson had been left in charge of the fort while the men were gone. Some of the children inside were her own.

③ MEMORY MASTER

1. Washington District became part of which state?
2. What was the journey to the Cumberland settlements like for the Donelson Party?
3. What is the settlement at French Lick called today?

PEOPLE TO KNOW

William Campbell
Charles Cornwallis
Samuel Doak
Patrick Ferguson
Overmountain Men
Mary McKeehan Patton
John Sevier
Isaac Shelby
George Washington

PLACES TO LOCATE

Appalachian Mountains
King's Mountain

WORDS TO UNDERSTAND

surrender

The British March into the Mountains

While the settlers were starting new lives on the French Lick, the American Revolution still raged in the colonies. The British decided to march south. British General Charles Cornwallis led his troops into Georgia. He expected to find many Loyalists who would help him quickly defeat the Patriots. For a while, that is exactly what happened. Then things changed.

Patriots began moving into the mountains to keep from getting captured by the British. Major Patrick Ferguson, one of Cornwallis's best soldiers, went over the mountains to catch the Patriots. As he and his men traveled, they told settlers the war was over. This was not true, but the Wataugans did not know what to believe. They thought Ferguson might be lying, so they refused to *surrender.*

The Overmountain Men

Major Ferguson grew frustrated with the settlers. He threatened to destroy the entire Watauga settlement if they did not surrender. The settlers began to worry that the Cherokees would help the

When the war moved west, the Overmountain Men were quick to respond. They drove the British south of Georgia.

British. A group of men decided it was better to go out and meet Ferguson than wait for his army to invade. John Sevier, Isaac Shelby, and William Campbell organized a group called the Overmountain Men.

Preparing for Battle

The Overmountain Men and their families began preparing for war. One woman, Mary McKeehan Patton, had learned how to make gunpowder. She knew the men would use a lot of gunpowder, so she made more than 500 pounds of it. Other women sewed clothing and packed food for their husbands, sons, fathers, and brothers to take with them. Winter was coming, and the men needed warm clothing. No one knew how long they would be gone.

When the preparations were finished, the Overmountain Men met at Sycamore Shoals. They did not look like soldiers. They had no uniforms, so they wore hunting clothes. The only weapons they carried were hunting knives and rifles. Reverend Samuel Doak, a Presbyterian minister, said a prayer and blessed the men.

What Do You Think?

Why do you think these men were called the Overmountain Men? What other group has "Overmountain" in its name?

Linking the Present to the Past

The words spoken by Reverend Doak before the Battle of King's Mountain remain precious to many Tennesseans. During the 21st-century war in Iraq, a captain from East Tennessee hung Doak's words in a meeting room in Iraq. Here is an excerpt from the sermon:

My countrymen, you are about to set out on an expedition which is full of hardships and dangers, but one in which the Almighty will attend you . . . Your brethren across the mountains are crying . . . . God forbid that you shall refuse to hear and answer their call . . . Go forth then in the strength of your manhood to the aid of your brethren, the defense of your liberty and the protection of your homes. And may the God of Justice be with you and give you victory.

Reverend Samuel Doak

Battle of Kings Mountain

South Carolina

One hundred fifty years after the Battle of King's Mountain, President Herbert Hoover visited the battle site. He said, "It was a little army and a little battle, but it was of mighty [importance]."

OUR LAND OUR LIVES

The Overmountain Men had spent many years in the mountains. They knew how to climb rocks and find hidden caves and hollows. The British soldiers were mostly American Loyalists from the South. They were not used to the mountains. They often slipped and fell. The Overmountain Men never got lost, and they knew how to walk through the forests without making a sound. Their years in the Appalachians taught them the skills they needed to win the Battle of King's Mountain.

The Battle of King's Mountain

The Overmountain Men did not wait for Major Ferguson's troops to find them. Instead they crossed the mountains and went looking for the British. They found more than 1,000 British soldiers on King's Mountain, a narrow ridge in South Carolina. Ferguson was confident the Wataugans would not be able to push his soldiers from the mountain.

The Overmountain Men climbed the ridge. Then they hid behind trees, logs, and rocks. They tried to move up the mountain three times. Each time, the British pushed them back down. But each time the Wataugans recovered and tried again.

When the Overmountain Men reached the top of the ridge, Ferguson's men had no way to escape. They were trapped on the ridge. Both groups fought hard, but the settlers defeated the British.

Victory!

The outcome of the Battle of King's Mountain surprised many people. As the Patriots celebrated, southern Loyalists grew discouraged. The victory was a turning point in the South because it helped the Patriots believe they could win the war.

General Cornwallis soon left the South. The Overmountain Men continued to fight alongside the Patriots until the end of the war. They fought both the British and the Indians.

More Trouble with the Cherokees

While the Overmountain Men were fighting at King's Mountain, the British urged the Cherokees to attack the Watauga settlements. The British believed Ferguson's troops would wipe out the men on King's Mountain. They wanted the Cherokees to wipe out the rest of the settlers.

After the battle, the Overmountain Men returned home for a while. Nancy Ward sent a message to John Sevier warning him of the upcoming attacks. Sevier decided to attack the Cherokees before the Indians attacked the settlements. Sevier's troops crossed the mountains and attacked several Cherokee towns. Then they marched into Chota, the Overhill Cherokee capital on the Little Tennessee River, but no one was there. The Cherokees had fled to safety.

EXPLORE TENNESSEE!

Did you know you can visit King's Mountain and see a reenactment of the battle? Each year, American, British, and Native American actors show what happened at the battle. They also show what life was like on the western frontier during the late 1700s.

Chota ●

TENNESSEE PORTRAIT

John Sevier
(1745–1815)

John Sevier was born in Virginia, but he moved across the mountains so he could have his own land. He married Sarah Hawkins, and they raised ten children. Sevier settled on a farm on the Watauga River, near the present-day town of Elizabethton. When the Revolutionary War began, he became a colonel in the North Carolina militia. His job was to protect the frontier settlements.

After Sarah died in 1780, Sevier married Catherine Sherill, the young woman he rescued from the Indians. She became known as Bonnie Kate Sevier. She already had 8 children, so the couple now had 18! The words on Bonnie Kate's gravestone describe how people remembered her: "brightest star among pioneer women of this state."

John Sevier is one of the most important men in Tennessee history. There are monuments to him at the Knox County Courthouse. The following words on Sevier's grave list many of the great things he did for our state:

John Sevier, pioneer, soldier, statesman, and one of the founders of the Republic; Governor of the State of Franklin; six times Governor of Tennessee; four times elected to Congress; a typical pioneer, who conquered the wilderness and fashioned a State; a protector and hero of King's Mountain; fought thirty-five battles, won thirty-five victories; his Indian war cry, "Here they are! Come on, boys!

When the war began, the British were certain they would win. Eight years later and against all odds, the British surrendered to George Washington and the Continental army.

"The World Turn'd Upside Down"

After the defeat at King's Mountain and several other battles, British general Cornwallis decided to go to Virginia. He did not know that France had sent a great fleet of ships to meet him. George Washington and his army then joined the French forces in Virginia. Washington's army and the French army and navy surrounded the British near Yorktown. The British troops were trapped.

General Cornwallis surrendered. As the British army departed, their band played a song called "The World Turn'd Upside Down."

The Treaty of Paris

After the war ended, the United States and Great Britain signed the Treaty of Paris. Once again, the Indian tribes were not invited to the meeting. Great Britain continued to control Canada, but the former 13 colonies were now an independent nation, the United States of America.

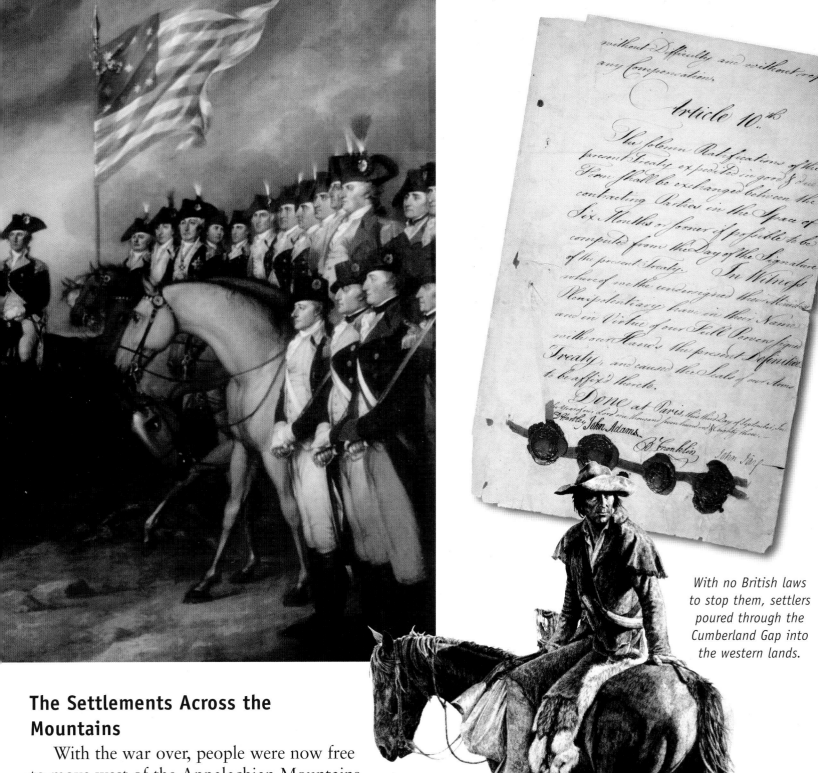

With no British laws to stop them, settlers poured through the Cumberland Gap into the western lands.

The Settlements Across the Mountains

With the war over, people were now free to move west of the Appalachian Mountains. British laws, such as the Proclamation Line, no longer stopped them. The Cherokees and other Indians realized the American victory meant they would be pushed even farther west. There were already two large settlements in Tennessee country: Watauga and Cumberland. The Indians now faced even more conflict over the land.

Life After the American Revolution

Look at this famous painting of Daniel Boone by George Caleb Bingham. Have you ever seen it before?

The painting shows the settlers in bright sunlight surrounded by dark, mysterious shapes. Perhaps this reflects both the hope and the fear they must have felt as they walked into a strange, new land. Only one person looks unafraid: Daniel Boone. His bright buckskin clothes and strong-minded expression make him look almost fearless.

If you look at the painting carefully, you can spot things that show how life changed because of the American Revolution. How is each of the things in the following list shown in the painting?

- American independence opened up the frontier for thousands of people. For many, that meant passage through the Cumberland Gap and into a new life.
- Independence meant a world without roads. The settlers had to clear their own trails.
- Independence meant going from British government to little or no government at all—at least until the settlers formed their own in places like Watauga and Cumberland.
- Independence meant new kinds of danger: Indians, wild animals, lack of food, clothes, and shelter.
- Independence meant women and children had new duties, including developing basic survival skills.
- Independence meant letting go of British traditions that had shaped people's lives for hundreds of years. It meant building an entirely new culture.

4 MEMORY MASTER

1. Who were the Overmountain Men?
2. Who won the Battle of King's Mountain?
3. What was the Treaty of Paris?

Chapter 6 Review

What's the Point?

As the 13 Colonies grew, Great Britain tried to control the people with more laws and higher taxes. Colonists were angry and began protesting. Across the Appalachians on the western frontier, the Cherokees signed the Treaty of Sycamore Shoals. It gave more than 20 million acres between the Cumberland and Ohio Rivers to a land company owned by Richard Henderson. After Thomas Jefferson wrote the Declaration of Independence, tensions rose, and fighting broke out in Lexington. The Cherokees joined the British in hopes of clearing settlers from the land. With help from the French, the colonists defeated the British. The United States of America was formed. Settlers were now free to move west.

Becoming Better Readers

John Sevier

As you read this chapter, you probably noticed that John Sevier appeared many times. What do you remember about John Sevier? On a piece of paper, draw a big circle. Then look back through the chapter for examples of how he made a difference in Tennessee history. Inside the circle, write short sentences about the things John Sevier did. After you have made these notes, write a paragraph about him. Describe his deeds, and explain how they affected Tennessee history.

Climbing to Connections

Outbreak of the American Revolution

1. Tell what the Sugar, Tea, and Stamp Acts were.
2. Summarize how the Sugar, Tea, and Stamp Acts contributed to the outbreak of the American Revolution.
3. Apply the motto "No Taxation without Representation" to what you learned about British control of the colonies.
4. What patterns do you see in the British actions and the colonists' reactions?
5. In one sentence, summarize the colonists' goals as they headed into the American Revolution. In a second sentence, write what the British were fighting for.
6. Do you think the colonists were justified in waging the American Revolution? Why or why not?

Before and After the American Revolution

Do you think the American Revolution made life better for American families? How? List at least three ways life in the United States improved as a result of the war.

Activity

Working Together

As people built this country, they had to work together to get things done. Choose one of the groups listed below. Think about one way they cooperated, and then act it out. See if your classmates can guess which group you are acting out.

- The Colonists
- The First Continental Congress
- The Overmountain Men
- The Cherokees
- The Patriots
- The Watauga Settlers

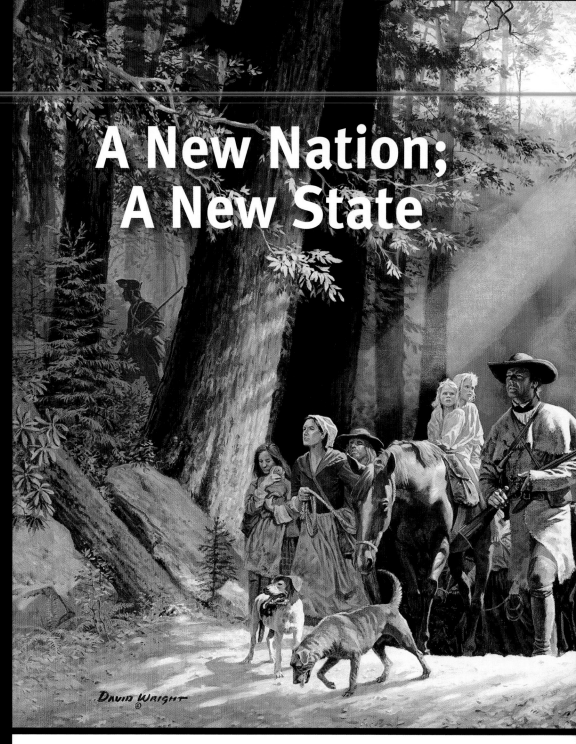

A New Nation; A New State

"*I have the pleasure of announcing to you, gentlemen, the admission of the State of Tennessee into the Federal Union . . . The period is at length arrived when the people of the South Western Territory may enjoy all the blessings and liberties of a free and Independent republic.*"

—John Sevier, Tennessee's first governor, 1796

How many children do you count in this painting? What do you think the long journey across the mountain wilderness was like for them?

Timeline of Events

1781
The U.S. Congress creates the Articles of Confederation.

1780   1782   1784   1786

1784
North Carolina offers to give its western lands to the U.S. government. The State of Franklin applies for statehood.

198

Chapter 7

After the American Revolution, the 13 states became one nation. But the United States was different from other nations in the world. It did not have a king. In the United States, the people were allowed to choose their leaders.

Across the Appalachian Mountains were the Watauga and the Cumberland settlements, which threatened the Indian way of life. The Indians often attacked the settlers, hoping to drive them back across the mountains.

1789
Nine states ratify the U.S. Constitution. George Washington becomes the first president of the United States.

1794
The first General Assembly of the Southwest Territory forms.

1796
Tennessee becomes the 16th state.

1788 — 1790 — 1792 — 1794 — 1796

1791
The territorial capital moves to Knoxville. The Cherokees sign the Treaty of Holston.

87
...ngress passes the ...rthwest Ordinance. ...e Constitutional ...nvention is held in ...iladelphia.

1790
The U.S. Congress creates the Territory South of the River Ohio. William Blount starts a territorial capital at Rocky Mount.

PEOPLE TO KNOW

William Cocke
Benjamin Franklin
Watauga settlers

PLACES TO LOCATE

Cumberland settlements
Virginia

WORDS TO UNDERSTAND

Articles of Confederation
cede
executive branch
federal
judicial branch
legislative branch
legislature
popular sovereignty
repeal
republican

Governing the States and the Nation

The American Revolution gave birth to many new ideas. The Declaration of Independence talked about rights of life and liberty. It talked about equality and said people had a right to decide who their leaders would be.

Americans did not want a government like Great Britain's. They felt the British king and Parliament had too much power. Americans wanted a government that let the states control the laws that affected them. But they also knew they needed to work together. They knew they needed a central government to protect the country from foreign attacks.

Congress began governing the new nation by asking the states to write state constitutions. National leaders told the states that their power to make laws came from the people who lived there. This idea is known as *popular sovereignty.* It was—and still is—very important to our country.

This building is a replica of the colonial capitol building in Williamsburg, Virginia.

A Republic

Virginia was the first state to adopt a *republican* constitution. Republican means the power lies with the citizens, and the people elect representatives to make decisions for them. The other states quickly held conventions to write republican constitutions as well.

Each new state constitution called for a *legislature* and a governor. A legislature, or *legislative branch* is a group of people who have the power to make laws. The legislature had more power than the governor.

A List of Rights

One of the main reasons the colonies separated from Great Britain was because people's rights had not been respected. Many people were worried that the new American government would also fail to respect these rights. To make sure this didn't happen, some state constitutions had a list of rights the government could not take away.

The Articles of Confederation

For over a year, the members of Congress talked about how to form a central government. Many members of Congress feared it would become too strong. They argued about how to pay for it. The states also had different ideas about how many votes each state should have. The states with many citizens wanted more votes in Congress than the states with fewer citizens. These smaller states worried that the large states would have too much power. The small states thought every state should have the same number of votes in Congress.

The delegates finally created a document called the *Articles of Confederation.* It said the states would sometimes help each other, but no state or government had power over another one. Each state was in charge of its own laws and citizens.

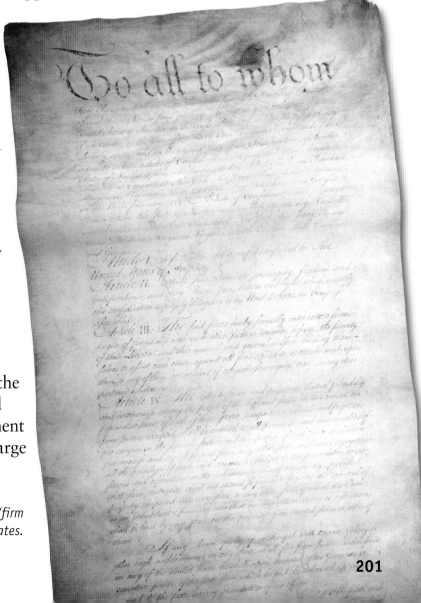

The Articles of Confederation created a "firm league of friendship" between the 13 new states.

What Do You Think

What does "power from the people" mean to you? Do you think it is important for our government's power to come from the people? Why or why not?

The central government created under the Articles of Confederation was not a *federal* government. A federal government is a national government that has power over the states. Under the Articles of Confederation, Congress had very little authority, but it was allowed to:

- manage relations with other countries
- print money
- borrow money
- supervise the delivery of mail
- help resolve boundary disputes

Under the Articles of Confederation, Congress:

- Could not raise taxes.
- Would not have an *executive branch* to carry out the laws.
- Would not have a court system, or *judicial branch,* to interpret the laws and settle arguments between the states.

When the Articles of Confederation were finished, the document went to every state for approval. Even though the Articles created a weak government, every state approved it. It was exactly what most people thought the country needed. But now the United States was more like 13 separate nations than one.

Minted from May of 1776 to January of 1779, this is the Continental Dollar. Printed on one side of the coin are the words "WE ARE ONE." How does that conflict with what you have read about the Articles of Confederation?

North Carolina Makes an Offer

After the war, the national government needed money. The Articles of Confederation did not give Congress the power to collect taxes, so it had no way to raise money. Congress finally asked several states to *cede* (give) their western lands to the national government. Then the government would be able to raise money by selling the land to settlers.

In June of 1784, the state of North Carolina offered to cede its western lands to the government. Its leaders felt this was a good idea because they were tired of fighting Indian wars. Congress had one year to accept North Carolina's offer.

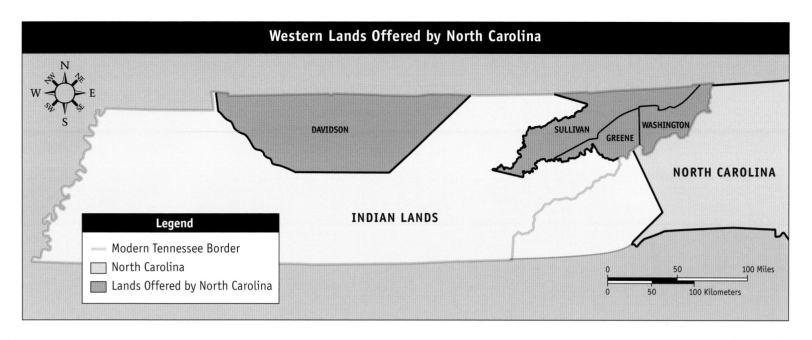

Western Lands Offered by North Carolina

DAVIDSON

SULLIVAN

GREENE

WASHINGTON

NORTH CAROLINA

INDIAN LANDS

Legend
— Modern Tennessee Border
☐ North Carolina
▨ Lands Offered by North Carolina

0   50   100 Miles
0   50   100 Kilometers

Forming a New State

As soon as news of the offer reached the western settlements, the leaders at Watauga held a meeting. They decided they wanted to form a new state. They sent a letter to Congress asking it to accept North Carolina's western lands. Then the group began making plans to write a constitution and hold elections.

The Wataugans were excited about the new state. For many years, they had felt North Carolina leaders ignored them. They were also upset because North Carolina had given western land (instead of money) to men who had fought in the war. Many settlers had planned to claim this land themselves. Becoming a state would give the people who lived in the settlements more power to take care of their own problems. They would not have to wait for decisions from leaders who were hundreds of miles away.

The frontier stretched on for miles. It was a long, rugged trip to see state leaders in North Carolina.

The State of Franklin

In November of 1784, the North Carolina legislature *repealed* (took back) its offer to give up the western lands. People living in the settlements were outraged. They knew land speculators had bought much of the land given to soldiers. They also knew the land speculators felt the land was worth more if it was part of North Carolina. The settlers believed the speculators had convinced North Carolina leaders to keep the western lands.

Declaring Independence from North Carolina

The Watauga settlers sent delegates to represent them at a meeting in Jonesborough. The delegates voted to form a separate state from North Carolina—even though state leaders were against the idea. Since no one from the Cumberland settlements was there, the new state would be only Sullivan, Greene, and Washington Counties.

The delegates wrote a document much like the Declaration of Independence. They listed the reasons they wanted to become a new state. They also wrote a constitution and held elections for a state legislature.

The delegates decided to name the new state Frankland, which means "the land of the free." Some people did not like this name, so

Activity

Wataugan Request

The Wataugans wanted the territory to become the state of Franklin. Choosing their words carefully, they wrote to the North Carolina legislature. Read the following sentence from their letter:

A decent respect to the opinions of mankind make it proper that we should manifest to the world the reason which induced us to a declaration.

1. Read this sentence to yourself three times.
2. Use a dictionary to look up any words you don't know.
3. Rewrite the sentence in your own words.
4. Share your sentence with the class.

The State of Franklin was named for Benjamin Franklin, one of the most respected political leaders in the nation.

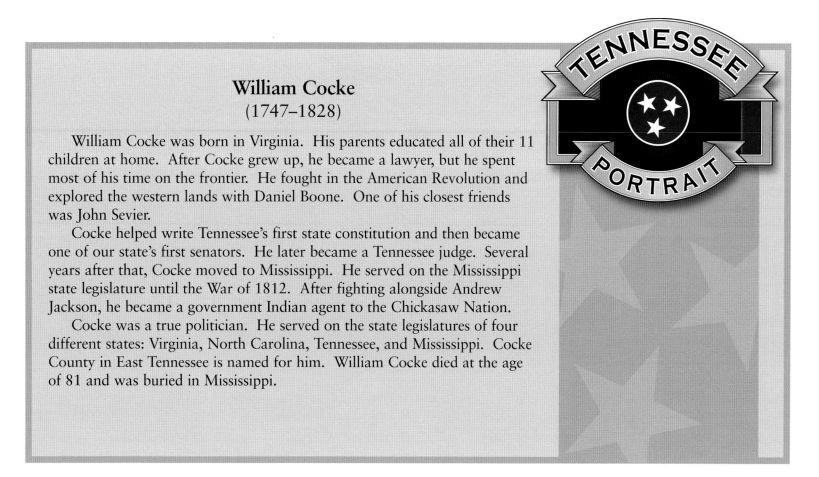

William Cocke
(1747–1828)

William Cocke was born in Virginia. His parents educated all of their 11 children at home. After Cocke grew up, he became a lawyer, but he spent most of his time on the frontier. He fought in the American Revolution and explored the western lands with Daniel Boone. One of his closest friends was John Sevier.

Cocke helped write Tennessee's first state constitution and then became one of our state's first senators. He later became a Tennessee judge. Several years after that, Cocke moved to Mississippi. He served on the Mississippi state legislature until the War of 1812. After fighting alongside Andrew Jackson, he became a government Indian agent to the Chickasaw Nation.

Cocke was a true politician. He served on the state legislatures of four different states: Virginia, North Carolina, Tennessee, and Mississippi. Cocke County in East Tennessee is named for him. William Cocke died at the age of 81 and was buried in Mississippi.

so the group finally settled on Franklin. William Cocke, a Wataugan, traveled east to urge Congress to make Franklin a state.

Seeking Statehood

At first, it seemed as if Congress supported the idea of statehood. Nine states had to vote "yes" for Franklin to become a state without North Carolina's approval. But when the vote was taken, only seven states voted for the idea.

William Cocke discussed the problem with Benjamin Franklin. Franklin advised him to meet with North Carolina leaders again. Cocke tried to convince state leaders to give up the western lands, but again they refused.

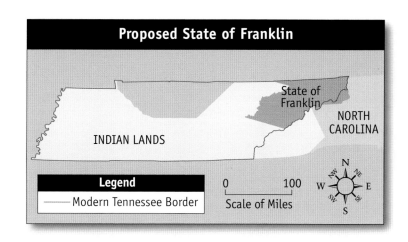

Proposed State of Franklin

State of Franklin

NORTH CAROLINA

INDIAN LANDS

Legend
—— Modern Tennessee Border

0   100
Scale of Miles

What Do You Think?

How do you think our state would be different today if it had become the state of Franklin?

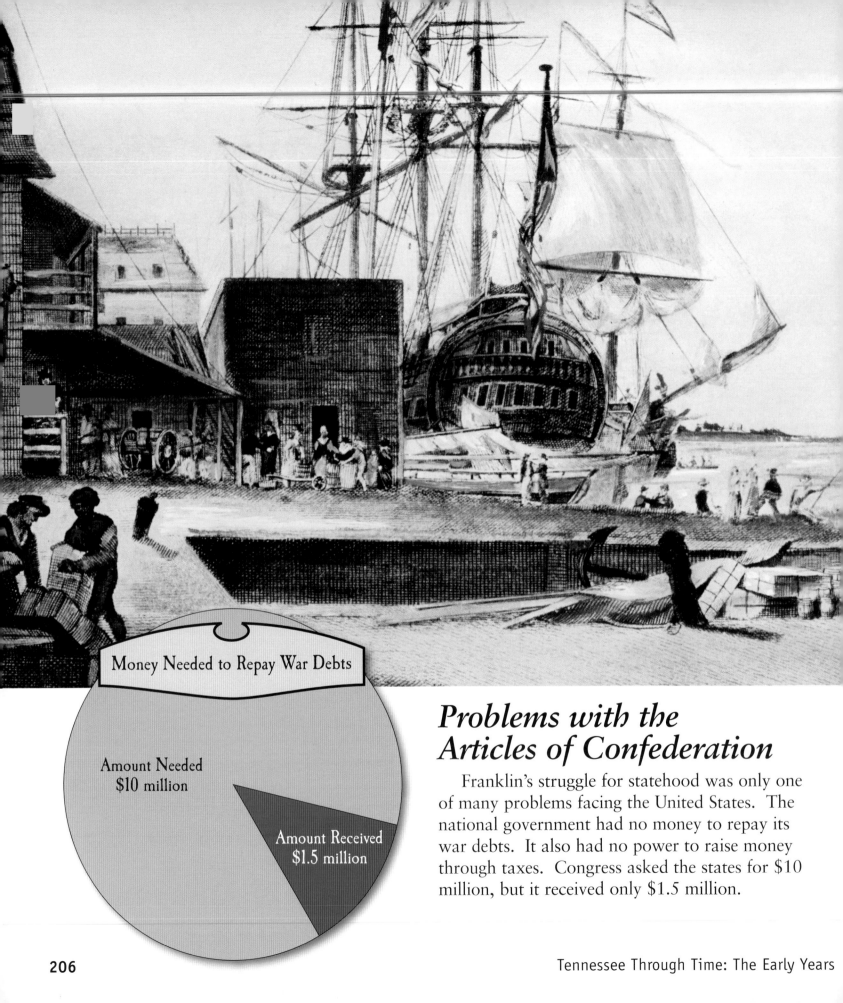

Money Needed to Repay War Debts

Amount Needed
$10 million

Amount Received
$1.5 million

Problems with the Articles of Confederation

Franklin's struggle for statehood was only one of many problems facing the United States. The national government had no money to repay its war debts. It also had no power to raise money through taxes. Congress asked the states for $10 million, but it received only $1.5 million.

Docks were usually busy places. When foreign countries bought fewer goods, sellers earned less money, and workers lost their jobs. The economy slowed and everyone suffered.

Goods traveling across the country were taxed differently in every state.

State Taxes

Most states taxed goods passing through the state. Congress had no power to stop them. Some people could not afford the taxes, so they bought fewer goods. As stores sold fewer goods, people earned less money. Soon people in every state were buying and selling fewer goods and earning less money.

Protection of Rights

Many Americans began complaining about state government. They said the states were not protecting their rights. They realized the government formed under the Articles of Confederation was not working well. Americans began talking about creating a new federal government that had more power.

Foreign Trade

The Articles of Confederation gave most government power to the states. Congress had the power to make agreements with other nations, but it could not make the states obey them. Trade agreements varied widely from state to state. Many countries decided not to trade with the United States anymore. This meant Americans could not sell their goods to people in other nations. It also meant Americans could not buy things from other countries.

1 MEMORY MASTER

1. What is popular sovereignty?
2. What did leaders in the Watauga settlements want to do with North Carolina's western lands?
3. What was one example of how the Articles of Confederation were not working?

PEOPLE TO KNOW

Benjamin Franklin
Alexander Hamilton
James Madison
William Paterson
Roger Sherman
George Washington

PLACES TO LOCATE

Philadelphia, Pennsylvania

WORDS TO UNDERSTAND

ambassador
amendment
anti-Federalist
checks and balances
compromise
debate
Federalist
periodical
Preamble
ratify
separation of power

Philadelphia, PA ●

Tennessee

The Delegates Gather in Philadelphia

Congress asked the states to send delegates to a meeting in Philadelphia to strengthen the Articles of Confederation. Every state except Rhode Island sent delegates to Philadelphia. The delegates met in the Pennsylvania State House (now Independence Hall), the same building where the Declaration of Independence had been signed. The meeting lasted almost four months. It became known as the Constitutional Convention. It is one of the most important meetings in American history.

George Washington

The delegates who went to Philadelphia were well known throughout the states. Perhaps the most respected person there was General George Washington. His presence at the meeting gave people confidence. Washington led the troops that defeated the British in the American Revolution. After the war, he returned to his farm in Virginia. Most Americans trusted him.

James Madison

James Madison was another Virginian at the convention. In the years after the war, Madison studied republican governments throughout history. He read books about ancient Greek and Roman governments. By the time he arrived in Philadelphia, he had already written a plan for a new government. Madison's plan became known as the Virginia Plan.

Alexander Hamilton

Alexander Hamilton was a delegate from New York. He had been an aide to General Washington during the war. Hamilton admired Great Britain's government. He wanted a strong central government.

Benjamin Franklin

At 81 years old, Benjamin Franklin was the oldest delegate. He was in poor health, but he had good ideas about government. Every

Do you think the delegates always agreed with one another? What do they look like they are doing in this painting?

year for 25 years, he had written a new issue of *Poor Richard's Almanack*. The magazine was very popular and sold thousands of copies each year. Franklin had become famous.

Several important people were missing from the meeting in Philadelphia. John Adams and Thomas Jefferson were serving as U.S. **ambassadors** to Great Britain and France. There were also no women, Native Americans, or blacks. The 55 delegates were all powerful white men.

Poor Richard's Almanack *was a newspaper magazine. It was so important to the colonists that some people made fabric covers to protect copies of it.*

The Meeting Begins

Once the Constitutional Convention began, the first thing the delegates did was elect George Washington as the convention president. Every single delegate voted for him.

Next, the men agreed to keep their discussions secret until the meetings were over. They wanted to talk about many different kinds of government, but they didn't want to upset or scare anyone. Even though it was a hot and humid summer in Philadelphia, they kept the windows closed.

The delegates then took a very daring step. They decided to ignore their instructions from Congress. Instead of strengthening the Articles of Confederation, they decided to create a completely new Constitution.

What Do You Think

Would you like to have been a delegate at the Constitutional Convention? Do you think it would be hard to decide how our government should operate? What would you have said at the meetings?

The Virginia Plan

The Virginia delegates presented James Madison's Virginia Plan. It said government power came from the people. It also said the people should elect representatives to make decisions for everyone. Large states would have more representatives than small states.

The Virginia Plan also described a system of government in which power was divided between the state and the national government. The national government had three branches: **legislative**, **executive**, and **judicial**. Each branch had certain duties. This was known as *separation of power.* Power would be separated, or divided, so no single branch had too much.

The Virginia Plan made sense to people who wanted a stronger national government. Others were afraid it gave the national government and the large states too much power.

Checks and Balances

To make sure that no branch of the government became too powerful, the Virginia Plan included *checks and balances.* Each branch had the power to check, or stop, the actions of the other branches. In this way, power among the branches stayed balanced.

Action	Power to Check
Legislative branch makes laws.	Judicial branch decides what the laws mean and if they conflict with the Constitution.
	Executive carries out the laws.
Executive branch makes treaties with other countries.	Legislative branch approves treaties.
Executive branch writes the budget.	Legislative branch approves the budget.
Executive branch can veto bills.	Legislative branch can reverse a veto with a 2/3 majority vote.
Executive powers are held by one person: the president.	Legislative branch can take a president to trial for breaking a law.
Executive branch chooses judges.	Legislative branch approves choices for judges and can remove judges for breaking laws.

The New Jersey Plan

William Paterson did not like the Virginia Plan. He was from New Jersey and did not want small states to have too little power. Paterson presented the New Jersey Plan. It strengthened the powers of Congress, but every state had the same number of representatives. The delegates from Pennsylvania and Virginia did not like the New Jersey Plan. They felt larger states should have more congressmen than smaller states.

The biggest difference between the two plans had to do with the number of representatives in Congress. The Virginia Plan proposed that the number of representatives be based on the population of the state. Larger states would have more than smaller states. Paterson and other delegates from smaller states wanted equal representation. They wanted every state to have equal voting power in Congress.

Virginia, 1787 Population 747,000

New Jersey, 1787 Population 184,000

The Great Compromise

By the middle of June, it was very hot in Philadelphia. Many of the delegates were tired of being in meetings. They wanted to go home, but they were still arguing about representation.

Finally Roger Sherman of Connecticut presented a *compromise.* He proposed that Congress have two parts: a **House of Representatives** and a **Senate**. In the House of Representatives, the population of the states would determine the number of representatives. Larger states would have more than smaller states. In the Senate, each state would have two members. Every state would be equally represented in the Senate. The delegates agreed to Roger Sherman's plan, which became known as the Great Compromise.

Roger Sherman was a shoemaker, a lawyer, and a judge. He was one of the signers of the Declaration of Independence.

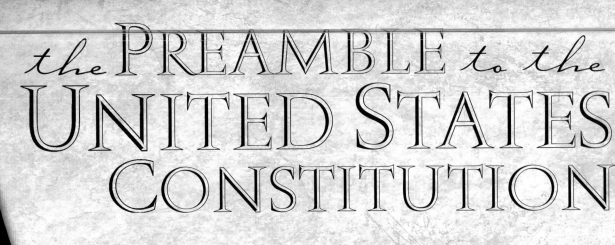

the PREAMBLE to the UNITED STATES CONSTITUTION

The *Preamble* of the Constitution explains why the Constitution was written. It is one very long sentence. It lists six goals for our Constitution.

We, the people of the United States, in order to form a more perfect Union, establish justice, insure domestic tranquility, provide for the common defense, promote the general welfare, and secure the blessings of liberty to ourselves and our posterity, do ordain and establish this Constitution for the United States of America.

To Form a More Perfect Union

The Constitution gives the national government power to correct problems that arose under the Articles of Confederation. *Amendments,* or changes, to the Constitution protect basic freedoms and civil rights. The delegates wanted the United States to be a "more perfect" union of states.

To Establish Justice

The Constitution provides for a system of courts. These courts decide what laws mean, punish lawbreakers, and make sure every American is treated fairly. The U.S. Supreme Court is the highest court in the land.

To Insure Domestic Tranquility

One of the delegates' major goals was to maintain law and order. The Constitution gives the government power to keep the peace. The U.S. Armed Forces protect life and property. State troopers, county sheriffs, and city police officers help enforce laws. The federal government lends a hand when floods, hurricanes, forest fires, and other natural disasters occur.

To Provide for the Common Defense

The colonies had already fought in several wars, including the Revolutionary War. To keep the nation safe in the future, the Constitution gives Congress power to raise an army and navy.

What Do You Think?

How does the government provide for your general welfare? Does it improve your fortune, health, happiness, and success? How?

To Promote the General Welfare

The Constitution gives Congress power to provide for the "general welfare" of the people. Welfare is good fortune, health, happiness, and success.

To Secure the Blessings of Liberty

"Give me liberty or give me death!" said Patrick Henry, a Patriot, during the American Revolution. Liberty is the freedom to live as you please as long as you obey the laws. The Constitution protects our liberties in many ways. It limits the power of government and guarantees our right to vote.

Linking the Present to the Past

Today, Congress runs many programs the delegates never could have imagined. Some of the most important programs focus on Social Security, public education, school lunch, and public health.

The Constitution of the United States

The meetings to write the Constitution lasted four long months. By the time the meetings ended, many delegates had already gone home. Only 39 of the original 55 delegates actually signed the final document.

The final United States Constitution was shorter than most state constitutions because the delegates didn't want it to have too many details. They wanted the rules to be flexible. They stressed basic principles and ideas. This allowed the Constitution to change as the country's needs changed. As a result, our Constitution is as fresh and useful today as it was when it was new.

Ratifying the Constitution

The next step in creating the new government was getting the states to *ratify,* or approve, the Constitution. Once nine states approved the document, it could become the law. The delegates went home and began trying to gather support.

In every state, people read rough copies of the Constitution. They gathered in homes, town squares, taverns, and other meeting

The Founding Fathers knew the Constitution would never be approved if people did not like it. The Preamble speaks to the common man. It clearly states that the U.S. government would be of the people, not of a king.

places to talk about it. The Constitution shocked many people. They thought it was too much of a change.

In some states, there were great *debates.* Americans split into two groups. The *Federalists* supported the Constitution. The *anti-Federalists* didn't because they believed it took too much power from the states. Many citizens also believed the Constitution did not respect some important rights.

James Madison promised to add a Bill of Rights that would make sure people's rights were protected. Even though the Bill of Rights wasn't written until after the Constitution was signed, Madison's promise made the difference in several states. All the states—except North Carolina and Rhode Island—ratified the U.S. Constitution. Those two states finally ratified it about two years later.

One of the signers of the U.S. Constitution was William Blount from North Carolina. Several years later, Blount moved across the mountains into what is now Tennessee.

A Bundle of Compromises

By the time it was finished, the Constitution had become a "bundle of compromises." In every section, the delegates made compromises. No state got everything it wanted. But everyone who signed the Constitution had great faith in it. They felt it was fair and would prevent any group from gaining too much power.

As the delegates were signing the document, Benjamin Franklin made a comment that became famous. Pointing to the empty chair where George Washington had been sitting, he said, "I have often . . . in the course of the session . . . looked at that sun behind the President without being able to tell whether it was rising or setting. But now at length I have the happiness to know it is a rising and not a setting sun." Benjamin Franklin believed the new government had a bright future.

George Washington sat in this chair for nearly three months during the Constitutional Convention. You can see it at Independence Hall in Philadelphia, Pennsylvania.

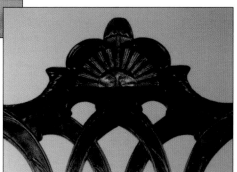

2 MEMORY MASTER

1. What did the delegates at the Constitutional Convention plan to do with the Articles of Confederation?
2. What is the system of checks and balances?
3. What was the Great Compromise?

PEOPLE TO KNOW

John Adams
Alexander Hamilton
Thomas Jefferson
Henry Knox
Pierre L'Enfant
George Washington

PLACES TO LOCATE

New York City
Washington, D.C.

WORDS TO UNDERSTAND

Bill of Rights
cabinet
criticize
graffiti
jury
mall
oath of office
privacy
trial

Our nation's capital moved from city to city for many years. In 1785, the capital moved to New York City. Five years later, it moved back to Philadelphia. Where is our nation's capital today?

People flocked around George Washington everywhere he went—even to church!

The First President of the United States

When George Washington was elected the first president of the United States, no one was surprised. Every single member of the election committee had voted for him. John Adams became vice president.

At the time, Washington was 57 years old. He did not want to leave his home, but he knew the new country needed him. He felt it was his duty to help. Washington traveled from his home in Virginia to New York City, the nation's capital at the time.

Celebrating George Washington

President Washington stopped at each town along his journey to New York City. Americans built bonfires, sang songs, and even lit fireworks as he passed through their towns. Thousands of people hoped to catch a glimpse of the president. They lined the dirt roads and threw flowers in his path.

When Washington arrived in Philadelphia, he got out of his carriage and rode a white horse. People cheered and waved as he crossed decorated bridges. Eight days later, Washington arrived in New Jersey. He traveled across the Hudson River toward New York City in a barge covered with more decorations. The sounds of booming cannons and ringing church bells filled the air.

Washington's Inaugural Address

On April 30, 1789, George Washington placed his hand on a Bible and swore to uphold the Constitution as president of the United States. Washington was aware that what he did that day was very important. He knew he was setting an example that future presidents would follow.

After Washington took the *oath of office,* he gave a speech. He had thought a lot about what he wanted to say during his speech. He even wrote it down so he would not forget anything important. He wanted to tell the people of his hopes for the new government.

Washington's speech became known as the First Inaugural Address. Here is part of what he said: "I dwell on this prospect [of a successful new nation] with every satisfaction which an ardent love for my Country can inspire."

George Washington's horse, Nelson, carried him through most of the American Revolution and to his inauguration.

What Do You Think ?

If you had a chance to talk to George Washington today, what would you say? What questions would you ask? Why do you think people thought he was such a great hero?

PASSPORT TO HISTORY

Inaugural Reporter

Pretend you were there when Washington gave his first speech as president. Answer the following questions to get a stamp in your passport:

1. What are some of the sights and sounds you saw?
2. Who was in the crowd? How did the crowd react to the speech?
3. What was the tone or mood of the speech?
4. What was the main message?
5. What things did Washington **not** say in his speech?

The Bill of Rights

During Washington's speech, he reminded Congress of James Madison's promise to write a **Bill of Rights.** Madison was now a member of the House of Representatives. He studied the Virginia Bill of Rights and asked members of Congress for other suggestions. He then wrote ten amendments that became the Bill of Rights.

1st Amendment

Freedom of religion: You can worship as you wish, or not at all. The government cannot choose one religion for the whole country.

Freedom of speech: You can express your opinion about any subject without being arrested. You can even **criticize** the government. But what you say can't cause danger or harm to others.

Freedom of the press: The government cannot tell people what they can or cannot print in newspapers or books.

Freedom of assembly: You have the right to join and meet with any group. However, you cannot commit crimes with the group.

2nd Amendment

Right to bear arms: You can own guns to protect yourself and to participate in other legal activities.

3rd Amendment

Right to not have soldiers in your home during peacetime: In the past, kings had forced citizens to feed and house soldiers not only during wars but in also times of peace.

4th Amendment

Freedom from improper search and seizure: You have a right to **privacy.** But if the police have reason to think you have something illegal in your home, they can get a search warrant and search your home.

5th, 6th, and 7th Amendments:

These have to do with rights people have if they commit crimes. They include the right to a speedy **trial** and a trial by a **jury.** A jury is a group of people who decide the outcome of a trial.

8th Amendment:

No cruel or unusual punishment is allowed.

9th Amendment:

People have other rights not named in the Bill of Rights.

10th Amendment:

A great deal of power will remain with the states. The people did not want the federal government to have all the power.

What Do You Think?

Does freedom of speech mean you can draw **graffiti** on public property? Does it allow you to tell lies that harm others? How can we use our freedoms so they don't hurt anyone else?

KEEP OUT!

Tennessee Through Time: The Early Years

The Executive Branch Begins

The new nation faced many problems, and President Washington knew he needed help. He organized the executive branch of the new government by creating three departments: the Treasury, the Department of State, and the Department of War. Alexander Hamilton became the Secretary of the Treasury; Thomas Jefferson became the Secretary of State; Henry Knox became the Secretary of War; Edmund Randolph became the Attorney General.

The Federalists and the Republicans

President Washington had carefully chosen brilliant leaders for his *cabinet* positions. He was surprised and disappointed when Alexander Hamilton and Thomas Jefferson began arguing about almost everything. Both men understood the importance of their jobs, but they had different opinions about how the government should operate.

Hamilton and Jefferson were very different from one another. Hamilton, who was short and very tidy, believed the country needed a strong central government. Jefferson, who was tall and often poorly groomed, believed the states should have more power. Their arguments led to two political parties. Hamilton's party was the Federalists. Jefferson's was the Republicans.

This is the first presidential cabinet. From left to right, George Washington, Henry Knox, Alexander Hamilton, Thomas Jefferson, and Edmund Randolph.

Our Nation's Capital

The new country needed a capital city. George Washington took the oath of office in New York City, but the national government then moved back to Philadelphia. In 1790, Congress passed a law that said the capital city would be on the Potomac River between Maryland and Virginia. It would cover ten square miles.

Washington chose the exact piece of land. He called the newly created town the Federal City. Others called it the District of Columbia. "Columbia" was a popular nickname for America after the American Revolution. It was in honor of Christopher Columbus.

The U.S. Capitol Building in Washington, D.C., is one of the most famous buildings in the world. Have you ever been there?

Washington, D.C.

Washington asked Pierre L'Enfant, a French architect and engineer, to plan the new capital city. L'Enfant wanted a city with wide streets; a large, open *mall* (public area); a beautiful mansion for the president's family; and a spacious capitol building. L'Enfant chose a famous hill as the site for the capitol building. At the bottom of the hill was the long, open mall.

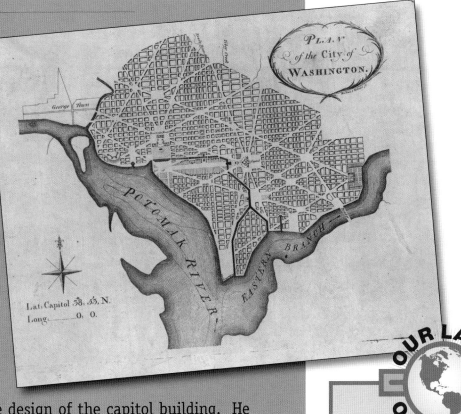

George Washington then held a contest for the design of the capitol building. He chose a plan by Dr. William Thornton. Thornton designed a grand building with three sections. In the center was a large dome that could be seen for miles around. On one side of the dome was a long wing for the U.S. House of Representatives. On the other side of the dome was a wing for the U.S. Senate.

Congress first met in the new capitol building in November of 1800, but the building was not finished. It took more than 34 years to complete. By the time it was finished, it already needed to be enlarged. After George Washington died in 1799, the capital city was renamed Washington, District of Columbia—or Washington, D.C., for short.

The site of our nation's capital was chosen by George Washington. He may have chosen it because it was a beautiful place. He may have chosen it because the Potomac River made it easy to reach. Many believe he chose it because it was midway between the northern and southern states. What do you think?

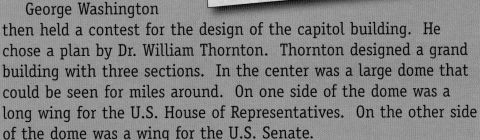

③ MEMORY MASTER

1. Name the first president and vice president of the United States.
2. What were the names of the first two political parties?
3. What name was finally chosen for our nation's capital?

Linking the Present to the Past

Do the Southwest Territory's boundaries look familiar to you? They should! They are our state's boundaries today.

Four Counties in the West

Across the Appalachians, the western settlers were trying to decide what to do. John Sevier and a few others still wanted to become a separate state, one that would now include the Cumberland settlements. Other settlers, however, decided to accept the fact that they lived in North Carolina.

During and after the American Revolution, North Carolina had divided Washington County into smaller counties: Washington, Sullivan, Greene, and Davidson. People in every county were unhappy with the state government. They felt North Carolina was not doing enough to protect them from the Indians.

The Territory South of the River Ohio

North Carolina was one of two states that had not ratified the U.S. Constitution when it was first presented. But in November of 1789, North Carolina became the 12th state to approve the Constitution. Three weeks later, the North Carolina legislature finally ceded its western lands to the national government. Congress accepted the land right away. It created the Territory of the United States South of the River Ohio, or the Southwest Territory.

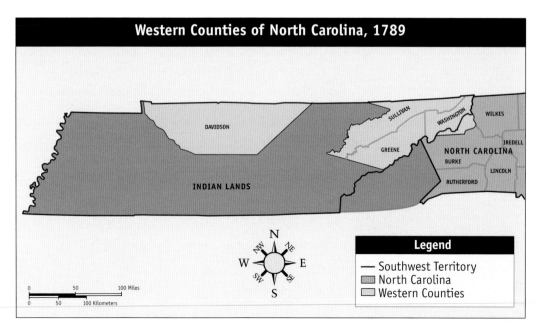

Western Counties of North Carolina, 1789

Legend
— Southwest Territory
North Carolina
Western Counties

The Northwest Ordinance

Many territories wanted to become states, but while their population stayed low, they had to remain territories. The president chose a governor, a secretary, and a body of judges to make all the laws for the territory.

A new law, the Northwest Ordinance, created a way for territories to become states. The Northwest Ordinance said that when a territory had 5,000 men (slaves, women, and children were not included in this number), it should form a House of Representatives, or General Assembly. When the population reached 60,000, the territory could apply for statehood.

William Blount Becomes Territorial Governor

President Washington appointed William Blount to two important positions. He became governor of the Southwest Territory and superintendent of Indian affairs. Blount and his brother owned large pieces of land in the Southwest Territory, but they had never visited the region.

Blount knew he needed the support of the people in the territory. As soon as he became governor, he traveled westward across the Appalachians and met with John Sevier. He set up a temporary territorial capital at Rocky Mount.

Gathering Support

William Blount visited every county and met with local leaders. In each place, he told the settlers that North Carolina had finally ceded its western lands to the government. The land was no longer part of North Carolina. In the Cumberland settlements, Blount stayed with James and Charlotte Robertson. The Robertsons liked him so much that they named their new baby William Blount Robertson. The people in the territory liked him too. They felt he was honest and fair.

Linking the Present to the Past

George Washington appointed three judges for the Southwest Territory. They were David Campbell and Joseph Anderson in the eastern counties and John McNairy in the Cumberland settlements. Can you find these names on a modern map of Tennessee? Each of these men has a county named after him.

The only county in Tennessee named for a woman is Grainger County. It was named for Mary Grainger, William Blount's wife.

William Blount
(1749–1800)

William Blount was born to a wealthy North Carolina family. He served during the American Revolution and fought in one battle with George Washington's troops. For the next several years, Blount helped enlist and supply soldiers to fight the British.

During the war, Blount married Mary Grainger. They had six children. After the war, Blount left the military. He served six years in the North Carolina legislature and two years in the Continental Congress. Blount then attended the Constitutional Convention and signed the U.S. Constitution. At first, he wasn't sure he wanted to sign it. Then he saw the delegates from the other states signing the document. He didn't want North Carolina to be the only state without a signature.

In 1790, Blount traveled into the western lands as governor of the Southwest Territory. He settled at Rocky Mount and then built a frontier mansion in Knoxville. Blount helped write the first Tennessee state constitution. He then became a U.S. Senator for Tennessee. Even though he was dismissed by the U.S. Senate, he came back to Tennessee and served in state government for another two years.

EXPLORE TENNESSEE!

The Rocky Mount Museum

Would you like to travel back in time and see what the Southwest Territory's first capital was like? You can! In Piney Flats, you can visit the William Cobb home, which is now the Rocky Mount Museum. This is the place where Governor Blount set up the first capital in our state.

The museum at Rocky Mount is called a Living History Site. That is because workers dress and behave as though it is 1791. If you visit the museum, you can see what daily life was like over 200 years ago. You can make candles or decorate with stencils. You can practice writing with a quill pen or learn to cook over an open fireplace. You can even learn how to mold pewter into cups, pitchers, plates, or silverware.

Indians and the Southwest Territory

William Blount knew the most serious problem facing the settlers was the ongoing battle with the Indians. The Cherokees were angry because settlers kept moving onto land that had been promised to them. The Chickamaugas, Creeks, Chickasaws, and Choctaws were angry too. They had all signed treaties that were supposed to protect their lands. But the settlers ignored the treaties and moved onto the Indian lands anyway.

A New Treaty

William Blount met with Cherokee leaders near James White's Fort, where the Holston and French Broad Rivers come together. Blount offered to pay the Cherokees $1,000 each year if they would allow white settlers to remain in the Southwest Territory. Blount and the Cherokees then signed the Treaty of the Holston.

After the treaty was signed, more settlers moved into the Southwest Territory. They also moved onto lands not protected by the treaty, taking land that belonged to the Indians.

A group of Cherokees traveled to Philadelphia to talk with President Washington and Secretary Knox about their problems. Knox increased the amount paid to the Indians each year, but he did not ask the settlers to move. Knox also ordered the settlers to stop attacking the Indians. Still, there were more battles. With each one, the Indians lost more land.

What Do You Think ?

Imagine you are a Cherokee leader. You have signed many treaties with government leaders, but settlers keep moving onto your land. You don't know where you and the rest of your people will live now. What do you think you should do?

A Capital for the Southwest Territory

William Blount decided to build the permanent capital for the Southwest Territory at White's Fort. He named the capital city after Secretary of War Henry Knox. The name of the capital became Knoxville.

EXPLORE TENNESSEE!

The Blount Mansion

Would you like to see the Blount's mansion? The house, located in downtown Knoxville, has been turned into a museum. It has a parlor, a hall, a kitchen, a large bedroom, and an office. The house also has a wing that may have once been used as slave quarters.

Working Toward Statehood

The Southwest Territory grew rapidly. Soon it held elections for a General Assembly. The assembly met the following year in Knoxville.

The General Assembly chose Dr. James White of Davidson County as its delegate to the U.S. Congress. White owned the fort where the last Cherokee treaty had been signed and land in the Cumberland region. He had also served in Congress as a representative for North Carolina. Shortly after arriving in Philadelphia, White sent word to Blount that the Southwest Territory should begin working toward statehood. Vermont and Kentucky had already been admitted as new states. White thought the Southwest Territory should become a state too.

Voting for Statehood

By 1795, the Southwest Territory had grown even more. In less than four years, the number of people living there had doubled! The General Assembly asked settlers to vote about statehood. The vote showed most people wanted the territory to become a state.

The people who opposed statehood lived in the Cumberland settlements. They were afraid their taxes would go up if the territory became a state. They were also concerned that the people in the eastern regions of the state would gain too much power.

A State Constitution

Governor Blount made plans for a constitutional convention to write a constitution for the new state. Each county sent five representatives to the meeting. The representatives used the

Our state is named for the beautiful Tennessee River.

Pennsylvania and North Carolina state constitutions as models. They also decided to name the state for its most important feature, the Tennessee River. The new state would be called Tennessee.

Joseph McMinn was one of the representatives at the convention. He traveled to Philadelphia to get approval for statehood for Tennessee. James White believed the process would be easy since two new states had already been admitted. But by 1796, things in Philadelphia had changed.

The Federalists vs. the Republicans

The two political parties, the Federalists and the Republicans, argued about almost everything. Tennessee was caught in the middle of the feud. John Adams, a Federalist, was running for president against Thomas Jefferson, a Republican. The Federalists want to delay statehood for Tennessee because they thought Tennesseans would vote for Thomas Jefferson. The Republicans wanted Tennessee's support so they argued for statehood.

Finally the Republicans offered a compromise. The compromise was that Tennessee would have three electoral votes—even though it should have had four. When Federalists accepted the compromise, Joseph McMinn breathed a sigh of relief. Tennessee could finally become a state.

Tennessee Becomes a State

On June 1, 1796, President George Washington signed the bill that made Tennessee the 16th state in the Union. William Blount and William Cocke became Tennessee's first U.S. senators. Andrew Jackson became the state's first U.S. representative, and John Sevier became the first governor. It was the beginning of a new era. What would the future hold for the young state?

④ MEMORY MASTER

1. What did the government call the land south of the River Ohio?
2. Who was the governor of the Southwest Territory?
3. What delayed statehood for Tennessee?

Linking the Present to the Past

The Republican representative who offered the compromise was Albert Gallatin of Pennsylvania. Years later, the Tennessee town of Gallatin was named in his honor.

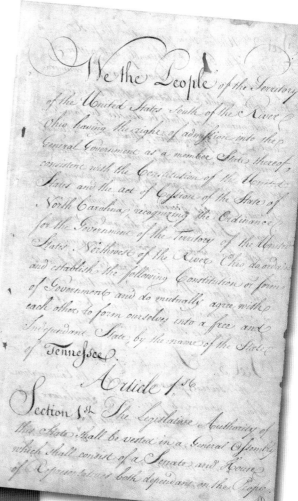

The first Tennessee Constitution said that anyone who denied God could not serve in the state government.

Chapter 7 Review

What's the Point?

The Watauga settlements tried but failed to become the state of Franklin. Under the Articles of Confederation, the new nation struggled with the problems of a weak central government. State delegates met at a Constitutional Convention and wrote the Constitution of the United States. The Constitution created three branches of government with checks and balances. George Washington became the nation's first president. Washington, D.C., became the nation's capital. People in the Watauga and Cumberland settlements were unhappy with the North Carolina government. North Carolina ceded the western lands to the U.S. government, which created the Southwest Territory. Finally the territory's population was large enough to apply for statehood. On June 1, 1796, Tennessee became the 16th state in the United States.

Becoming Better Readers

Reasons for the Constitution

Have you ever wondered what it was like at the Constitutional Convention? Pretend you were there. Make a list of three reasons you think the Articles of Confederation needed to be replaced. Now think about why the Constitution was necessary. List five reasons. Be a careful reader, and look for things the Constitution had that the Articles of Confederation didn't have. Think about ways the delegates worked together to get the Constitution written.

Climbing to Connections

John Sevier

The following quote by John Sevier appears at the beginning of this chapter. Read it again, and then answer the following questions.

I have the pleasure of announcing to you, gentlemen, the admission of the State of Tennessee into the Federal Union . . . The period is at length arrived when the people of the South Western Territory may enjoy all the blessings and liberties of a free and Independent republic.

1. What event does John Sevier announce in this quote?
2. Describe what Sevier means by "enjoy all the blessings and liberties of a free and Independent republic."
3. Complete this sentence: Sevier was the State of Franklin's one and only _____, Tennessee's first _____, a United States _____, and a _____.
4. How are all of John Sevier's titles connected?
5. If Sevier had not been Tennessee's first governor, what would be different today about Tennessee history?
6. Sevier wanted Tennessee to become a state separate from North Carolina. Do you think that was a good idea? Why or why not?

Evaluation Station

Bill of Rights Class Discussion

Do you remember what the first ten amendments to the Constitution are called? The Bill of Rights! Reread page 218 on the Bill of Rights. Discuss with your class why the Bill of Rights was needed.

As a class, examine the First Amendment:

- What is free speech?
- How might people have different opinions concerning freedom of speech?
- Is there a way to resolve opposing viewpoints concerning freedom of speech? How?

Activity

Tennessee Is Born

Organize a Tennessee Statehood Day—even if you can't celebrate the day on June 1st! In a group choose one of the following categories: games, activities, contests, speeches, food, or something else to celebrate Tennessee. Then make a list of your ideas, things you will need, and things you will do. If everyone does his or her part, your class will have a wonderful party for Statehood Day!

"The roads were [filled] with movers during the summer months—great top-heavy . . . wagons drawn by oxen . . . gentlemen astride blooded horses, rawboned farmers on hairy plow-nags, peddlers and merchants . . . immigrants too poor to afford [even a few] belongings and children on their backs—all moving west toward the promised land in Tennessee."

—Anonymous,
early 19th century

Middle Tennessee blossomed in the years after statehood. By 1801, more than 60 percent of the population lived in Middle Tennessee.

Timeline of Events

1800
Thomas Jefferson is elected president of the United States.

1804–1806
Lewis and Clark explore the Louisiana Territory.

1800   1802   1804   1806

1801
Archibald Roane becomes governor of Tennessee.

1803
The United States purchases the Louisiana Territory. John Sevier begins a second term as governor of Tennessee.

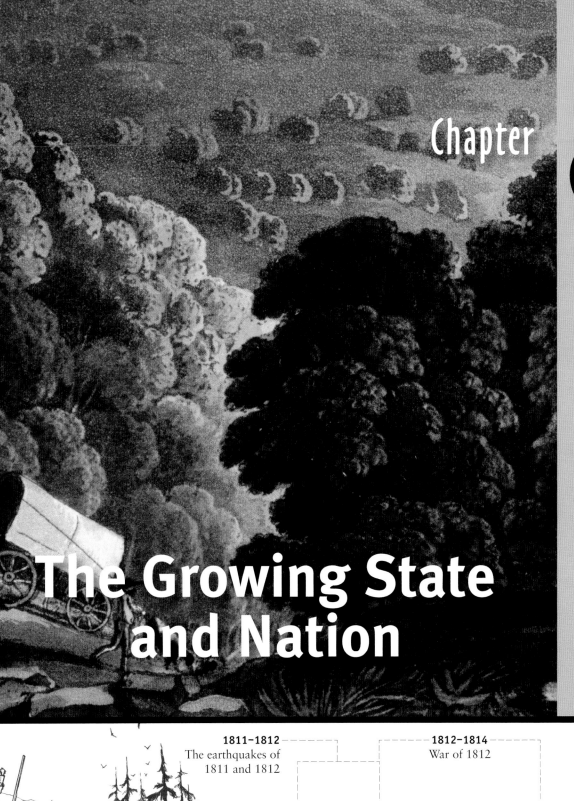

Chapter

8

After statehood, more settlers moved to Tennessee. They built small towns and large cities. Then the United States bought the Louisiana Territory. This land doubled the size of the nation. When our nation went to war with England again, many men from our state volunteered to serve. They were led by Tennessean Andrew Jackson.

The Growing State and Nation

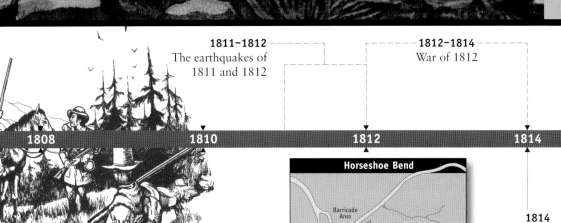

1811–1812
The earthquakes of 1811 and 1812

1812–1814
War of 1812

1808   1810   1812   1814

Horseshoe Bend

Barricade Area

Tohopeka Village

Tallapoosa River

N W S E

1814
Francis Scott Key writes "The Star-Spangled Banner."
Battle of Horseshoe Bend

The Journey to Tennessee

After Tennessee became a state, settlers poured into the region. They did not come for adventure. They came because they wanted land for their families. Most of the land belonged to the Cherokees and Chickasaws, but settlers believed they had the right to take it.

Most wagons were pulled by oxen. This was because oxen are much stronger than mules or horses.

Some of the earliest settlers in Tennessee were African Americans. Although there were a few free blacks, most were slaves. They had no choice about where to live. They went wherever their owners took them.

Traveling in the Wilderness

When Tennessee first became a state, only one or two roads connected it to other states. There were few real roads between the settlements within the state either. Settlers had cleared trails, but tree stumps made the trails difficult to use. Frequent rains created deep, muddy holes. It was so hard to take wagons across the trails that people usually walked or rode horses instead. Whenever they could, settlers traveled by water because it was faster, safer, and easier.

Can you guess what the two pieces of bent wood sticking up from this wagon were used for?

Linking the Present to the Past

For many years, settlers traveled on dirt trails, or *traces*. A trace is a path, trail, or road made by passing animals and people. The settlers cut down trees to clear trails, but stumps still stuck out of the ground. Over years of use, wagon wheels carved deep ruts in the road. As wagon wheels cut deeper into the ground, the bottoms of the wagons began brushing the tree stumps. Sometimes a tree stump stopped a wagon right in its tracks. People called this "getting stumped." Have you ever heard someone say they were stumped? It usually means the person is stuck and can't think of a new idea.

This family's cabin is not quite finished. Where do you think they slept at night?

Life on the Frontier

Life on the frontier took hard work. Every member of the family had to help. Men hunted and cleared the land. Women cooked, sewed, spun wool or cotton into thread, and wove cloth. They also planted gardens, churned butter, and made soap. Parents and older brothers and sisters taught small children how to care for animals and do other chores. Even the youngest members of frontier families quickly learned how to survive in the wilderness.

Choosing a Place to Live

The first thing a frontier family had to do was choose a spot for its home. Much of the land was covered by dense forests. Settlers had to cut down hundreds of trees to make room for cabins, fields, and forts.

Families needed fresh water, so they built their cabins near streams or springs. Many people built their homes on hills too. They wanted a good view of the land all around. Another common place to build a cabin was near stations, or forts. Family members could run to the fort for protection during Indian attacks.

What Do You Think?

Settlers cleared trees from hundreds of acres of land. What do you think they did with all those trees?

Tennessee Through Time: The Early Years

Building a Cabin

The earliest houses on the frontier were log cabins. Have you ever seen a log cabin? Most log homes were not very big. That is because a wall could only be as long as the tallest, straightest trees men could find.

Logs don't fit perfectly together, so there were gaps in the walls. Families filled the gaps with *chinking* of mud or clay to keep out cold air. In warm weather, families removed the chinking. Then air blew through the cracks and cooled the cabin.

After the men finished the cabin, they cut out doors and windows. They placed the door on the south side because the sun warmed that side during the cold winter months. The last thing frontier builders built was a chimney for the fireplace. They did not attach it tightly, so the family could knock it off in a hurry if the cabin caught fire.

Making Frontier Furniture

Furniture on the frontier was simple and homemade. Almost every home had at least one bed. The mattress was filled with corn husks and straw. Featherbeds were much softer, but few people could afford them. Some people made bedding of chicken feathers, but goose feathers were best. Most families also had a table and benches and some kind of *cupboard*. A cupboard is a cabinet with shelves for storing dishes. Frontier homes didn't have closets. People stored their clothes in chests or hung them on pegs on the wall.

This is a dog-trot cabin. Dog-trot cabins are actually two small cabins connected by one roof. The open space between the two cabins creates a breeze, so the area is shady and cool. Dogs trotted through the space, so people began calling this type of cabin a dog-trot cabin. Dogs and their owners escaped the summer heat by relaxing in the shade of the dog trot.

Maple Syrup Time

One favorite fall activity was making syrup from the sap of maple trees. Frontier families went out early in the morning and drilled small holes in the bark of maple trees. After drilling each hole, the children gently tapped a spout into the tree. The spout had a little hook that held a bucket.

Throughout the day, children lugged the heavy buckets of clear sap back to the cabin. Mother poured it into a huge pot over the fire. She spent hours stirring the sap to make sure it did not become too hot. If it cooked too long, it turned to sugar. Then Mother was disappointed because the syrup was ruined. But the children were thrilled. They knew Mother would pour the sugar into molds and make maple sugar candy! Whether the sap became syrup or sugar, everyone was happy that they had a way to sweeten their food.

Families that lived far away from streams had to draw water from a well every day. Have you ever carried a bucket of water?

Women on the Frontier

Frontier women took care of the family and the home. There were few doctors, so frontier women cared for the elderly and the ill and even delivered new babies.

Food

On the frontier, making a meal was hard work. A frontier woman spent many hours each day preparing food for her family.

All farm families in Tennessee raised corn, the most important crop on the frontier. Sometimes women roasted it over a fire. Other times they dried it and took it to a mill, where it was ground into meal. Women used the meal to make cornbread or mush. Sometimes they poured mush into a pan and let it sit until it became firm. Then they sliced it and fried it in bacon grease. Farm families also fed corn to their animals.

Squash, pumpkins, and potatoes were other important crops. The settlers dried peas, beans, and apple slices to eat during the winter months. During the summer, mothers sent

What Do You Think?

How do you think the settlers learned to grow squash, corn, and beans? Who first grew these crops?

their children out into the woods with baskets so they could gather berries and nuts. Sometimes frontier fathers carefully gathered honey from wild bees.

Farm Animals

Many settlers raised animals, especially hogs and chickens, for food. The men also hunted wild turkeys, rabbits, squirrels, deer, and even bear. A well-fed family ate meat three times a day. When the weather turned cold, frontier men and women worked together to butcher the animals. The women then salted and smoked the meat to keep it from spoiling. Most settlers had cows, but they did not use them for meat. If a family owned a cow, they drank its milk and used its cream to make butter and cheese.

Clothing

Women made almost all of the clothing worn by people in frontier Tennessee. They grew *flax,* a tall, thin plant that looked like wheat. The tiny flax *fibers* grew in a zigzag pattern. This rough pattern helped the fibers stick together when they were twisted. Many fibers twisted together made linen thread.

After the women spun the flax and sheep's wool into thread, they wove it into fabric. The fabric was called linsey-woolsey because it was made of linen and wool. Many early settlers came to Tennessee with only the clothing they were wearing. The process of growing flax, spinning thread, weaving cloth, and sewing clothes took almost a year!

Frontier families had no place to buy shoes. Instead, they made *moccasins* from soft animal leather. As soon as the weather was warm, children stopped wearing their moccasins. They went barefoot—even to school.

Soap

Frontier women made their own soap. All year long, they saved ashes from the fireplace. They kept the ashes in barrels and put water in the barrels. The ashy liquid that oozed out the bottom of the barrels was called lye. Frontier women put lye in big kettles, added animal fat, and cooked the mixture over the fire. After it cooled, they molded the gooey liquid into bars of soap.

This is linsey-woolsey. All fabric was precious to people on the frontier.

This is a wooden butter churn. Frontier children poured cream into the bucket, set a lid in place, and moved the churn up and down. In time, the cream turned into butter.

This is lye soap. How do you think it smelled? Some families added color or scents to the soap.

Tennessee's first mountain settlers played banjos and developed their own style of music. Today, it is known as bluegrass. It is one of America's most popular forms of music.

Everyone joined in the fun at frontier parties.

Fiddle music can be soft and slow or lively and quick. Have you ever heard fiddle or violin music?

Frontier Entertainment

Music was an important part of life from the earliest days in Tennessee. Everyone on the frontier loved to sing and tell stories. There were no radios, televisions, or CD players, so people got together and entertained one another. They sang **hymns** and **ballads** they knew before they moved west. Hymns are religious songs, and ballads tell stories.

A favorite musical instrument was the **fiddle** (violin). If no one had a fiddle, settlers made their own instruments. Some people learned how to play beautiful music on a washtub bass, a cigar-box banjo, a jug, or even a saw!

At frontier parties, people danced and played music. Others sat quietly, listening to stories, legends, and **tall tales.** Tall tales are stories of people who can do things that are impossible. Tall tales are more than just fun. They usually teach a lesson too.

Linking the Present to the Past

Can you imagine life without music? Music was as important to frontier folk as it is to us today. The 2002 Tennessee quarter shows a fiddle, a guitar, and a trumpet. It celebrates our state's musical heritage—from frontier fiddles to modern guitars!

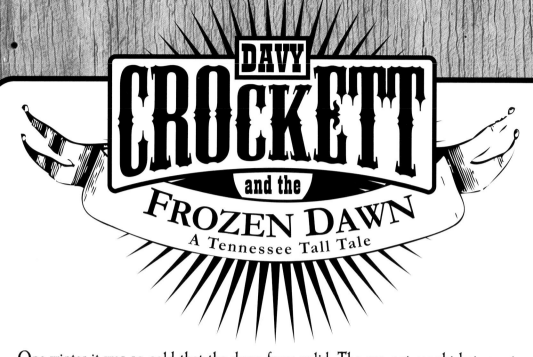

DAVY CROCKETT and the FROZEN DAWN
A Tennessee Tall Tale

One winter it was so cold that the dawn froze solid. The sun got caught between two ice blocks, and the earth iced up so much that it couldn't turn. The first rays of sunlight froze halfway over the mountain tops. They looked like yellow icicles dripping towards the ground.

Now Davy Crockett was headed home after a successful night hunting when the dawn froze up so solid. Being a smart man, he knew he had to do something quick or the earth was a goner. He had a freshly killed bear on his back, so he whipped it off, climbed right up on those rays of sunlight and began beating the hot bear carcass against the ice blocks, which were squashing the sun. Soon a gush of hot oil burst out of the bear, and it melted the ice. Davy gave the sun a good hard kick to get it started, and the sun's heat unfroze the earth and started it spinning again. So Davy lit his pipe on the sun, shouldered the bear, and slid himself down the sun rays before they melted. He took a bit of sunrise home in his pocket.

Retold by S. E. Schlosser

Education on the Frontier

Education was important to people in Tennessee. Before the region became a state, the territorial government passed a law that stated,

Religion, Morality, and Knowledge being necessary to good Government and the happiness of mankind, schools and the means of education shall be forever encouraged.

Most early settlers could read and write and owned several books. Before the first schools were built, mothers taught children at home.

Blount College

When Blount College opened in Knoxville, it was the first college in the United States that taught girls and boys in the same classroom. It was not long, however, until girls were sent to "female seminaries." In the seminaries, girls learned how to read and write. They also learned how to take care of a home. Blount College later became East Tennessee College. Today, it is the University of Tennessee.

The *Blue-Backed Speller*

Noah Webster, a teacher in Connecticut, realized that many people did not spell words the same way. He decided to write a spelling book. It became known as the *Blue-Backed Speller* because it had a blue binding. Webster's spelling book taught people all across the country to spell words the same way.

Many Tennessee families owned a *Blue-Backed Speller*. They used it to teach their children to read. Schools even held spelling contests called spelling bees. Spelling bees became a favorite frontier activity. Does your school have spelling bees?

More than 100 million Blue-Backed Speller books have been sold.

The first school in Memphis was the Male Academy, which opened in 1833. It was a log cabin on Court Square. The first public school in Chattanooga was Howard. It opened in 1865.

The First Schools

Presbyterian ministers opened the first two schools in Tennessee. Reverend Samuel Witherspoon Doak started the first one, Martin Academy, in Watauga. Martin Academy later changed its name to Washington College.

Reverend Thomas Craighead moved to the Cumberland settlements and opened Davidson Academy. Davidson Academy later became Cumberland College. Then it became the University of Nashville. In 1875, it became George Peabody College for Teachers.

What Do You Think?

In early Tennessee, some school teachers were ministers. Others were parents of students or people chosen by town leaders. They were not trained to be teachers. Today, teachers have to go to college for at least four years. They must spend time in a classroom with an experienced teacher. Why do you think it is important for teachers to be trained? What makes some teachers better than others?

EXPLORE TENNESSEE!

Doak House Museum

You've read about Reverend Samuel Doak in earlier chapters of this book. His son, Reverend Samuel Witherspoon Doak, brought the Presbyterian religion to our state and started our first school. Today, you can visit Samuel Witherspoon Doak's house in Greeneville. It is on the Tusculum College campus in Greeneville. The Doak House Museum has many artifacts that tell about education and religion in the Southwest Territory.

Linking the Present to the Past

Today, the school that began as Davidson Academy is part of Vanderbilt University.

Early Towns in Tennessee

As the population of Tennessee grew, towns began to appear. Settlers wanted to sell their products and buy the things they needed. River towns, such as Knoxville and Nashville, became important trading centers.

For a while, Knoxville grew faster than Nashville. Within a short time, however, Nashville had more than 100 homes, 15 stores, and a public square with a courthouse. Towns such as Dandridge, Jonesborough, Greeneville, Kingston, Rogersville, and Clarksville grew quickly too.

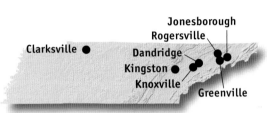

Have you ever been to Jonesborough, Tennessee's oldest town? This is what it looked like when it was new.

John and Luraney Oliver
(Birth and death dates unknown)

John and Luraney Oliver were a poor young couple with a new baby. They needed a place to live and land of their own. A friend told them about a place called Cades Cove in the Smoky Mountains of East Tennessee. The Olivers decided to go.

The Olivers carried only a few things on the 100-mile walk to Cades Cove. Luraney was expecting another baby, and it took the couple over a week to make the journey. Once they got to Cades Cove, they began clearing the land. They also built a cabin. It took so long that the Olivers did not have time to gather and store food for the winter.

The cold winds began to blow, and the little family grew hungry and scared. They did not know if they would survive. But nearby Indians had been watching the Olivers. They Indians were kind and generous. They shared their food with the little family. In the spring, other families arrived. Over time, the mountain community grew.

The Olivers raised nine children and had a good life at Cades Cove. As their children married, they stayed in East Tennessee. In fact, members of the Oliver family lived at Cades Cove for over 115 years!

TENNESSEE PORTRAIT

Native Americans and settlers worked together. They depended on one another to provide the things they wanted and needed.

Tennessee Through Time: The Early Years

Travel and Trade

The rivers of Tennessee were the best way to move things from place to place. People sent corn, whiskey, tobacco, furs, iron, and flax by boat. In Middle Tennessee, goods went down the Cumberland or Tennessee Rivers to the Ohio River. From there, they sailed down the Mississippi River to Natchez, Mississippi or New Orleans, Louisiana. The journey took more than two months. After the goods were sold, the merchants returned to Tennessee on the Natchez Trace.

Pikes

As towns grew, people built roads between them. These roads were often called *pikes.* For example, the road connecting Knoxville to Kingston was the Kingston Pike. The road connecting Nashville to Gallatin was called the Gallatin Pike. The word "pike" was short for "turnpike," which meant a toll road. A *toll* is a fee travelers have to pay to use a road.

1 MEMORY MASTER

1. What kind of houses did people on the frontier build?
2. Where was the first school in Tennessee?
3. What is a pike?

Linking the Present to the Past

Many roads in Tennessee today are still called pikes, but people don't have to pay to use them anymore. Have you ever taken a drive on Granny White Pike? It was named for Granny White, a woman who ran an inn near Nashville and died in 1816.

PEOPLE TO KNOW

Napoleon Bonaparte
William Clark
Thomas Jefferson
Meriwether Lewis
James Monroe
Sacagawea

PLACES TO LOCATE

Appalachian Mountains
Columbia River
France
Louisiana Territory
Mississippi River
Missouri River
New Orleans, Louisiana
North Dakota Territory
Pacific Ocean
Rocky Mountains
St. Louis River

WORDS TO UNDERSTAND

keelboat
Louisiana Purchase
pole

The Louisiana Purchase

At the time of statehood, Spain still controlled the Mississippi River and a huge piece of land west of it. This western land was called the Louisiana Territory. Spain also controlled the Mississippi River's largest port city, New Orleans. Tennesseans used the Mississippi River to take goods to market in New Orleans. From there, large ships carried the goods to the states along the Atlantic Coast.

Tennesseans worried that Spain might try to stop them from using the river. Then farmers and businessmen would have to carry goods across the Appalachian Mountains. Since it was a long, dangerous trip, Tennesseans would not be able to sell as many goods.

Making an Offer

Napoleon Bonaparte, a powerful French leader, took the Louisiana Territory from Spain. President Thomas Jefferson feared

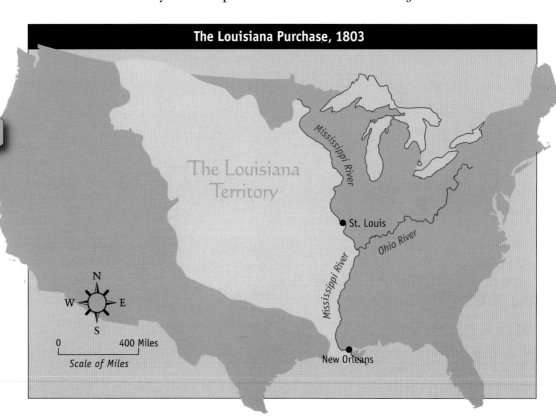

The Louisiana Purchase, 1803

The Louisiana Territory

Mississippi River

St. Louis

Ohio River

Mississippi River

New Orleans

N
W E
S

0   400 Miles
Scale of Miles

James Monroe did not have a chance to ask President Jefferson for permission before he signed the Louisiana Purchase Treaty. With the stroke of a pen, Monroe spent $15 million and doubled the size of the United States.

Linking the Present to the Past

Have you ever visited any of the following places? If you have, then you have been in the Louisiana Territory!

- Louisiana
- Arkansas
- Missouri
- Iowa
- Minnesota west of the Mississippi River
- North Dakota
- South Dakota
- Nebraska
- Kansas
- Oklahoma
- Northern Texas
- Northeast New Mexico
- Eastern sections of Montana, Wyoming, and Colorado

Napoleon might close the Mississippi River and the city of New Orleans to Americans. Jefferson also worried that France might try to take control of the entire United States.

Jefferson sent James Monroe to talk with Napoleon. Monroe offered to pay $2 million to buy the east bank of the Mississippi River. Monroe was shocked when Napoleon offered to sell him the entire Louisiana Territory! The United States paid $15 million for nearly 530 million acres of land. This was called the *Louisiana Purchase.* It doubled the size of the United States and made it one of the largest countries in the world.

Lewis and Clark

The United States now owned the Louisiana Territory, but no one knew how big it was. Thomas Jefferson wanted a group of explorers to travel up the Missouri River, across the Rocky Mountains, and down the Columbia River. Jefferson hoped the explorers would find a water route to the Pacific Ocean. He also wanted to learn more about the plants and animals in the region. Were they different from those in the rest of the United States?

Jefferson knew many Indian tribes lived in the territory. How did these tribes live? What languages did they speak? Were they different from the tribes that lived east of the Mississippi River? Jefferson wanted to get to know the western Indians so Americans could trade with the Indians.

Jefferson chose Meriwether Lewis to lead an expedition through the Louisiana Territory. Lewis asked Jefferson to choose William Clark, from Kentucky, to help him lead. Lewis and Clark had become friends while serving in the army. Both men knew a great deal about surviving in the wilderness. They also knew how to draw maps. Mapping new lands was one of the most important reasons for the trip.

Meriwether Lewis

William Clark

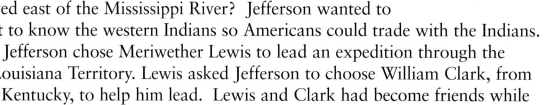
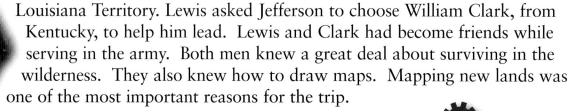

TERRIFIC TECHNOLOGY

Several years before Lewis and Clark's journey, an important timekeeping machine was invented: the chronometer. With this piece of equipment, Lewis and Clark were able to map the land.

To measure longitude, explorers needed an exact way to measure time. The rocking motion of ships, horses, and wagons stopped even the best clocks. The chronometer was a clock that was not affected by movement. As long as the chronometer was wound every day, it kept perfect time—no matter where it was.

Equipment and Supplies

Lewis and Clark planned to travel during every season. Here are a few of the things they packed:

- 150 yards of cloth to be sewn into tents and sheets
- 12 pounds of soap
- 193 pounds of "portable soup" (a thick paste made of beef, eggs, and vegetables)
- 3 bushels of salt
- writing paper, ink, and crayons
- 15 rifles
- 420 pounds of sheet lead for bullets
- 176 pounds of gunpowder
- 600 "Rush's pills" (laxatives)
- four-volume dictionary

Items to Offer as Gifts to the Indians:

- 144 pocket mirrors
- 4,600 sewing needles
- 144 small scissors
- 10 pounds of thread
- silk ribbons
- many yards of brightly colored cloth
- 288 knives
- 8 brass kettles
- 33 pounds of tiny colored beads

Lewis and Clark's Backpacks

If people looked through your backpack, what would they learn about you? Historians can tell a lot about the trip Lewis and Clark made by studying the things they took with them. Each item is a clue. Pretend you are a historian and you are opening Lewis and Clark's "backpacks."

To get a stamp in your passport, make a copy of this chart. Then choose three items from the equipment and supplies list and three items from the list of things they planned to offer as gifts to the Indians. List the six items you chose in the first column of your chart. Next to the item, write what it is used for. Then write how you know that. The first one has been done for you. Fill in the chart for each item.

Item	What Is It Used For	How We Know
Writing paper, ink, and crayons	To record what they discovered on their expedition	They used these items to write in journals, make maps, and draw sketches.

The Corps of Discovery

Lewis and Clark needed strong men to make the journey with them. Lewis said he wanted "good hunters, stout, healthy, unmarried men, [used] to the woods, and capable of bearing [tiredness]." They finally chose 43 men to join their team.

Some of the men Lewis and Clark chose were friends from the army. They also chose a gunsmith, a carpenter, a cook, and a few woodsmen and hunters who knew how to trap animals. Two team members spoke several languages. Clark took York, his slave, as a member of the expedition. Thomas Jefferson called the group the Corps of Discovery.

Preparing for the Expedition

Once the group was formed, Lewis and Clark set up camp across the Mississippi River from St. Louis. The team spent the winter at the camp preparing for the journey. They read articles about the land written by early explorers. Lewis already knew a lot about science. He studied the stars, plant life, and medicine. No one knew how long the journey would take or what the men might find.

During the winter, the men built a large boat for the trip. The boat, a *keelboat,* was very unusual. It could be rowed, sailed, *poled,* or towed. It had a large, flat bottom and a single sail. Traveling against a river's current required a crew of at least 22 men.

The Journey Begins

By May of 1804, the preparations were finished. Lewis and Clark led their team out of St. Louis and up the Missouri River. Along the way, they saw several empty Indian villages. Smallpox had killed all the people who once lived there.

The group traveled through the summer and fall. When winter came, they stopped in the North Dakota Territory and camped at a Mandan Indian village. The Mandans had traded with Europeans for many years, so they were not afraid of explorers. During the winter, the Mandans gave them food. They also taught the explorers about the Rocky Mountain region.

Sacagawea

During the winter, the Corps of Discovery hired a trapper to guide them through the next part of their journey. The trapper brought along his 16-year-old Indian wife, Sacagawea. Sacagawea was a member of the Shoshone tribe.

The expedition left St. Louis, Missouri, on May 14, 1804. William Clark wrote in his journal that there was a *"jentle brease."*

When she was 12, she had been kidnapped by another tribe. That tribe sold her as a slave to the trapper. During the winter, Sacagawea had a baby boy.

When spring arrived, the group began traveling up the Missouri River again. At first, neither Lewis nor Clark wanted to travel with a mother and her child. They soon learned, however, that the Indians they met were friendlier because Sacagawea and the baby were with them. When the explorers met the Shoshone, Sacagawea discovered the chief was her brother. The Shoshone chief greeted Lewis and Clark warmly. He also gave them horses and guides.

Some members of the Corps of Discovery did not want Sacagawea or her baby to go with them.

The Growing State and Nation

Can you imagine traveling west until you reached the Pacific Ocean? How do you think Corps of Discovery members felt when they saw the ocean?

Searching for the Pacific

Crossing the Rocky Mountains was the most difficult part of the journey. The men had to lead the horses up dangerous, rocky paths, and it was hard to find food in the rugged mountains. When the group reached a river in today's Idaho region, they built canoes. The men hoped the river would lead them to the Pacific Ocean.

In November of 1805, the Corps of Discovery finally reached the Pacific Ocean. Their journey over the mountains proved there was no water route to the Pacific Ocean. The explorers spent the winter in the region that is now the state of Oregon.

Coming Home

In the spring, the tired explorers began their long journey home. When they reached St. Louis, they were greeted with parades and celebrations. The men were heroes because their journey had been a

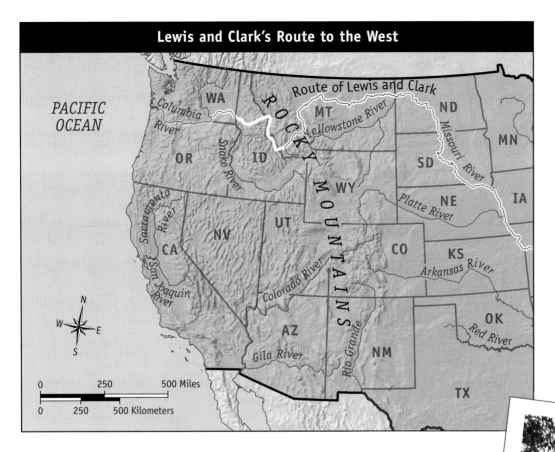

Lewis and Clark's Route to the West

PACIFIC OCEAN

WA
OR
ID
MT
ND
MN
SD
WY
NE
IA
NV
UT
CO
KS
CA
AZ
NM
OK
TX

Route of Lewis and Clark
Columbia River
Snake River
Sacramento River
San Joaquin River
Colorado River
Gila River
Rio Grande
Yellowstone River
Missouri River
Platte River
Arkansas River
Red River
ROCKY MOUNTAINS

N
W E
S

0   250   500 Miles
0   250   500 Kilometers

What Do You Think ?

After Lewis and Clark explored the West, thousands of settlers followed them. They built homes and cleared millions of acres for farms. There was plenty of room to grow. How would life in the United States be different if our country had not purchased the Louisiana Territory?

huge success. They had mapped the West and learned much about it. They knew it had good land for homes, farms, and large settlements.

Lewis and Clark learned much about the natural resources in the Louisiana Territory. They brought back plants and animals that were strange and new to most Americans. They explained how the land, water, minerals, plants, and animals could bring the United States great wealth.

Thomas Jefferson named Meriwether Lewis governor of the Louisiana Territory. Three years later, Lewis decided to travel to Washington, D.C. He died while passing through Tennessee. He is buried along the Natchez Trace.

2 MEMORY MASTER

1. What event doubled the size of the United States?
2. What are the names of the two men who led a journey to explore the Louisiana Territory?
3. Who was Sacagawea?

Meriwether Lewis was governor of the Upper Louisiana Territory when he died in Tennessee. This monument to him can be seen along the Natchez Trace Parkway.

PEOPLE TO KNOW

Willie Blount
Creek Indians
Sam Houston
Andrew Jackson
Francis Scott Key
Dolley Madison
James Madison
Red Eagle
Archibald Roane
John Sevier
Tecumseh
Eli Whitney

PLACES TO LOCATE

Baltimore, Maryland
Mississippi River
New Orleans, Louisiana
Tennessee River

WORDS TO UNDERSTAND

anthem
boll
gin
impressment
rivalry
war hawk

The Settlers Spread Out

The state of Tennessee grew rapidly as people moved westward. In 1800, the population was 105,000. Ten years later, it had more than doubled.

After the cotton gin was invented, more people wanted to plant cotton. But in the settled regions of the state, it was too cold to grow the crop. The western regions, however, had just the right climate. Settlers moved west to the land between the Tennessee and Mississippi Rivers and planted thousands of acres of cotton.

TERRIFIC TECHNOLOGY

The Cotton Gin

Cotton is a plant that grows fluffy, white fibers in sections called **bolls.** The bolls also contain dozens of seeds. The seeds have to be removed before the fibers can be spun into thread. For thousands of years, cotton seeds had to be pulled out by hand. This was very slow, boring work.

About 200 years ago, a man named Eli Whitney invented a machine that quickly removed the seeds from the cotton. The machine was called a cotton **gin.** "Gin" was short for "engine." With a cotton gin, one person could do as much work as 50 people who were working by hand.

Sevier and Jackson

After John Sevier served three terms as governor, Archibald Roane became the new governor. At the time, Andrew Jackson was a land speculator. Jackson had a quick temper. He seemed always ready to settle his differences by fighting.

Sevier and Jackson both wanted to become the major general of the state militia. They ran against one another in an election, but there was a tie. Jackson and Roane were close friends, so the governor gave the job to Jackson.

After Jackson became major general, Sevier became so angry that a *rivalry* developed between the two men. It also strengthened a growing rivalry between East Tennessee and Middle Tennessee. This struggle between the regions grew much stronger as the years passed.

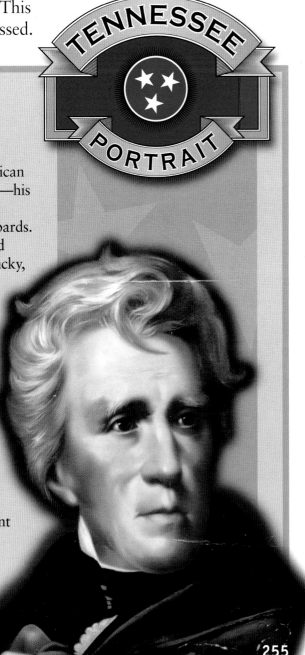

Andrew Jackson
(1767–1845)

Andrew Jackson was born in the backwoods of South Carolina. His father died before he was born. As a young man, he fought in the American Revolution and became a prisoner of war. He lost the rest of his family—his mother and two brothers—during the war, so he hated the British.

Shortly after arriving in Tennessee, Jackson met Rachel Donelson Robards. She had come to the Cumberland settlements with her parents, John and Rachel Donelson. Rachel Robards had been married to a man in Kentucky, but she believed they were divorced. She had moved back to Tennessee to live with her mother.

Jackson and Rachel fell in love. Three years later, they went to Natchez, Mississippi, and got married. When they returned to Nashville, they learned that Rachel was not divorced from her first husband! After he finally gave her a divorce, she and Jackson married for a second time. Jackson's enemies never forgot about Rachel's mistake. Over the years, they brought it up many times. This hurt Rachel and deeply angered Jackson.

As a delegate from the Cumberland settlements, Jackson helped write the state's first constitution. He then became the district attorney in Nashville, where he built a successful law practice. Once Tennessee became a state, Andrew Jackson was chosen as the state's first representative to the U.S. Congress. He went on to become an important military leader and the seventh president of the United States.

The Earthquakes of 1811 and 1812

"At Knoxville, the quaking of the earth . . . lasted more than three minutes. The rattling of the windows and furniture of the houses were such as to awaken almost every family. This was about two in the morning."

—Samuel Mitchell, 1815

A fur trader traveling on the Mississippi River during the earthquakes later wrote, "So great a wave come up the river that I never seen one like it at sea. It carried us back north, up-stream, for more than a mile. The water spread out upon the banks—covering three or four miles inland." Today, the water that spread out for miles is Reelfoot Lake.

Tecumseh, a powerful Shawnee war chief in the Northwest, told Americans that great earthquakes would occur along the Mississippi River. He said they would come during the winter of 1811 and 1812. He also said the earthquakes would destroy the white people. The settlers who lived in the region did not know what an earthquake was.

Exactly as Tecumseh foretold, the earthquakes came: two in December, one in January, and one in February. The earth shook violently and opened deep cracks in the ground. Trees bent over and snapped. Many houses crumbled, and there were terrible mud slides. In some places, the land rose or fell 20 feet!

Huge waves on the Mississippi River sank boats and crashed others against the shore. Much of the land flooded, and the river actually flowed in a different direction for a while. Reelfoot Lake in West Tennessee was formed when the Mississippi River shifted. Today, it is the largest natural lake in Tennessee.

Modern-day scientists believe the earthquakes of 1811 and 1812 were the strongest quakes to ever occur in North America. The earthquakes rang church bells as far away as Boston, Massachusetts, and caused damage in Washington, D.C., and Canada. But they did not destroy the white people.

What Do You Think

Can you imagine living through such terrible earthquakes? What do you think it would be like? Where would you go for protection? What would you do to try to stay safe?

The Battle of Tippecanoe was the first battle of the War of 1812.

Trouble for the Creeks

The Creeks and the Chickasaws still lived in southern and western Tennessee. They watched as more and more settlers moved onto their lands. They realized the settlers would soon cross Tennessee's border to plant cotton in Alabama and Mississippi. The Indians were afraid they would lose even more land.

A Visit from Tecumseh

Tecumseh traveled from the Northwest to the South to meet with the Chickasaws, Cherokees, and Creeks. He tried to convince them to join with his tribe to fight the settlers. The Creeks took matters into their own hands and began crossing the Tennessee border and stealing from farmers. The settlers grew angry and finally asked the state government to send the militia.

While Tecumseh was in the South, American soldiers destroyed several Shawnee settlements in northern Indiana. This attack became known as the Battle of Tippecanoe.

When Tennesseans learned Tecumseh had visited the South, they grew very worried. They did not want the Indians to work together or fight back. The settlers just wanted the Indians to leave.

Tecumseh was a noble soldier and warrior. He never allowed prisoners to be tortured or abused.

The British captured American soldiers and encouraged Indians to attack settlers.

The British Make Trouble for Tennessee

In Europe, a war between France and Great Britain raged. Leaders in both countries wanted the United States to help them, but American leaders did not want to choose sides. They wanted to stay friendly with both countries. Soon British ships began capturing American sailors as they sailed across the Atlantic Ocean. The British forced the Americans to work for them. This practice was called *impressment.*

When ships full of Tennessee goods were stopped at sea, people in Europe could not buy the goods. Many people in our state lost money because the demand for Tennessee goods dropped. That made prices drop. Whenever there is less demand for goods, prices for the goods go down. This is called the law of supply and demand.

The War of 1812

Over the years, several states had elected new members to the U.S. Congress. Many of these new leaders wanted to go to war with Great Britain. They also wanted to attack the Indians and drive them farther west. These men were young and had not fought in a war. They did not understand how bloody and terrible war was.

People began calling them *war hawks.* Tennessee's three congressmen and two senators were war hawks.

President James Madison agreed with the war hawks. He sent a message to Congress asking members to declare war. After a long debate, Congress finally declared war on both the British and the Creek Indians. It was called the War of 1812.

Tennessee Volunteers Again

As soon as Congress declared war, Billy Phillips, a young jockey, jumped on his horse in Washington, D.C., and took off for Tennessee. He arrived in Nashville shouting, "Here's the stuff! War with England! War!" Everyone was excited. Cities and towns across the state held big parties and celebrations.

Tennessee's new governor was Willie Blount (William Blount's half brother). He and Andrew Jackson immediately sent messages to President Madison. They told the president that Tennessee was ready to fight.

What Do You Think ?

Imagine you are a member of the U.S. Congress prior to the War of 1812. Would you have been a war hawk? Why or why not?

Linking the Present to the Past

Thousands of Tennessee men were quick to respond when asked to fight. Their willingness to serve set a pattern for other wars to come. It also helped Tennessee earn its state nickname: the Volunteer State.

Tennesseans have a long history of volunteering for service. What does this say about our state? This painting shows Andrew Jackson and the Tennessee Volunteers.

War with the Creeks

While the country prepared for war with Great Britain, the conflict with Indians in Tennessee grew worse. The Creeks knew soldiers were planning to attack, but they were divided about what to do. Some Creeks wanted peace with the settlers. Others, such as Chief Red Eagle, wanted to attack white settlements. Red Eagle's group was known as the Red Sticks because they carried war clubs painted the color of blood.

In August of 1813, the Red Sticks attacked a group of white settlers in Alabama. They killed more than 500 men, women, and children. When news of the attack reached Tennessee, Governor William Blount was furious. He wanted to wipe out the Creeks.

Governor Blount called for 1,500 men to help General Andrew Jackson fight the Creeks. More than 2,500 men volunteered. Jackson and John Cocke organized the large company of soldiers and headed for Alabama. Many Cherokee warriors joined them. They wanted to fight the Creeks too.

Chief Red Eagle's English name was William Weatherford.

The Battle of Horseshoe Bend

After several small battles, the Red Sticks knew the Tennessee militia was planning a major attack. The Red Sticks chose a spot near a Creek village in a bend of the Tallapoosa River. They thought the river would protect them from the back. The Red Sticks built a thick, log wall for protection and waited for Jackson's troops to attack.

Early in the morning, two of Jackson's cannons began firing at the wall. At the same time, Cherokees swam across the river and attacked the Creeks from the back. Sam Houston, a young soldier from East Tennessee, led some of Jackson's men over the wall. The Creeks were trapped between Jackson's soldiers and the Cherokees.

When the battle was over, more than 750 Creek warriors were dead. Jackson lost only 50 men, but another 150 men were wounded. One of the injured men was Sam Houston, who later became an important political leader.

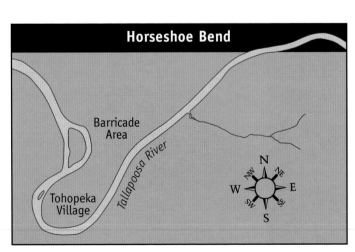

Horseshoe Bend

Barricade Area

Tallapoosa River

Tohopeka Village

The Battle of Horseshoe Bend took place near Tohopeka Village.
Fifteen Creeks died for every one American who died.

General Jackson was surprised that Red Eagle showed so much courage. He did not take the chief prisoner. Chief Red Eagle lived out the rest of his life as a peaceful farmer.

Chief Red Eagle Surrenders to Jackson

Chief Red Eagle was not at Horseshoe Bend on the day of the battle. When he learned about it, he realized he was defeated. Red Eagle walked into Jackson's headquarters in Alabama. He surrendered and agreed to give 22 million acres of land to the United States. The chief asked for only one thing. He wanted Jackson to do whatever he could to protect the remaining Creek women and children.

"Old Hickory" Returns to Tennessee

Andrew Jackson received a hero's welcome when he returned to Nashville. During the war with the Creeks, Jackson's men began calling him Old Hickory. They said he was as tough as an old hickory tree. Across the state, people talked about Andrew Jackson. They were thrilled that he had led the Tennessee volunteers to victory.

The Burning of Washington, D.C.

While Red Eagle was surrendering in Tennessee, leaders in Great Britain were deciding to send more soldiers to North America. The powerful British navy planned to attack cities along the Atlantic Coast. One of these cities was our nation's capital, Washington, D.C.

In the summer of 1814, the British sailed into the capital city. They burst into the House of Representatives and burned all the furniture. Dolley Madison, the wife of President James Madison, was alone at the White House. When she learned the British were headed toward her, she cut a painting of George Washington out of its frame. Then she rolled up the canvas and carried it with her as she left town. She also saved the Declaration of Independence and several other important papers.

What Do You Think ?

Why do you think Dolley Madison took the portrait of George Washington? Do you think the British would have wanted to destroy it? Why?

Dolley Madison would not leave the White House without the painting of George Washington. She also stuffed a carriage with important government papers.

The British army was too small to take control of the entire city of Washington, D.C. They decided instead to do as much damage as they could.

Our National Anthem

A few weeks after the British stormed the nation's capital, they attacked Baltimore, Maryland. The United States had built a fort in Baltimore Harbor to protect the city from attack. It was this fort the British were attacking. Francis Scott Key, a young American lawyer, was on a ship that was trying to reach Baltimore. His boat was not allowed to sail into the harbor until the battle was over.

Through the night, Francis watched the attack. He could only see the flag flying over the fort by the light of blasting bombs and cannons. After the battle ended, the night was too dark for Francis to tell if the flag was still there. He had to wait until the light of morning.

The Dawn Breaks

From the ship's deck, Francis watched and waited for sunrise. When the dawn broke, he could see the American flag still waving over the fort. His heart soared. The United States had won the battle!

Francis wrote a poem that explained how he felt that morning. His brother-in-law set the words to music. Then a music publisher named it "The Star-Spangled Banner." In 1931, "The Star-Spangled Banner" became our country's national *anthem.*

Francis Scott Key had a wife, six sons, and five daughters waiting for him at home.

The British attack Baltimore Harbor.

Pretend you have been gone for a while and cannot get home because your town is under attack. Would you be worried about your family and friends? How would feel when the sun rose and you could finally see the U.S. flag? That is how Key felt when he wrote the "Star-Spangled Banner."

The Star-Spangled Banner

O say, can you see, by the dawn's early light,
What so proudly we hailed at the twilight's last gleaming?
Whose broad stripes and bright stars, through the perilous fight,
O'er the ramparts we watched, were so gallantly streaming!
And the rockets' red glare, the bombs bursting in air,
Gave proof through the night that our flag was still there:
O say, does that star-spangled banner yet wave
O'er the land of the free and the home of the brave?

The Battle of New Orleans

After the American victory over the Creeks at Horseshoe Bend, President Madison made Andrew Jackson major general of the U.S. Army. The war with Great Britain was still being fought, and Madison feared the British navy was going to attack New Orleans. Madison ordered Jackson to go to Louisiana. When Jackson arrived in New Orleans, he quickly organized an army. One of his soldiers was a famous pirate named Jean Lafitte. The troops set up camp along the Mississippi River just outside the city.

In January of 1815, the British army attacked the camp. But Jackson's soldiers were armed and ready. In less than two hours, the Americans defeated the British. The British lost more than 2,000 soldiers, but the United States lost only 71. Jackson's army stayed in New Orleans for the next three months. During that time, the U.S. Army lost more soldiers to disease than it had lost to battle.

Jackson Becomes Famous

News of the victory at the Battle of New Orleans spread quickly across the country. In every state, people said Andrew Jackson was a great hero. Some said he was our country's second George Washington. They said the War of 1812 was the second war for independence from Great Britain. Andrew and Rachel Jackson attended many parties and became very famous. What would his fame mean for his future? What would it mean for the state of Tennessee?

③ MEMORY MASTER

1. Which representative to Congress became the seventh president of the United States?
2. What event created Reelfoot Lake?
3. What did the war hawks want?

The Battle of New Orleans was actually a series of battles in December of 1814 and January of 1815.

The Battle of New Orleans was a huge victory, but it did not have to be fought. Two weeks before the battle, the United States and Great Britain had signed a treaty that ended the war. No one in America knew about the treaty because it was signed in Paris, France. It took weeks for news to travel across the vast Atlantic Ocean.

Chapter 8 Review

What's the Point?

Tennessee grew rapidly as settlers moved west looking for land. People built cabins, raised animals, made clothes, and grew food. Cities grew larger as travel and trade along the rivers became important businesses. The United States doubled in size when it bought the Louisiana Territory, which was explored by Lewis and Clark. More settlers moved to western and southern Tennessee to plant cotton in the warmer climate. This caused problems with the Creeks and Chickasaws, who lived there. The Indians eventually moved out of Tennessee. The United States fought and won the War of 1812 against Great Britain.

Becoming Better Readerss

Tall Tales

Frontier parties were full of dancing, music, and storytelling. One type of story told was a tall tale. Have you ever read a tall tale about characters like Paul Bunyan or Sally Ann Thunder? Take your reading a step further by reading a tall tale. Then share your tall tale with the class as if you were a storyteller at a frontier party. Here are a few tall tale books you can check out from your school or local library:

200 Years through 200 Stories by Anne Klebenow
American Tall Tales by Adrien Stoutenburg
American Tall Tales by Mary Pope Osborne
Cut from the Same Cloth: American Women of Myth, Legend, and Tall Tales by Robert D. San Souci
Frontier Tales of Tennessee by Louise Davis
Paul Bunyan by Steven Kellogg
Tennessee Tales the Textbooks Don't Tell by Jennie Ivey

Climbing to Connections

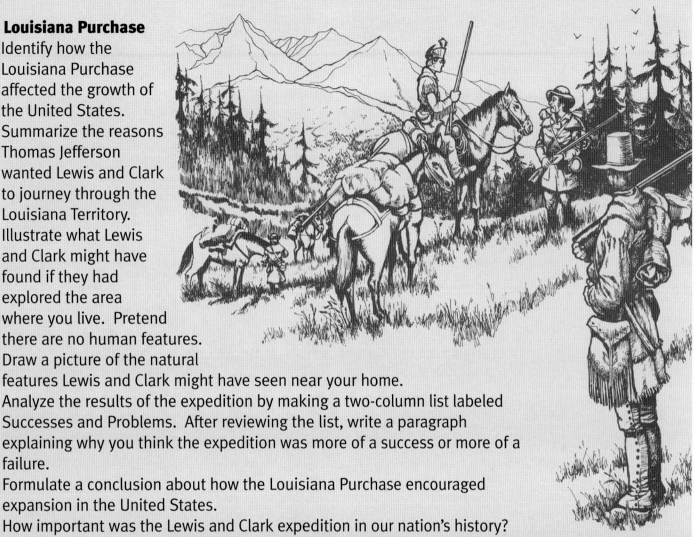

The Louisiana Purchase

1. Identify how the Louisiana Purchase affected the growth of the United States.
2. Summarize the reasons Thomas Jefferson wanted Lewis and Clark to journey through the Louisiana Territory.
3. Illustrate what Lewis and Clark might have found if they had explored the area where you live. Pretend there are no human features. Draw a picture of the natural features Lewis and Clark might have seen near your home.
4. Analyze the results of the expedition by making a two-column list labeled Successes and Problems. After reviewing the list, write a paragraph explaining why you think the expedition was more of a success or more of a failure.
5. Formulate a conclusion about how the Louisiana Purchase encouraged expansion in the United States.
6. How important was the Lewis and Clark expedition in our nation's history? Do you think it was necessary? Why or why not?

Evaluation Station

The Main Event

Now that you have read the chapter, go back to the timeline on the opening pages. Talk about the events on the timeline with a partner. Think about why each event was important. Then decide with your partner which was the most important event in the chapter. How did this event affect other events in our state's or nation's history? How would our lives be different today if that event had not happened?

"*When a people has their head in the lion's mouth, [good sense] requires them to take it out with great care. We are all [waiting] in great suspense to hear our final doom.*"

—*Cherokee Chief John Ross before removal, 1838*

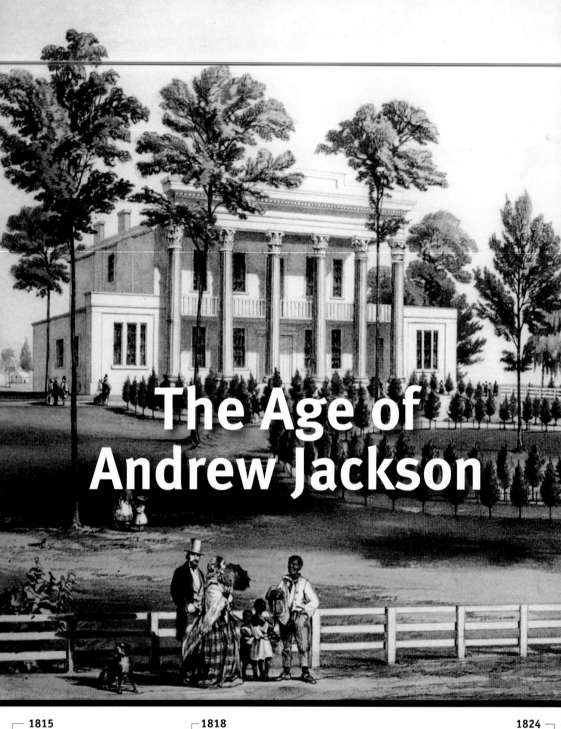

The Age of Andrew Jackson

Andrew Jackson's Nashville home, the Hermitage, opened as a museum over 100 years ago. Since that time, more than 15 million people have visited.

Timeline of Events

1815
The Manumission Society of Tennessee is established.

1818
Andrew Jackson fights the Seminole Indians in Florida.

1824
Andrew Jackson loses his first campaign for president of the United States.

| 1816 | 1818 | 1822 | 182 |

1819
The Panic of 1819
The first steamboat arrives in Nashville.
The first anti-slavery newspaper in the United States is published at Jonesborough.

1821
Sequoyah develops a written Cherokee language.
Andrew Jackson becomes the territorial governor of Florida

After the War of 1812, there was a new spirit and energy in the United States. The war had been a great victory. People were proud to be Americans, and Andrew Jackson was a national hero. Many Tennesseans wanted him to become president of the United States. The Cherokees did not like Jackson, however, because he wanted them to move out of Tennessee and Georgia.

1825
Frances Wright establishes Nashoba in West Tennessee.

1828
Andrew Jackson is elected president.

1830
Congress passes the Indian Removal Act.

1836
David Crockett dies in Texas at the Battle of the Alamo.

1838
The Cherokees leave Tennessee on the Trail of Tears.

1826 **1828** **1830** **1832** **1834** **1836** **1838**

1833
A cholera epidemic kills thousands.

1835
The U.S. Senate approves the Treaty of New Echota, forcing the Cherokees to leave Tennessee.

1834
Tennessee adopts a new state constitution.

1837
Andrew Jackson completes his second term as president.

Constitution.
of the
State of Tennessee.

Growth in the New Century

Tennessee grew rapidly after the War of 1812. Many people who planned to move to the West decided to stay in Tennessee. In 1810, our state's population was 216,000. Over the next ten years, that number nearly doubled. Knoxville and Nashville became large cities, and other towns along the rivers grew too. The population of Middle Tennessee grew larger than that of East Tennessee.

The Jackson Purchase

Andrew Jackson was a national hero after the victory at the Battle of New Orleans. People in every state knew his name. The new president, James Monroe, sent Jackson and a group of Tennessee Volunteers to Florida to drive out the Seminole Indians. When the United States later purchased Florida, President Monroe asked Jackson to be its territorial governor.

General Andrew Jackson and his troops prepare to attack the Seminole Indians in Florida.

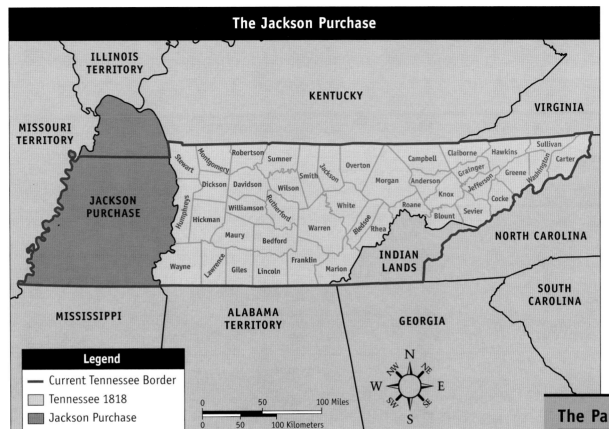

The Jackson Purchase

Legend
— Current Tennessee Border
☐ Tennessee 1818
☐ Jackson Purchase

Even though Jackson was in Florida, he was still working as a land speculator. He and several other speculators wanted to own much of the fertile land between the western section of the Tennessee River and the Mississippi River. The land belonged to the Chickasaws. But Jackson knew people would pay a lot of money for it because it would be a good place to grow cotton. The state needed the money to pay debts.

The Chickasaws did not want to give up the land. President Monroe sent Jackson and Isaac Shelby, a Kentuckian, to talk with four Chickasaw chiefs. They finally agreed to sell their western lands for $300,000. This sale was called the Jackson Purchase. It added land to both Tennessee and Kentucky.

Linking the Present to the Past

Today, many Native Americans believe the Chickasaws never would have agreed to sell their land unless they were forced. They also say the Chickasaws never received the money they were promised for the Jackson Purchase.

The Panic of 1819

As the population of the state grew, the demand for land increased. This caused the price of land to rise. Banks in Knoxville and Nashville loaned money to people so they could buy land. When the banks began having problems, it created money problems for nearly everyone. People became nervous and stopped buying goods. When no one buys goods, money becomes scarce. This is called an *economic panic.*

Settling West Tennessee

State leaders created 16 new counties out of the land gained through the Jackson Purchase. With West Tennessee now open for settlement, people began moving across the Tennessee River. In 1819, John Overton, Andrew Jackson, and James Winchester established the city of Memphis along the Mississippi River. The land was ideal for growing cotton because summers in the region were long and hot.

As West Tennessee grew, the three Grand Divisions—East Tennessee, Middle Tennessee, and West Tennessee—began to compete for power. The Indian tribes were almost gone. White Americans claimed nearly all the land east of the Mississippi River.

Counties of West Tennessee, 1819

Obion | Weakley | Henry
Dyer | Gibson | Carroll | Benton
Lauderdale | Haywood | Madison | Henderson
Tipton
Fayette | Hardeman | McNairy | Hardin

— Current Tennessee Border

Counties Created from Jackson Purchase

0   25   50 Miles
0   25   50 Kilometers

John Overton, Andrew Jackson, and James Winchester chose the site for Memphis because it sat high on a Chickasaw Bluff. Even when the Mississippi River flooded, the water never reached the top of the bluff. It was a perfect place to build a port city.

OUR LAND OUR LIVES

Located on the Mississippi River, Memphis became the largest port city in Tennessee.

Travellers Rest

Judge John Overton's home at his plantation, Travellers Rest, has been restored and turned into a museum. The house shows what life was like in Middle Tennessee from the Native American period through the Civil War. Reenactors, dressed in costume, tell stories about the landowners, slaves, and other people who visited or lived at Travellers Rest. The plantation is historic and educational, but it is also fun. There are programs and tours for students, teachers, scouts, and even senior citizens! Travellers Rest is said to be the oldest house open to the public in Nashville.

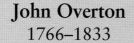

TENNESSEE PORTRAIT

John Overton
1766–1833

John Overton was one of Andrew Jackson's closest friends. Overton was born in Virginia, but he went to law school in Kentucky. After graduation, he moved to Tennessee and set up a law practice. When Overton was nearly 30, he became a tax collector in the Southwest Territory. This was a hard job because people did not like to pay taxes.

After Tennessee became a state, Overton became a land speculator. He bought and sold thousands of acres of land in Middle and West Tennessee and became very wealthy. In 1804, Overton became a judge and made many important decisions about the land. He also owned many large banks. In addition, Overton was a successful planter. His enormous cotton and fruit plantation near Nashville is called Travellers Rest.

Overton got married when he was 54. His 37-year-old bride, Mary, was a widow with five children. Together the Overtons had three more children. Mary Overton was a devoted mother who knew how to make medicine from herbs. Most families at that time lost one or more children to disease, but all eight of Mary's children lived to adulthood.

Overton owned 5,000 acres of the land on which Memphis was built. He was one of Andrew Jackson's closest advisors and worked to strengthen the city for the rest of his life. Overton and Jackson remained friends until Overton died.

Sequoyah

After the Chickasaws left, the only Indians still living in Tennessee were the Cherokees. Sequoyah was a Cherokee warrior who had fought with General Jackson at the Battle of Horseshoe Bend. During the war, Sequoyah and other Cherokee soldiers could not write letters to their families because Cherokee was only a spoken language. There was no way to write in Cherokee.

Talking Leaves

Sequoyah's father was a white man from Virginia. He gave Sequoyah the English name George Gist. As a child, Sequoyah watched white settlers read words from "talking leaves" (books). Some Cherokees believed reading was magic, but Sequoyah didn't think so. He knew there must be a way to learn how to do it. He finally learned that the settlers used letters to represent sounds. Then they put the letters together to create words and the words together to describe ideas.

Creating the Signs

At that time, none of the Indian languages in North America were written. All Indian stories and legends were passed down

Sequoyah wanted his people to be able to read and write in Cherokee. How would your life be different if you could not read or write?

EXPLORE TENNESSEE!

Sequoyah Birthplace Museum

The only tourist site in Tennessee owned by the Cherokees is the Sequoyah Birthplace Museum in Vonore. The museum preserves Cherokee culture and honors Sequoyah. Each year, the museum holds many events, including a Fall Festival, a Statehood Day celebration, a Little Tennessee River Music Festival, and a Sequoyah Remembrance Day.

Vonore ●

through speaking. Sequoyah wanted his people to be able to record ideas, so he began working on a way to write in Cherokee.

At first, Sequoyah tried to use the English alphabet, but this did not work. The Cherokees used many sounds that white settlers did not use. In fact, Sequoyah discovered that the Cherokee language had 86 different sounds! It took him more than 12 years to design a symbol for each one.

When Sequoyah was finished, he tested his *syllabary* on his daughter. She quickly learned to read and write. This encouraged him to teach the syllabary to a few Cherokee leaders. They were amazed at how easy it was to learn.

Sequoyah's syllabary was a huge success. The Cherokee Nation adopted it as its official language. It was the first written language of Native Americans living in North America. The Cherokee government began publishing a newspaper, *The Cherokee Phoenix*.

The Cherokee Phoenix *still prints articles in both Cherokee and English.*

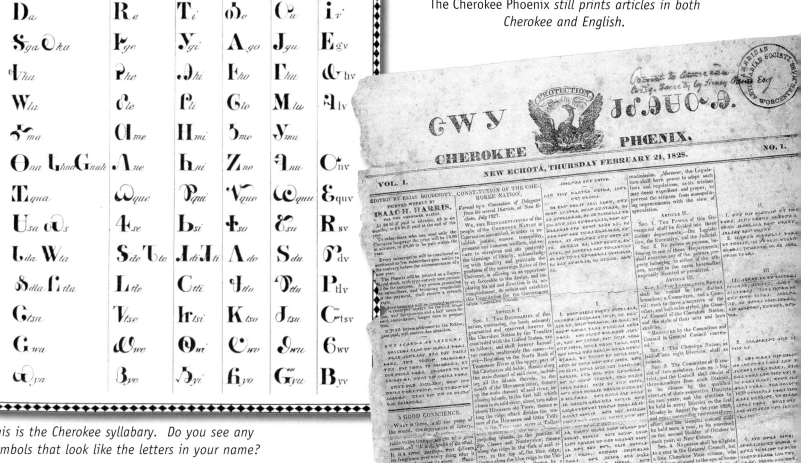

This is the Cherokee syllabary. Do you see any symbols that look like the letters in your name?

Most of the workers in this mill are women. Can you tell what they are making?

A Changing Way of Life

During this period of history, most people in Tennessee continued farming. As the size of farms grew, families produced more crops than they could use. They sold their extra crops and used the money to buy things they did not make themselves. New businesses sprang up all over the state. This was the beginning of the *Industrial Revolution,* a time when business and industry developed rapidly.

Mass Production

One of the things people started buying was fabric. Spinning thread and weaving cloth took many hours. In cities, cotton mills quickly produced hundreds of yards of fabric. This is called *mass production.*

Since the mills made so much fabric, it did not cost very much to buy. (Did you remember that high supply equals low price?) Almost everyone could afford to buy fabric. Women still had to sew clothing, but they no longer had to make their own cloth.

Iron

Many tools people used were made of iron. A large supply of iron *ore* was found on the western Highland Rim. After the ore was taken from the ground, workers melted it. Then they poured it into molds of all sizes and shapes. Many of these workers were slaves. Some of them became very skilled and were able to earn their freedom. Tennessee's iron deposits had supplied Jackson's army with cannonballs during the War of 1812.

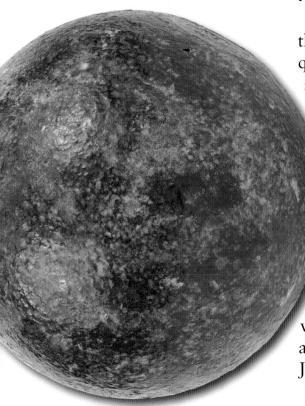

The iron in this cannonball may have come from Tennessee's Highland Rim.

This mill is at Cades Cove. Early mills were powered by water, but later mills used steam or electricity.

Gristmills

Some families owned land that had rivers or streams on it. They built *gristmills* on the rivers. A gristmill is a building with a huge waterwheel. Water from the river made the waterwheel go round and round. The turning wheel moved a large millstone, which ground wheat and other grains into flour. Workers then poured the flour into wooden barrels. Farmers no longer ground their own flour. Instead, they took it to a nearby mill and paid the miller to grind it for them.

THE Great American
STEAMBOAT
★ ★ ★

For many years, people used keelboats to move goods up and down the Mississippi, Tennessee, and Cumberland Rivers. Keelboats were hard to use. They tipped over easily. Piles of furs, iron tools, and other goods spilled into the river. People needed a better way to travel and move goods.

The first steamboat to arrive in Nashville was the *General Jackson* in 1819. But eight years earlier, the *New Orleans* steamed down the Mississippi past Memphis. By the 1830s, steamboats were a common sight up and down Tennessee's great rivers. Soon steamboats traveled from Nashville to New Orleans. They also carried goods from Pittsburgh, Cincinnati, and Louisville to Nashville. Nashville became a large trading center.

Some steamboats were huge. They had giant paddlewheels, engines that spewed thick smoke, and enough room for 400 passengers. These big boats were like floating palaces. They had carpeted floors in the guest rooms and sparkling lights in the dining rooms.

Steamboats were safer than keelboats, but traveling on them was still sometimes dangerous. The rivers had sandbars, underwater trees, and other hazards. Steamboat pilots had to learn every twist and turn of the rivers. Another problem was that the boats could explode when their steam engines overheated. In 1865, a large steamboat named the *Sultana* exploded on the Mississippi River, a few miles north of Memphis. The boat was overcrowded, and more than 1,700 people died. It was the largest sea disaster in U.S. history.

How a Steam Engine Works

TERRIFIC TECHNOLOGY

Water

Smokestack

Firebox

Steam from the water moves the piston.

Piston

The piston moves back and forth, pushing and pulling the driveshaft.

The moving driveshaft turns the paddlewheel on the back of the boat.

The Age of Andrew Jackson

Some people attended camp meetings every year. They visited with friends and family before and after the preaching. How many tents can you count in this painting?

St. Mary's Catholic Church

Most of the early settlers in Tennessee were Protestants. Then in 1820, the city of Nashville built a bridge across the Cumberland River to connect Nashville with Edgefield. Many Irish Catholics went to Middle Tennessee to help build the bridge, and they decided to stay. Soon the Catholics built a church, the Holy Rosary, in downtown Nashville. About 30 years later, St. Mary's Church replaced the Holy Rosary. It was the first permanent Catholic church in Nashville.

Revivals and Camp Meetings

During this period of rapid growth and change, Methodist, Baptist, Presbyterian, and other **Protestant** preachers began arriving in Tennessee. People sometimes called them "circuit riders" because the preachers rode from town to town, preaching along the way.

Some preachers stayed in one place for a while and gave sermons every day. Large groups of people gathered to hear the sermons. The meetings were called **revivals.** They were also called camp meetings because people who lived far away set up tents and stayed overnight.

During the camp meetings, preachers gave long sermons. Some lasted four hours! There was a great deal of singing, and sometimes bands played. Many people committed to changing their lives and were **baptized.**

1 MEMORY MASTER

1. What is an economic panic?
2. What did Sequoyah create?
3. What is mass production?

Slavery on the Rise

As more farmers planted cotton, they needed more workers. In Tennessee and throughout the rest of the South, the number of slaves grew quickly. Our state's location in the middle of the nation made it a place where people came to buy and sell slaves. There were slave markets in both Nashville and Memphis, and a few Tennesseans grew wealthy in the slave trade.

The Grand Divisions and Slavery

Tennessee was different from most southern states because the way people felt about slavery depended on where they lived. The geography of each Grand Division changed the economics and politics of the region.

East Tennessee had mostly small farms because the land had many ridges, valleys, and mountains. Most families were able to run their farms by themselves, so there were very few slaves. Most East Tennesseans were against slavery.

Middle Tennessee had larger farms and a few plantations, so there were more slaves. Some Middle Tennesseans were for slavery. Others were against it.

Because West Tennessee had flat, rich land, farming was the most important business in the region. Plantations covered hundreds of acres. The slave population was very large. There were also many free blacks living in towns and cities in West Tennessee. Most white West Tennesseans supported the practice of slavery.

CITY DIRECTORY. 251

FORREST & MAPLES,
SLAVE DEALERS,
87 Adams Street,
Between Second and Third

MEMPHIS, TENNESSEE,

Have constantly on hand the best selected assortment of

FIELD HANDS, HOUSE SERVANTS & MECHANICS,
at their Negro Mart, to be found in the city. They are daily receiving from Virginia, Kentucky and Missouri, fresh supplies of likely Young Negroes.

Negroes Sold on Commission,
and the highest market price always paid for good stock. Their Jail is coming Three Hundred, and for and safety, is the best arra Union. Persons wishing ted to examine their st elsewhere.

They have on hand at present, Fifty likely young Negroes, comprising Field hands, Mechanics, House and Body Servants, &c.

Farms Using Slave Labor

West	Middle	East
40%	**25%**	**8%**

PEOPLE TO KNOW

Elihu Embree
Frances Wright

PLACES TO LOCATE

Memphis
Nashville

WORDS TO UNDERSTAND

abolish
abolitionist
antislavery
conductor
emancipate
manumission
overseer
patroller
reformer
station
Underground Railroad

A Hard Life

Some slave owners in Tennessee treated their slaves very badly. Others treated them almost like family members. A few hired cruel *overseers* to manage their workers. Fear of punishment or death kept most slaves from trying to run away. They also did not want to leave friends and family behind.

On the Farm

Many slaves lived on farms or plantations and worked in the fields. They worked from sunup to sundown. Most slave owners gave their slaves plenty of food because they wanted the slaves to remain strong and healthy. However, some slaves were hungry almost all the time. Slave families were often split up when one member of the family was sold to a different owner. Parents lived in fear that their children would be sold far away from them.

Southern landowners did not know who would work in the fields if slaves were freed.

Slaves had to obey every order their owner or overseer gave them. They were not allowed to make decisions for themselves.

Slave owners did not allow slaves to read and write. One Dickson County slave recalled, "The white folks didn't want us to learn nothing. And if a slave picked up a little piece of paper, they would yell, 'Put that down, you! You don't want to get in our business.'" Some slaves secretly learned to read and write anyway. A few even managed to use those skills to get out of slavery.

In the City

Many slaves lived in cities and became skilled workers. City life gave them more chances to learn and to earn their freedom. Slaves became carpenters, road builders, weavers, cooks, musicians, and more. In some towns, there were no special areas set aside for slaves, so whites and black slaves lived close together.

Religion

Religion was an important part of a slave's life. Faith in God gave the people hope that one day they would be free. As they worked in the fields, they sang songs about freedom. These songs, called negro spirituals, were based on Bible stories. Slave owners didn't like the songs. They didn't want their slaves singing, praying, or even thinking about freedom.

One Tennessee slave said, "The white folks wouldn't let the slaves pray. If they got to pray, it was while walking behind a plow. White folks would whip the slaves if they heard them sing or pray."

What Do You Think ?

Why do you think slave owners did not want their slaves to be able to read? Does the ability to read give people power? Why?

Elihu Embree
(1782–1820)

Elihu Embree was born in Pennsylvania to Quaker parents who were strongly against slavery. When Elihu was eight years old, his family moved to East Tennessee. He and his brother Elijah built a successful iron business. They owned an iron mine, a business that made goods from iron, and 260 acres of land on the Nolichucky River.

When Embree was 20, he married Annes Williams, but she died a few years later. Then he married Elizabeth Worley, a slave owner. Embree sold Elizabeth's slaves, who were all members of one family. He later bought back the slave family because he wanted to set them free.

Embree had stopped practicing the Quaker religion, but when he turned 30, he went back to it again. He became a leader of the Manumission Society of Tennessee. *Manumission* means freeing from slavery. The society worked to try to end slavery by freeing one slave at a time.

In 1819, Embree began publishing the first antislavery newspaper in the United States. It was called *The Manumission Intelligencer*. The next year, the paper's name changed to *The Emancipator*. To *emancipate* means to set free. Embree wrote that slave owners were "monsters in human flesh." He sent copies of the newspaper to the governors of all the slave states.

Embree spent all his time and money on the newspaper and on fighting slavery. The family was almost broke when Elizabeth suddenly became sick and died. Less than six months later, Embree got sick and died too. He was only 38 years old. His home in Telford was the site of a Civil War battle. Many believe it was also a hiding place for runaway slaves.

Arguments over slavery grew so intense that people began drawing guns on their friends and neighbors.

The Antislavery Movement

As revivals, camp meetings, and religion became more popular, some people began to think our country should change. They wanted it to become a fairer, better place. These people were called **reformers** because they wanted to "re-form" the country.

One thing many reformers wanted to change was slavery. They believed owning another person was wrong. The people against slavery wanted to **abolish,** or end, slavery. They were called **abolitionists.**

As **antislavery** efforts increased, slave owners defended slavery. They argued that the Bible supported slavery. They said slavery was good for slaves because blacks couldn't survive without help.

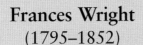

Frances Wright
(1795–1852)

Frances Wright was from Scotland. She came to the United States for a visit and decided to stay. Many people did not like her because she spoke her mind. At that time, American women did not often speak out in public. Wright hated slavery. She made many speeches in public about the evils of slavery.

Wright wanted to create a place where slaves could live freely. She also wanted to educate and prepare them for life as free citizens. She bought land near Memphis and called the settlement Nashoba, the Chickasaw word for "wolf." Then Wright and her sister bought 15 slaves and moved them to the settlement where they could live freely. They began to farm and build a community.

Wright became sick shortly after starting Nashoba. She returned to Scotland for treatment. While she was gone, people who lived near Nashoba began complaining about the community. They did not like blacks and whites living together. Many people who had donated money to help run Nashoba stopped supporting it.

When Wright returned, she decided her experiment was a failure. She did not think she could give her slaves freedom in the United States, so she took them to Haiti. The governor of Haiti gave them land and their freedom. Wright was thrilled that her slaves were finally free.

● Nashoba

Wright spent her entire family fortune on Nashoba.

Railroad A Way to Freedom

Underground Railroad Routes

CANADA

Boston •

Detroit • Buffalo • New York •

Chicago • Wheeling

Cincinnati • Alexandria •

St. Louis • Parkersburg

Fort Donelson

Memphis • Charleston •

Atlantic Ocean

Houston • New Orleans •

Gulf of Mexico

THE BAHAMAS

MEXICO

CUBA

Legend
General routes of escape

Slave state—slavery permitted

Free state—slavery prohibited

Slaves hated slavery and wanted to be free. Even though they were afraid, thousands ran away to freedom in the North. Some runaways traveled through Middle or East Tennessee. Others traveled as stowaways on boats headed up the Mississippi River from Memphis and other southern cities. As soon as they crossed the Ohio River into Illinois or Indiana, they were free. Other runaways climbed the rugged Appalachians to freedom in Pennsylvania.

These escape routes became known as the **Underground Railroad.** The Underground Railroad was not really underground, and it was not really a railroad. It was a secret system run by whites and free blacks who joined together to help slaves escape.

The journey to freedom on the Underground Railroad was long and dangerous. Sometimes owners chased runaway slaves. If the runaways were caught, the slave owners punished them. A few went to jail. Others were beaten to death. Sometimes owners sold slaves who had tried to run away. These slaves often never saw their families again.

Conductors and Secret Codes

Men called *patrollers* searched for runaways, so slaves had to travel mostly at night. The runaways used the moon and stars, especially the North Star, to guide them. They also looked for secret codes from songs people sang, marks on trees, and other hidden signals. The codes helped the runaways find their way. They also warned of danger.

During the day, slaves hid in forests or the homes of people who helped them escape. These people were called *conductors.* Conductors hid runaway slaves in safe places called *stations.* Many stations had secret passageways, hidden staircases, or underground rooms.

The Underground Railroad in Tennessee

Over a period of 60 years, nearly 100,000 slaves escaped using the Underground Railroad. One route passed through the ridges and valleys of East Tennessee. Slaves from Alabama and Georgia hid in caves, barns, and homes on their journey northward. A Quaker family named Griffitts built a house near the Little Tennessee River in East Tennessee. The home became a station on the Underground Railroad. And in Friendsville, a Quaker family hid food and supplies for runaways in a cave.

② MEMORY MASTER

1. Why did people in the three Grand Divisions of Tennessee feel differently about slavery?
2. What did reformers want to abolish?
3. What was the Underground Railroad?

A Symbol for the Nation

The United States was young and growing strong. It had a bright future. Americans began saying Andrew Jackson was a symbol for the nation. He was young and strong, energetic and smart. Americans felt our country was all of those things too. Many historians call these years the Age of Andrew Jackson.

Andrew Jackson's friends wanted him to become president. In 1823, the General Assembly appointed Jackson to the U.S. Senate. His friends hoped being a senator would help other Americans learn more about him.

The Election of 1824

In some ways, Jackson was very different from the other men who had been president. He was not well educated or from an eastern state. He was, however, a wealthy landowner.

When it came time for the presidential election, there were four candidates:

- Andrew Jackson, from Tennessee
- John Quincy Adams, the son of President John Adams, from Massachusetts
- William H. Crawford, from Georgia
- Henry Clay, Speaker of the U.S. House of Representatives, from Kentucky

The Electoral College voted, but none of the candidates received enough votes to become president. The U.S. Constitution said the members of the House of Representatives had to choose the president by voting on the top three candidates. They were Jackson, Adams, and Crawford.

In the House election, John Quincy Adams received the most votes. He became president even though

Andrew Jackson

Henry Clay

John Quincy Adams

William H. Crawford

Jackson had received more votes from the people. The election angered many Tennesseans. They felt the presidency had been stolen from Andrew Jackson.

Andrew Jackson Becomes President

The Tennessee General Assembly still wanted Andrew Jackson to become president. Before the next election, state leaders helped him with a long *campaign.* A campaign is a time when candidates post signs, hand out brochures and letters, give speeches, and attend meetings to educate voters about their position on the issues. During the three-year campaign, the people who supported John Quincy Adams said terrible things about Andrew and Rachel Jackson's marriage. Rachel was very embarrassed and upset by the gossip.

Rachel Jackson Dies

Andrew Jackson won the election by a large vote, but Rachel was worn out. On December 22, 1828, she had a heart attack and died. She was only 60 years old. Jackson was heartbroken. He blamed Adams's supporters for Rachel's illness and death. Now he had to go to Washington and serve as president alone. Jackson had Rachel buried in her garden at the Hermitage, their home in Nashville. The church bells of Nashville rang at her funeral, and thousands of people mourned her passing.

Rachel Jackson was buried in the long, white gown she had bought for Jackson's inauguration.

The Hermitage

The Hermitage is Andrew Jackson's home in Nashville. The first log home on the property was built by Nathaniel Hays. In 1804, Andrew and Rachel bought the plantation. They dressed up the log house with wallpaper and paint and planted large fields of cotton.

Over the years, the Jacksons' fortune grew. They built an entirely new house. They also added slave quarters, a cotton gin, a dairy, a carriage house, a formal English garden, a smokehouse, a large kitchen, a library, and a church.

Today you can visit the Hermitage. There is a large Visitor Center where you can watch a film about the Jacksons. You can also visit the original log house, a museum, and a gallery. You can take a tour through the house and garden, visit Andrew Jackson's tomb, and learn more about slavery, farming, and nature.

BORN TO COMMAND.

OF VETO MEMORY.

HAD I BEEN CONSULTED.

KING ANDREW THE FIRST.

This cartoon shows Jackson dressed as a king. He is standing on a shredded U.S. Constitution. What message does this cartoon send?

The Whigs

Andrew Jackson was a strong president. But many Americans did not like the things he did and said. They felt he had too much power. Newspapers published cartoons showing Jackson wearing a robe and crown like he was a king and gave him the nickname King Andrew. The people who were against him formed a new political party called the Whigs.

Many Tennesseans wanted Hugh Lawson White, from Knoxville, to be the next president. But Jackson believed Martin Van Buren, the vice president, should become president. Jackson's support of Van Buren made some Tennesseans so angry that they joined the Whig Party.

Jackson's party, the Democratic-Republicans, dropped "Republican" from their name. They began calling themselves Democrats. For the next 20 years, the state government was divided between the Democrats and the Whigs.

Linking the Present to the Past

Because Jackson, a Tennessean, began the Democratic Party, the Tennessee Democratic Party still holds an annual Jackson Day Dinner.

Cholera

Years ago, cholera was a deadly disease. Healthy people sometimes died only a few hours after getting sick with it. The cholera germ keeps the human body from absorbing liquids. People died of thirst even if they were drinking water.

In 1833, a terrible cholera epidemic swept through Tennessee. An **epidemic** is a time when many people have the same disease. Thousands of people died. Large cities grew quiet, and wagons traveled the streets gathering dead bodies. In some small towns, nearly everyone died. Here is part of letter from a man in Mount Pleasant during the cholera epidemic:

Linking the Present to the Past

In the 200 years since it first appeared, cholera has killed millions of people. Scientists now know it is spread through water. In the United States today, drinking water is cleaned and treated with chemicals. Cholera has become very rare and is easily cured.

Uncle Jack was in the neighborhood a few days ago trying to get a location near the Nashoba Springs for himself and a number of other families during the Epidemic—We were to have heard from him the next day but not a word has reached us since. I fear he or a portion of his family have been taken off by that fearful disease . . . Such times were never seen . . . Young Men and Ladies in the very bloom of health perhapse in one hour are no more. Business is almost entirely [stopped]. Nor can you see a face that looks bright, nor an Eye looks drye.

A New State Constitution

William Carroll helped establish Tennessee's first state prison.

What Do You Think ?

Why do you think the number of delegates from each region was so different? What does that tell you about the state at that time? Do you think the people from East and West Tennessee felt the number of delegates was fair? Why or why not?

William Carroll, the governor of Tennessee, was a popular leader. He had moved to Nashville as a young man and become a successful businessman. He served as an officer in the Tennessee militia and fought under Andrew Jackson in the War of 1812.

Carroll wanted the state government to create a public education system. He asked the General Assembly to sell some public lands to pay for schools. But the General Assembly did not want to put money into schools. It voted against state-funded education.

Frustrated by this and other problems, Governor Carroll convinced state leaders that Tennessee needed a new state constitution. The General Assembly called a constitutional convention in Nashville. Eighteen delegates came from East Tennessee, thirty from Middle Tennessee, and twelve from West Tennessee. Former governor Willie Blount was chairman of the convention.

Many convention delegates agreed with Governor Carroll's ideas about education. They added a section to the state constitution to create a common school fund that would pay for schools, teachers, and supplies. Even with the new section, it was many years before every county in Tennessee had a school.

A State Capital

Tennessee now had over 700,000 people, but it still had no permanent capital. Can you guess why the General Assembly could not agree on a capital city? The people who lived in East Tennessee wanted the capital to be near them. But the people who lived in Middle Tennessee wanted the capital in their region.

In the early years of statehood, General Assembly meetings moved from city to city. While John Sevier was governor, the state government met in Knoxville. Willie Blount then became governor and moved it to Nashville. After the War of 1812, the capital returned to Knoxville. It then moved to Murfreesboro. In 1826, the capital returned once again to Nashville.

The delegates talked about several cities, but they could not agree. They decided to delay the decision. They added a section to the new constitution that said the General Assembly had to select a capital city by 1843.

Most free blacks did not own 200 acres of land. They could no longer vote after the Constitution of 1834 was approved.

What Do You Think ?

Why do you think the delegates made it so difficult for free black men to vote? How does this show that feelings about slavery and blacks in general had not changed?

Slavery in the New Constitution

The delegates working on the constitution argued long and hard about slavery. Most East Tennesseans were against the practice, but West Tennesseans owned thousands of slaves. In the end, the state delegates added a section that said slavery could not be abolished unless slave owners agreed.

In Tennessee, free black men had been able to vote. But the new constitution changed that. It said only white males 21 years of age or older who owned at least 200 acres of land and had lived in the state for three or more years could vote.

Approving the New Constitution

After the delegates completed the new constitution, the people of Tennessee voted on it. All but four counties approved it, so the Constitution of 1834 became law.

The four counties that voted against the Constitution of 1834 were, Davidson, Robertson, Smith, and Williamson. They were all in Middle Tennessee.

More men from Tennessee died at the Alamo than from any other state.

Long before the Alamo was the site of a battle, it was a Catholic mission.

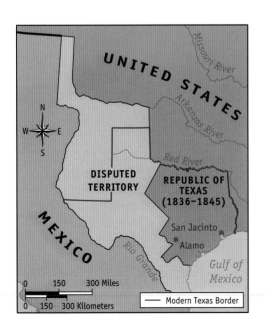

The Texas Revolution

While the Tennessee state delegates were working on the new constitution, settlers in Texas were trying to become a state. Texas was a territory that belonged to Mexico, but the Mexican government wanted Americans to move there. The soil in Texas was fertile and good for growing cotton and other crops. Thousands of Americans built homes, farms, and plantations there.

The Americans who moved to Texas were different from the people living in Mexico. Mexicans spoke Spanish, but Americans spoke English. The Mexican government had abolished slavery, but Americans brought slaves to work in the cotton fields. The settlers wanted Texas to separate from Mexico and become part of the United States.

The Texas settlers organized an army with former Tennessean Sam Houston as general. Mexican general Santa Anna came to Texas to stop the settlers from joining the United States, and fighting soon broke out. The Texas army lost a major battle at the Alamo. Then they fought another battle called the Battle of San Jacinto. As they fought, they cried, "Remember the Alamo!" Perhaps remembering their defeat at the Alamo helped them fight harder because the Texans won the Battle of San Jacinto.

After San Jacinto, the settlers expected the territory to become a state. But there was a problem. Congressmen from northern states did not want to admit another slave state into the Union. Texas instead became an independent country, the Republic of Texas.

David Crockett
(1786-1836)

David Crockett was born and raised in East Tennessee. When he was 20, he married Polly Finley. A few years later, Crockett, his wife, and their two boys moved to Middle Tennessee. Crockett joined the army and fought alongside Andrew Jackson at the Battle of Horseshoe Bend. After Crockett left the army, Polly gave birth to a baby girl and then died. A year later, Crockett married a widow, Elizabeth Patton, with two children.

Crockett wanted to be a government leader—maybe even president. He ran for a seat in the Tennessee legislature. The people of Tennessee liked Crockett and elected him. He served first in the Tennessee legislature and then in the U.S. House of Representatives.

Crockett did not think it was right to force the Indians off their land. His speeches upset Andrew Jackson and Governor William Carroll, and they stopped supporting him. Crockett ran for another term in the House, but he lost. He then decided to move to Texas. He still wanted to become president, and he believed Texans would help him become popular again. Sadly, Crockett was among 32 Tennesseans killed at the Alamo.

David Crockett is one of the most famous people from Tennessee. But it was not his political service or his death that made him famous. It was the many wonderful stories that he told and that have been told about him.

When people in the eastern United States learned about the Tennessee frontiersman who became a politician, they began writing about him. Some of their stories were true, but many of them were not. Some wrote that he could "run faster, jump higher, squat lower, dive deeper, stay under [water] longer, and come out drier than any man in the whole country." One story said he saved the world by unfreezing the sun. Another said he rode his pet alligator up Niagara Falls, one of the largest waterfalls in the world!

In the 1950s, the Walt Disney Company produced a movie and then a television show called *Davy Crockett*. Adults and children across the country loved it. Soon stores sold coonskin caps, fringed deerskin pants and jackets, lunch boxes, towels, wallets, and records of the show's song. Today, it's hard to know how many of the Davy Crockett stories are true, but they have helped people learn about the state of Tennessee.

TENNESSEE PORTRAIT

The Age of Andrew Jackson

Sam Houston
(1793–1863)

Sam Houston was born in Virginia and moved with his widowed mother to Tennessee. During his teen years, Houston left his family for long periods of time to live with the Cherokees. An Indian leader, Chief John Jolly, taught Houston how to speak Cherokee. The chief loved Houston and treated him as if he were his son. When Houston was 20, he left the Cherokees to work as a schoolteacher in Maryville.

Soon after the War of 1812 began, Houston joined the army. He fought alongside Andrew Jackson and was wounded at the Battle of Horseshoe Bend. He then became an Indian agent for the army. Two years later, he quit the army and began studying law. Houston opened a law office in Nashville and became attorney general. He remained close friends with Jackson, who helped him get elected to the U.S. House of Representatives. Houston served two terms in the House and then became governor of Tennessee.

After Houston's young wife suddenly left him, he quit his job as governor. He traveled to Oklahoma, rejoined the Cherokees, and married an Indian woman. Three years later, Houston left the Cherokees and his wife and moved to Texas.

Houston became a powerful military leader in Texas and led soldiers to victory in the Battle of San Jacinto. Texas was not yet a state, so the people elected Houston president of the Republic of Texas. He served two terms and worked with the U.S. government to help Texas become a state. At the age of 47, he married Margaret Lea. Over the years, Houston and his wife had eight children.

Houston won a seat in the U.S. Senate, where he served for 13 years, and then became governor of Texas. He was a slave owner, but he did not want slavery to spread into the western territories. He did not want the North and South to separate. He knew it would lead to war. Eight years before Abraham Lincoln said, "A house divided against itself cannot stand," Sam Houston said, "A nation divided against itself cannot stand."

When the state of Texas decided to leave the Union, Houston chose not to support secession. As a result, he was removed from the office of governor. He retired, moved back to his farm, and then died of pneumonia the following year.

Sam Houston's life is a good example of how quickly the nation changed during these years. He served his country from the early frontier days to the Civil War. He also helped Texas become a country and then a state. Texans have honored him by naming one of their largest cities, Houston, after him.

The Cherokees

By 1828, the Cherokee population (including black slaves) was nearly 16,000. The Cherokees organized a republican government, wrote a constitution, and elected a council to make decisions for the tribe. They also built a capital city, New Echota, in northern Georgia.

Landowners and Christians

The Cherokees began allowing their people to own land. Cherokee men became farmers and raised corn, tobacco, cotton, and other crops. They owned sawmills, blacksmith shops, cotton gins, and close to 2,000 slaves. Many Cherokees learned to speak English.

White missionaries taught the Indians about Christianity. Some Cherokees stopped practicing their ancient religion and became Christians. They even helped missionaries build churches.

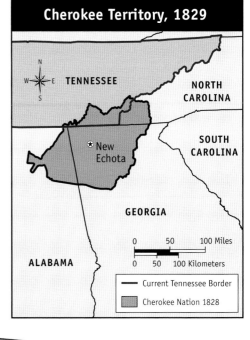

Cherokee Territory, 1829

This mission school had Cherokee, Creek, and white students.

This town was a Cherokee missionary station. Do you think the Cherokees wanted to live like the settlers? Why or why not?

Andrew Jackson and many other Americans felt the Cherokees were standing in the way of progress. Jackson began pushing for the Indian Removal Act after less than one year in office.

uncommitted to any other course than the strict line of constitutional duty; and that the securities for this independence may be rendered as strong as the nature of power and the weakness of its professor will admit, — I cannot too earnestly invite your attention to the propriety of promoting such an amendment of the constitution as will render him ineligible after one term of service.

It gives me pleasure to announce ... policy of ... for ... the removal

THE CASE

OF

THE CHEROKEE NATION

against

THE STATE OF GEORGIA:

ARGUED AND DETERMINED AT

THE SUPREME COURT OF THE UNITED STATES,

JANUARY TERM 1831.

WITH

AN APPENDIX,

Containing the Opinion of Chancellor Kent on the Case; the Treaties between the United States and the Cherokee Indians; the Act of Congress of 1802, entitled 'An Act to regulate intercourse with the Indian tribes, &c.'; and the Laws of Georgia relative to the country occupied by the Cherokee Indians, within the boundary of that State.

BY RICHARD PETERS,
COUNSELLOR AT LAW.

Philadelphia:
JOHN GRIGG, 9 NORTH FOURTH STREET.
1831.

The Indian Removal Act

The state of Tennessee wanted the Cherokees' land, so the government tried to convince them to move. Some packed up and headed west, but most did not want to leave. They wanted to stay on the land that had been their home for centuries.

The Cherokees hoped the governments of Tennessee and Georgia would help their territory become a state. But Andrew Jackson did not want the territory to become a state. He knew gold had been discovered on the land, and he wanted to sell it to white settlers.

Jackson asked Congress to pass a law that would force the Cherokees off their land. In 1830, Congress passed the Indian Removal Act. The only member of Congress from Tennessee to vote against the act was David Crockett.

The Cherokees Go to Court

The Cherokees felt the Indian Removal Act was unfair, so they sued the state of Georgia. This was because most Cherokee land was in Georgia. The case went to the highest court in the nation, the U.S. Supreme Court. The Supreme Court decided the Cherokees could keep their land.

Andrew Jackson refused to follow the Supreme Court's decision. He said the Indians had to leave Tennessee and move west. The Cherokees were not sure what to do. Chief John Ross believed they should stay in Tennessee. Another chief, Major John Ridge, felt they should move to the West.

The Treaty of New Echota

Government representatives went to New Echota to sign a treaty with the Cherokees. The treaty stated that the Cherokees would give up their eastern lands and move to the West within two years. The Cherokees would receive $5 million for the land.

John Ridge signed the treaty for the people he represented, but John Ross refused. Ross immediately traveled to Washington to work out a better agreement. President Jackson's staff refused to see

This is the title page of the U.S. Supreme Court record from the Cherokee's case against Georgia.

him. In 1836, the Senate approved the Treaty of New Echota by one vote. Some of the Cherokees began to move west, but Chief John Ross and many others refused to leave their homes.

The Trail of Tears

By 1838, thousands of Cherokees remained in Tennessee and Georgia. Chief John Ross did not believe the government would force them to leave. But he was wrong.

Collection Camps

In the spring of that year, General Winfield Scott and his soldiers moved 14,000 Cherokees and 2,000 black slaves to "collection camps." In the camps, thousands of people became sick and died. John Ross tried to work out an agreement with General Scott, but the government stood firm in its decision. The Cherokees soon realized there was nothing more they could do. Under the direction of armed soldiers, they began walking westward.

An *immigrant* is a person who has moved from one place to another place. An *emigrant* is a person who is moving from one place to another place.

The Trail of Tears

The Indian Removal Act forced more than 70,000 Indians off their homelands. How did Indians feel about this? Read the following quotes to learn about the Trail of Tears from some people who were there. Then, on your own paper, answer the questions that follow.

"Our poor emigrants, many of them quite naked, and without much shelter, must suffer, it is impossible to do otherwise."

—Army officer who traveled with the Choctaws

"The Cherokees are nearly all prisoners. They have been dragged from their houses, and encamped at the forts and military posts, all over the nation. In Georgia, especially, [many] were allowed no time to take any thing with them, except the clothes they had on. Well-furnished houses were left to plunderers, who, like hungry wolves, follow in the train of the captors."

—Evan Jones, missionary who traveled with the Cherokees

"They drove us out of our house to join other prisoners. . . . My father had a wagon pulled by . . . oxen . . . Eight of my brothers and sisters and two or three widow women and children rode with us. . . . My father and mother walked all the way. . . . The people got so tired of eating salt pork on the journey that my father would walk through the woods as we traveled, hunting for turkeys and deer which he brought into camp to feed us. . . . There was much sickness among the emigrants and a great many little children died of whooping cough."

—Rebecca Neugin, Indian

"Buried Nancy Bigbear[']s Grandchild. Marched at 9 A.M. . . . halted at Piney River, 1/2 after 3 . . . rained all day, encamped and issued corn only—no fodder to be had . . . 11 miles to day."

—diary of Captain B.B. Cannon, who led the first group of Cherokees

1. What were some of the Indians doing when the soldiers came?
2. What did the Indians have to leave behind?
3. What were some of the dangers on the journey?
4. Write two thoughtful sentences about what you learned from these quotes.

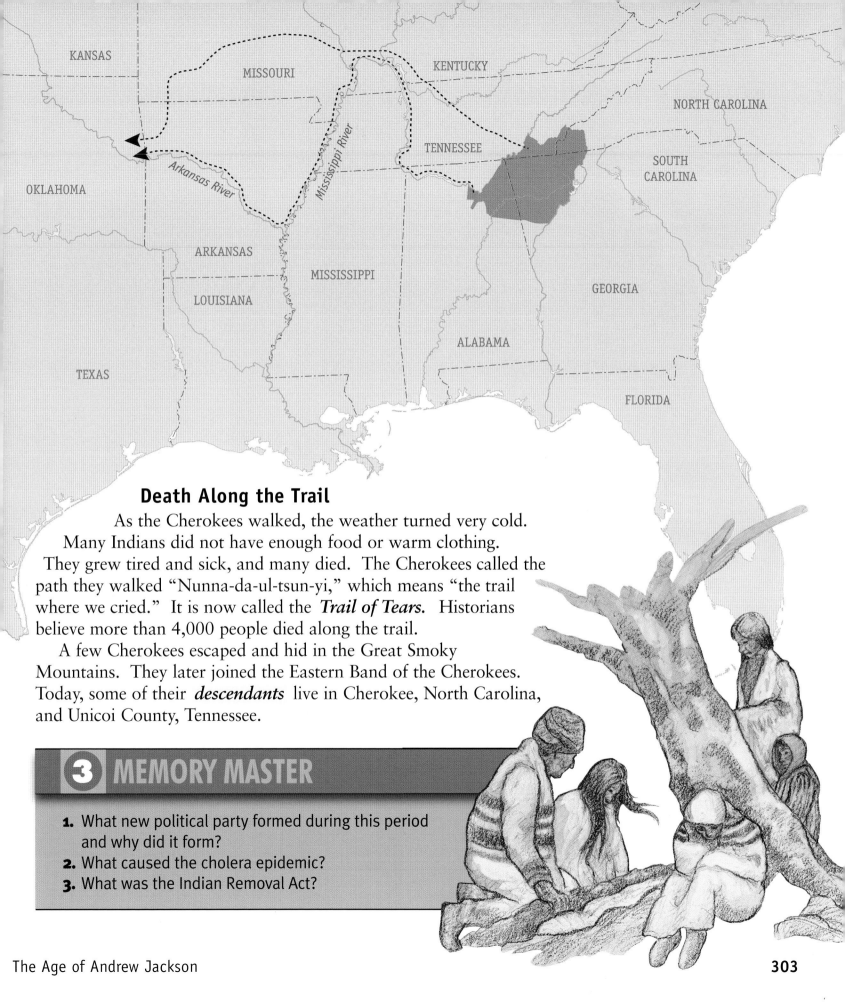

Death Along the Trail

As the Cherokees walked, the weather turned very cold. Many Indians did not have enough food or warm clothing. They grew tired and sick, and many died. The Cherokees called the path they walked "Nunna-da-ul-tsun-yi," which means "the trail where we cried." It is now called the *Trail of Tears*. Historians believe more than 4,000 people died along the trail.

A few Cherokees escaped and hid in the Great Smoky Mountains. They later joined the Eastern Band of the Cherokees. Today, some of their *descendants* live in Cherokee, North Carolina, and Unicoi County, Tennessee.

3 MEMORY MASTER

1. What new political party formed during this period and why did it form?
2. What caused the cholera epidemic?
3. What was the Indian Removal Act?

Chapter 9 Review

What's the Point?

In the years following the War of 1812, Tennessee's population doubled. The Jackson Purchase opened West Tennessee to white settlers. Business and industry grew, farmers sold their extra crops, steamboats improved travel, and mass production meant more goods for sale. The number of slaves living in Tennessee grew as more plantations were built. Abolitionists tried to end slavery and helped many slaves escape on the Underground Railroad. Andrew Jackson became president of the United States, and the Whig party formed. Tennessee adopted a new constitution, and a cholera epidemic spread across the nation. President Jackson signed the Indian Removal Act. Thousands of Indians died as they walked along the Trail of Tears.

Becoming Better Readers

Led to the Civil War	Did Not Lead to the Civil War

Interpreting a Timeline

You have probably noticed that reading a timeline is different from reading a story. A timeline is a list of facts that may or may not relate to one another. A story is a string of ideas that all work together. In both a timeline and a story, readers have to find clues that help answer questions. The timeline at the beginning of this chapter lists many events. Some of them led to greater conflict over slavery and, eventually, the Civil War. Others had nothing to do with the war at all. On your own piece of paper, make two columns. Label the first column "Led to the Civil War" and the second column "Did Not Lead to the Civil War." Then list each event from the timeline on pages 270-71 in the correct column. Share your columns with the class to see if your thoughts are the same.

Climbing to Connections

The Age of Andrew Jackson

1. Why was this period called the Age of Andrew Jackson?
2. Summarize three of Andrew Jackson's accomplishments.
3. Would Jackson's accomplishments be the same if he had been born during another time period? Why or why not?
4. Analyze why the United States was an important setting for the Age of Andrew Jackson.
5. Compare and contrast Jackson with his close friend Sam Houston. What did the two men have in common? What was different about them? List two examples of each.
6. Evaluate the life of Andrew Jackson. What did he do for Tennessee? What did he do for the United States? Was everything he did good for our country? Why or why not?

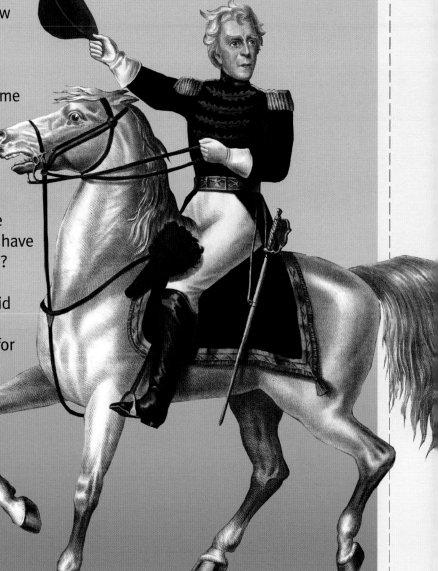

Evaluation Station

Voting "No!"

When Tennessee wrote a new constitution, four counties voted against it. The four counties were Davidson, Smith, Williamson, and Robertson. Locate these four counties on a map. By studying their location, what can you guess about them? Why do you think these counties voted against the new constitution? How do you think people in these counties felt when the state constitution passed anyway?

"*If there is no struggle,
there is no progress.*"

—Frederick Douglass

Tennessee's Antebellum Years

*Once the Cherokees were gone,
people began settling in the
southern part of East Tennessee.
They built homes on and around
Lookout Mountain.*

Timeline of Events

1837
Andrew Jackson returns
to Tennessee after eight
years as president.

1839
James K. Polk is elected
governor of Tennessee.

1845–1848
The Mexican War

1844
James K. Polk is elected
president of the United States.

1835

1840

1845

1843
Nashville becomes
the state capital.

1842
The first train in
Tennessee runs on the
LaGrange and
Memphis Railroad.

1845
Texas becomes a state.
Andrew Jackson dies
at the Hermitage.

Chapter

10

After the war with Mexico, the United States stretched from the Atlantic to the Pacific. Many Americans rushed to the West in search of gold. As the country expanded, people became more divided about slavery. Would the state of Tennessee join its southern neighbors in leaving the Union?

1850
California becomes a state.
An abolitionist newspaper begins printing chapters of *Uncle Tom's Cabin*.

1857
In the *Dred Scott* case, the U.S. Supreme Court decides blacks are not U.S. citizens and have no rights.

1861
Tennessee secedes from the Union.

1850   1855   1860

1848
The California Gold Rush begins.

1854
The Kansas-Nebraska Act passes.
Tennessee's first railroad, the Nashville and Chattanooga, is complete.

1847
The first telegraph comes to Tennessee.
More than 30,000 soldiers respond to James K. Polk's call for Tennessee volunteers to fight in the Mexican War.

1852
Uncle Tom's Cabin is published as a book, changing the way millions of Americans feel about slavery.

A New Tennessee Politician

Did you know Andrew Jackson was not the only man from Tennessee to become president? Another Tennessean, James K. Polk, became president too. A third Tennessean, Andrew Johnson, became president several years later. You'll read about him next year.

James K. Polk was born in North Carolina and moved to Middle Tennessee with his family as a young man. He then went to the University of North Carolina and returned to Nashville after he graduated. Polk studied law with Felix Grundy, one of the best-known lawyers in the state. Grundy encouraged Polk to run for office.

After serving in the state General Assembly, Polk won a seat in the U.S. Congress. Andrew Jackson was still president when Polk became Speaker of the House. The two men worked so closely together that people began calling Polk "Young Hickory." After Jackson left the White House, he wanted Polk to leave Washington and run for governor of Tennessee instead.

James K. Polk was the oldest of ten children.

James K. Polk Becomes Governor

James K. Polk and his wife, Sarah, enjoyed living in Washington, D.C. They didn't want to go back to Tennessee. Andrew Jackson talked with Polk for a long time and convinced him to return. Polk came home, ran for governor, and won. The Democrats were very happy.

The Whigs, however, were not happy. Two years later, they chose James Jones to run against Polk. Jones had little political experience.

He was known across the state as "Lean Jimmy" because he was tall and thin. People enjoyed the jokes he told about Governor Polk. The Whigs called Governor Polk "Little Jimmy" and criticized him. It was a bitter election, and Jones won.

After the election, half the men in the General Assembly were Democrats, and half were Whigs. The two parties couldn't agree on anything! They couldn't even agree on who to send to Washington, D.C. For two years, Tennessee had no representatives in the U.S. Senate.

Going Back to Washington

Polk ran for governor again in 1843, but Jones defeated him a second time. Polk returned to his law practice and began thinking about moving back to Washington. He hoped the Democrats would choose him to run for vice president.

Westward Expansion

In the 1840s, many Americans believed our country's destiny was to become much larger than it already was. They thought our country's borders should be the Atlantic and Pacific Oceans. This idea was called **westward expansion.** It was also called *Manifest Destiny.* Destiny means that something is supposed to happen.

Americans had already begun to move onto the land west of the Louisiana Purchase. Some settlers lived in Oregon, and thousands lived in Texas. People began to ask, "Should the United States try to expand its borders? How? What will happen to the people who already live in those regions?" These were difficult questions, and people disagreed about the answers.

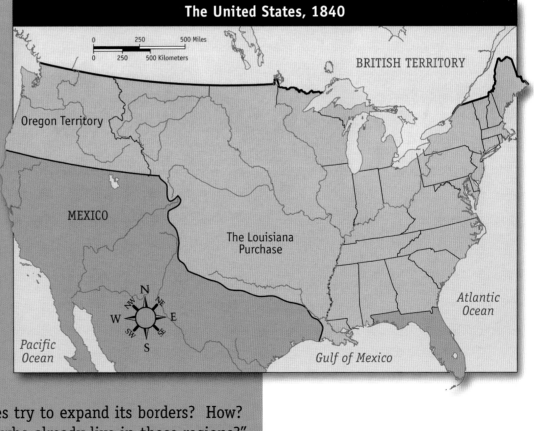

The United States, 1840

BRITISH TERRITORY

Oregon Territory

MEXICO

The Louisiana Purchase

Pacific Ocean

Gulf of Mexico

Atlantic Ocean

The Presidential Election of 1844

In 1844, the Democratic Party met to choose a candidate for president. Andrew Jackson told the Democrats they needed someone from the West, but they had a hard time choosing a candidate. After voting seven times, they finally settled on James K. Polk.

Many Democrats in Congress had never heard of Polk. They did not remember that he had once been Speaker of the House. He was known as the "dark horse" candidate because people thought he could not win the election. In a horse race, the dark horse is expected to lose. But the dark horse sometimes comes from behind to win.

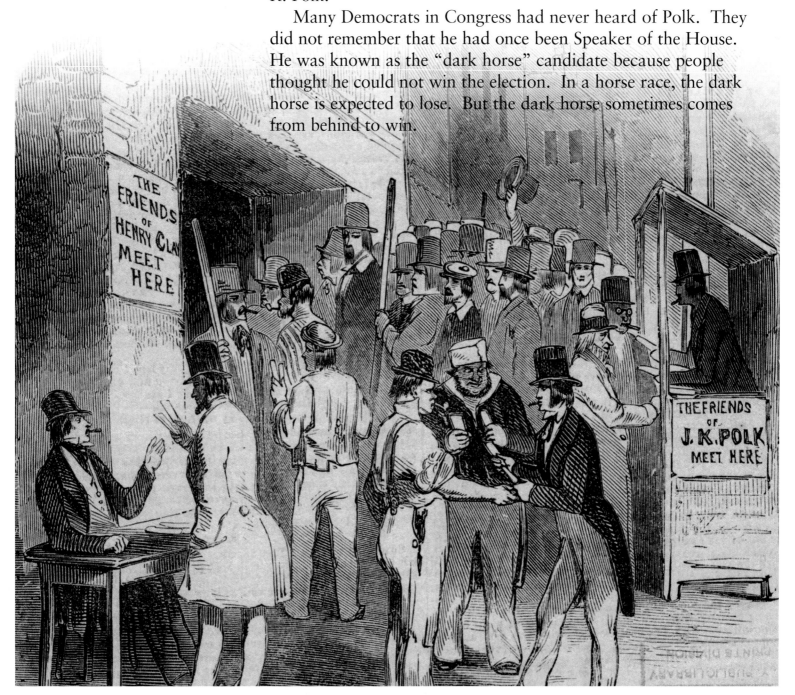

James K. Polk won the election of 1844 largely because most Americans believed in Manifest Destiny. They wanted the nation to stretch from sea to sea.

James K. Polk Becomes President

The Whigs nominated Henry Clay from Kentucky. Everyone thought he would win the election. Then a third political party, the Liberty Party, chose James G. Birney to run for president. Now there were three candidates.

Polk campaigned by telling voters that Texas should be admitted to the Union. At the beginning of the campaign, Clay said he was against statehood for Texas. Then he realized most people wanted Texas to become a state. During the campaign, he changed his mind and said he supported statehood. Birney campaigned by talking about abolishing slavery.

Many people who might have voted for Clay instead voted for Birney. It split the Whig Party's votes, so Polk won the election. Andrew Jackson was pleased that "Young Hickory" was the new president.

A Message Through a Wire

Think of all the ways you communicate today. How many times do you talk on the phone each day? Have you ever written a letter? Have you ever sent or received an e-mail? How about a text message?

One hundred and fifty years ago, **communication** was very different than it is today. The easiest way to send a message then was by using a **telegraph.** A telegraph machine sent a series of clicks over an electric wire. Different clicks stood for different letters. People on each end of the wire sent and received the clicks. Then they translated them into words. James K. Polk was the first president to have his inauguration reported by telegraph.

To build a telegraph system, workers first cut down trees and removed all of the branches. They put the tree trunks into holes in the ground and then strung wires on the tops of them. Telegraph wires connected towns that were hundreds of miles apart. The first telegraph message in Tennessee was received in 1848.

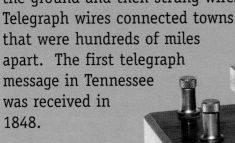

James K. Polk's Home

James and Sarah Polk's Columbia home is one of the most popular places to visit in Tennessee. It is now a museum that houses more than 1,000 items that belonged to the Polks.

During the summer, the museum offers week-long Polk Academy. Kids ages 10 to 12 have a chance to do things frontier children did. You can learn to make candles, soap, and goods made of tin. You can also play 19th-century games, dig for artifacts, and cook on an open hearth. You can even learn how to write with a quill pen!

The Mexican War

Soon after Polk became president, the Republic of Texas became the 31st state. Then the United States and Mexico began arguing about where the

The Volunteer State

Before the war with Mexico, newspapers had called Tennessee the "Volunteer State" because so many men had volunteered for military service. When Americans learned about Tennesseans' generous response to the call for help, everyone in the nation began calling Tennessee the "Volunteer State."

Texas border should be. U.S. officials said the southern border should be the Rio Grande River. But Mexico said the border should be the Nueces River, which was farther north.

Mexican soldiers traveled north of the Rio Grande River to show that Mexico planned to keep the land. President Polk sent U.S. soldiers to Texas to take the land back. After fighting broke out, Congress declared war on Mexico.

The Tennessee Volunteers

At this time, the U.S. Army was very small. Polk knew the troops needed help, so he called for volunteers. Many Texans had once lived in Tennessee. When they moved to Texas, they left

"After [repeated threats], Mexico has passed the boundary of the United States, has invaded our territory and shed American blood upon the American Soil. She has proclaimed that [fighting has begun], and that the two nations are at war."

—President James K. Polk, May 11, 1846

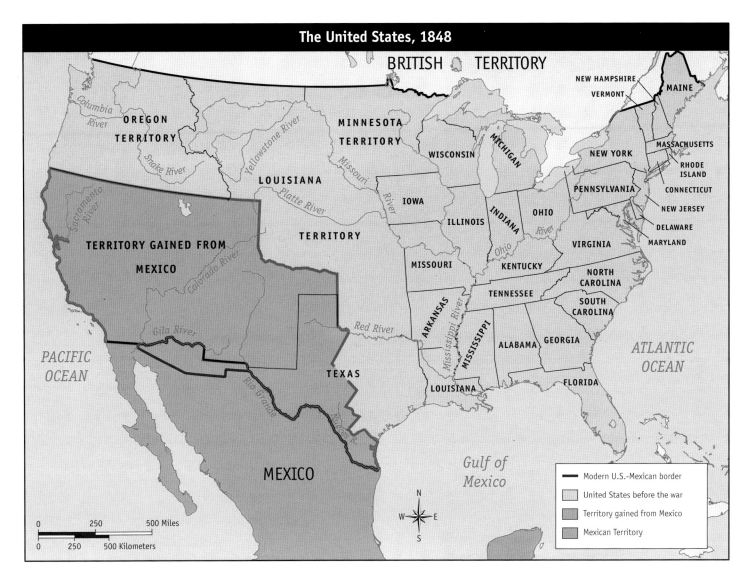

The United States, 1848

BRITISH TERRITORY

OREGON TERRITORY

MINNESOTA TERRITORY

WISCONSIN

MICHIGAN

LOUISIANA

IOWA

TERRITORY GAINED FROM MEXICO

TERRITORY

ILLINOIS
INDIANA
OHIO

MISSOURI

KENTUCKY

VIRGINIA

MISSISSIPPI
ARKANSAS

TENNESSEE

NORTH CAROLINA

SOUTH CAROLINA

ALABAMA
GEORGIA

NEW HAMPSHIRE
VERMONT
MAINE
NEW YORK
MASSACHUSETTS
RHODE ISLAND
CONNECTICUT
NEW JERSEY
DELAWARE
MARYLAND
PENNSYLVANIA

PACIFIC OCEAN

TEXAS

MEXICO

LOUISIANA

FLORIDA

ATLANTIC OCEAN

Gulf of Mexico

Columbia River · Snake River · Yellowstone River · Missouri River · Platte River · Sacramento River · Colorado River · Gila River · Rio Grande · Nueces R. · Red River · Mississippi River · Ohio River

0   250   500 Miles
0   250   500 Kilometers

N W E S

— Modern U.S.-Mexican border
☐ United States before the war
☐ Territory gained from Mexico
☐ Mexican Territory

friends and family behind. Polk asked for only 2,800 men, but more than 30,000 Tennesseans volunteered. They wanted to help protect Texas and their loved ones.

The United States Wins!

After two years of fighting, the United States defeated Mexico. The southern border of Texas became the Rio Grande River. Mexico also gave up all of the land between Texas and the Pacific Ocean.

Finally the United States stretched all the way to the Pacific Ocean. Manifest Destiny had been achieved. In the coming years, the states of California, New Mexico, Arizona, Nevada, and

Utah would be carved out of the land gained through the Mexican War.

Mexico lost nearly half of its land in the Mexican War.

Andrew Jackson Dies

Although he had always been energetic, Andrew Jackson was one of our country's unhealthiest presidents. He was tall and thin and had thick, red hair that turned gray as he aged. He often had headaches and stomachaches. In the most famous of the many **duels** he fought, a bullet struck so close to his heart that it could not be removed. Jackson had other old wounds, and one writer said he "rattled like a bag of marbles." Jackson had aches and pains for most of his life, and he sometimes shook and coughed up blood.

Jackson moved back to the Hermitage after completing his second term as president. He died eight years later. Two days after Jackson's death, he was buried next to his wife, Rachel, in the garden at the Hermitage. He was 78 years old.

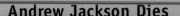

Andrew Jackson's last words were, "Oh, do not cry. Be good children, and we shall all meet in Heaven."

Nearly 10,000 people attended Andrew Jackson's funeral. His tomb is one of the most popular tourist locations in Tennessee.

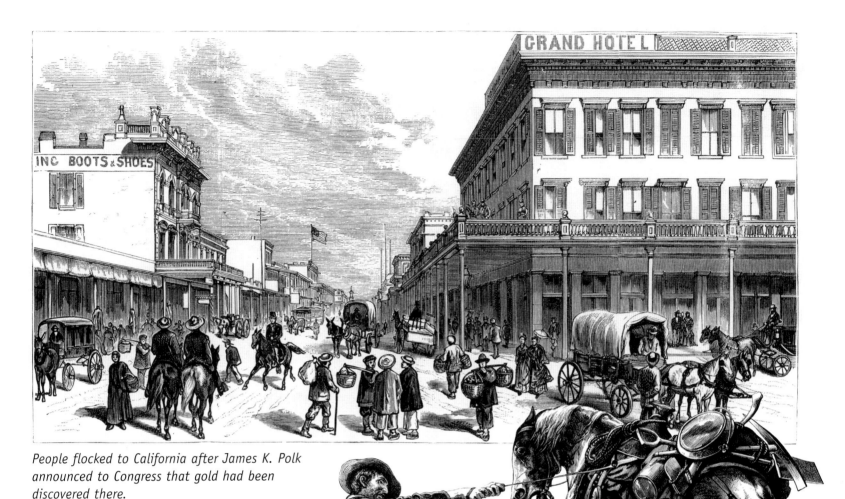

People flocked to California after James K. Polk announced to Congress that gold had been discovered there.

The California Gold Rush

After the Mexican War ended, hundreds of soldiers from Tennessee settled on land in California. They were there the next year when miners discovered gold. Over the next three years, more than 250,000 Americans rushed to California to look for gold. Among them were many young Tennesseans who hoped for instant wealth. Some later returned to Tennessee, but others remained in California. They ran hotels, restaurants, hardware stores, and other businesses.

The people who went to California looking for gold were called '49ers because they went to California in 1849. So many people moved to California that after one year the population was large enough for the territory to become a state.

Northerners hated the Fugitive Slave Act. They agreed to the law, but most refused to obey it.

What Do You Think ❓

Running away was only one way slaves fought back. Sometimes they worked very slowly or broke things. They also told jokes and stories or sang songs that made fun of their owners. Can you think of other ways slaves could fight back without their owners knowing it?

The Compromise of 1850

The question of statehood for California caused a great debate in the U.S. Congress. Members knew Southerners would want to move west and take their slaves with them. Many Congressmen did not want slavery to spread to the West. They didn't even want it to remain in the South! Members of Congress argued for weeks. Then they finally reached a compromise.

In the Compromise of 1850, Southerners agreed to support California as a free state. In exchange, Northerners had to agree to a new law called the Fugitive Slave Act. The law said Northerners had to help capture slaves who had run to freedom in the North. The Fugitive Slave Act was very upsetting to Northerners who wanted to abolish slavery.

The Power of a Book

After the Fugitive Slave Act passed, a woman named Harriet Beecher Stowe began writing about slavery. Her story was called *Uncle Tom's Cabin*. In the story, an abused slave named Eliza tries to run away to freedom. An antislavery newspaper printed one chapter of Stowe's story each week. Many people who read it realized for the first time how truly terrible slavery was.

After all the chapters were written, *Uncle Tom's Cabin* was printed as a book. Thousands of people read it and became very angry. Some people were angry because they thought slavery was evil and wrong. Others—especially slave owners—were angry because they didn't want people to learn about slave life. These men tried to have the book outlawed.

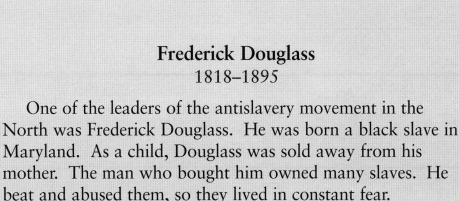

Frederick Douglass
1818–1895

One of the leaders of the antislavery movement in the North was Frederick Douglass. He was born a black slave in Maryland. As a child, Douglass was sold away from his mother. The man who bought him owned many slaves. He beat and abused them, so they lived in constant fear.

Douglass's owner sent him to work in Baltimore. There he learned to read and write. He also learned about freedom. After he returned to his owner, he suffered more beatings. He knew life could be better. He promised himself that one day he would be free.

Douglass finally escaped to Massachusetts. He began reading antislavery materials and joined antislavery groups. Then he wrote a book called *Narrative of the Life of Frederick Douglass: An American Slave*. It became a bestseller.

For the rest of his life, Douglass made speeches against slavery. When people heard him speak, they understood how cruel slavery really was. They were able to see how badly slaves were treated. By the time the Civil War began, Frederick Douglass was one of the most famous men in America.

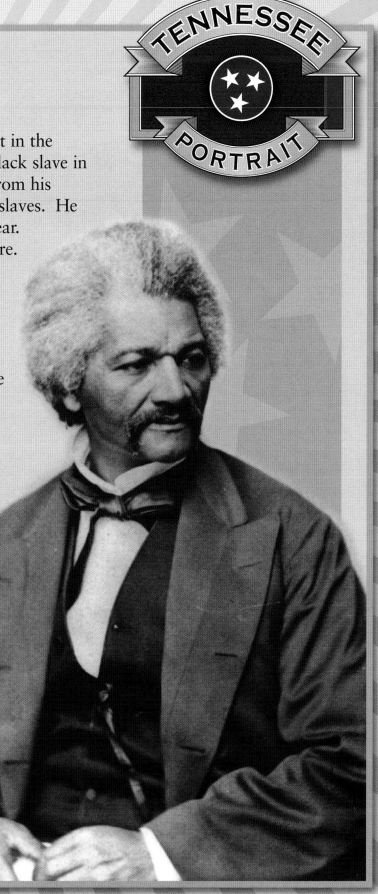

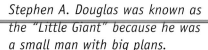
Stephen A. Douglas was known as the "Little Giant" because he was a small man with big plans.

The Kansas-Nebraska Act

One of the people who helped write the Compromise of 1850 was Stephen A. Douglas, a senator from Illinois. He was eager to organize the lands of the Louisiana Purchase. But southern politicians didn't want more free states. They slowed down the process so it took much longer for a territory to become a state.

Douglas thought he might get Southerners to cooperate if he gave them something they wanted. He proposed letting the people of each new territory decide whether to allow slavery. His proposal was called the Kansas-Nebraska Act.

Popular Sovereignty

The Kansas-Nebraska Act supported an idea called popular sovereignty. Popular sovereignty meant people who lived in the territories had the right to decide on the issue of slavery. Southern politicians liked that idea. They agreed to the Kansas-Nebraska Act.

Those who were against slavery were also against the Kansas-Nebraska Act. They did not want slavery to spread into the new territories. The act passed and opened Kansas and Nebraska to slavery. Northerners were outraged.

The Kansas-Nebraska Act is one of the most important documents in U.S. history. Many people believe this act led to the Civil War.

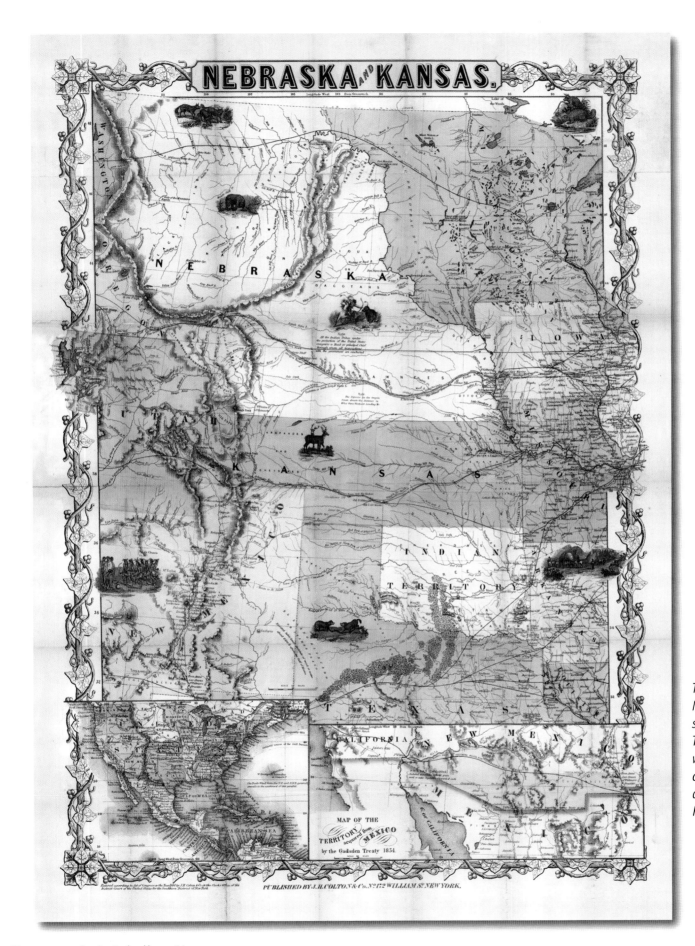

NEBRASKA AND KANSAS.

MAP OF THE
TERRITORY
acquired from MEXICO
by the Gadsden Treaty 1854

PUBLISHED BY J.H. COLTON & C°. N°172 WILLIAM St. NEW YORK.

The Kansas-Nebraska Act stirred up politics. The people who were against it came together and formed the Republican Party.

Dred Scott

Throughout the 1850s, members of the U.S. Congress argued about slavery. The issue was dividing the nation. Even members of the same political parties argued. The Whigs fought so much that the party split. Americans wanted someone to make a decision so people would stop arguing about it. In 1857, the U.S. Supreme Court did just that. The court case was called *Dred Scott v. Sandford*.

Dred Scott was a slave who lived in St. Louis, Missouri. He traveled with his owner and lived for a while in both Illinois and the Wisconsin Territory. Slavery was illegal in those places, so Scott thought he should be free. When his owner refused to free him, antislavery leaders found lawyers to help him. Scott then sued his owner.

Dred Scott first took his case to court in 1846. It climbed the courts for the next 11 years.

Climbing the Courts

Several courts decided that Dred Scott was free, but his owner disagreed. The owner kept taking the case to higher courts, hoping some judge would decide Scott was still a slave. Finally, *Dred Scott v. Sandford* went before the Supreme Court. Roger B. Taney was the chief justice of the Supreme Court. That means he was the leader of the judges. Taney did not own slaves, but he once had. Seven of the other nine judges on the Supreme Court—including one from Tennessee—were slave owners.

A Decision Is Made

After more than a year, the Supreme Court decided Dred Scott was still a slave. It also decided that all blacks, slave or free, were not citizens of the United States. Blacks could not take cases to court because they had no rights. The decision even said blacks were not included in the "all men are created equal" phrase in the Declaration of Independence.

Many people thought the Supreme Court's decision would end all the arguing, but it didn't. Instead it made the arguments about slavery much worse. Northerners and Southerners alike became angrier. They would not listen to one another. Both sides believed they were right.

Chief Justice Roger B. Taney was a former slave owner from Maryland.

John Brown's Raid

One Northerner who was angry about slavery was John Brown. Brown was an abolitionist from New York. He did not want slavery to be allowed in the territories or in future states. He wanted slavery to end forever.

In the fall of 1859, John Brown led a group of men, including five blacks, to Harper's Ferry, Virginia. There the men captured a storehouse full of guns and weapons. They planned to give the weapons to slaves so they could attack their owners. Federal troops found out about the raid and surrounded the storehouse. They captured John Brown and sent him to prison. A judge ordered that he be put to death.

Southerners were deeply troubled about what John Brown had done. They worried that other people would give weapons to slaves. The idea of slaves with guns terrified southern slave owners.

Just before he was hanged, John Brown said, "The crimes of this guilty land will never be [erased] but with blood."

Eight of the men with John Brown were killed or captured during the raid.

Virginia Hill
Birth and death dates unknown

Virginia Hill's story is a bit of a mystery. Some say she came from Virginia. Others say her name was Virginia. Some say she came from North Carolina. Others say her father was from North Carolina. Some say she bought 400 acres in Clay County. Others say she bought 2,000 acres there. But there is one thing everyone agrees about. Around 1830, a woman bought land in Tennessee, brought slaves to it, and then set them all free.

The community was called Free Hill because the people were free, and the land was hilly. The land was also far away from other towns and bordered by two rivers and a lake. Some said Free Hill was almost an island. That made it safe.

At its peak, Free Hill was a thriving community of 300 citizens. There were two grocery stores, three night clubs, two restaurants, two churches, and a school. The residents loved one another and became like one big family. People said it was a peaceful, comfortable place to live.

Linking the Present to the Past

Over the years, most isolated black communities disappeared, but Free Hill remains. Fewer than 100 people live there today, but it is still special to the people who moved away. Most return each year for a big reunion on the second Sunday of July.

1 MEMORY MASTER

1. What Tennessean became president after Andrew Jackson?
2. Why did most Northerners dislike the Fugitive Slave Act?
3. What was the decision in the *Dred Scott* case?

PEOPLE TO KNOW

William Strickland

PLACES TO LOCATE

Frankland
Jacksoniana
Memphis
Nashville

WORDS TO UNDERSTAND

antebellum

Tennessee's Population Grows

The 40 years before the Civil War are often called the *antebellum* years. "Antebellum" is a Latin word that means "before the war." During this time, the United States gained even more land. The country's population grew too.

One reason the population grew was because families from Europe moved to the United States. Many easterners moved west, and immigrants took the factory jobs they left behind. As the immigrants earned more money, they also began to move west.

West Tennessee and Memphis

West Tennessee grew much faster than the other two regions. Over a period of 20 years, the population of West Tennessee grew from 2,500 to 200,000. By 1860, Memphis was the largest city in Tennessee and the fifth largest city in the South. One visitor described Memphis as "the liveliest, raciest, richest, most energetic, and thrifty city within the limits of the Union."

The people who lived in Memphis came from all over the world. There were immigrants from Ireland, Germany, England, Scotland, Italy, and France. The city had almost 4,000 black slaves too. Most of the region's 100,000 slaves, however, lived outside Memphis on cotton plantations.

The Mississippi River brought people from all over the world to Memphis.

PASSPORT TO HISTORY

The Growing Slave Population

(Source: The U.S. Census Bureau)

Year	Total Population of Tennessee	Slave Population of Tennessee	Percent of Population Held as Slaves
1800	105,000	13,584	12.9
1810	261,000	44,734	17.1
1820	422,000	80,107	19.0
1830	682,000	141,647	20.8
1840	829,000	183,059	22.1
1850	1,002,717	239,459	23.9
1860	1,109,801	275,719	24.8

Historians use all kinds of evidence to study the past. Use this population chart to answer the following questions. Turn in your answers to get the last stamp in your passport to history.

1. During which year was the slave population in Tennessee the highest?
2. What pattern do you see in both the first and second columns?
3. By how much did the total population of Tennessee grow from 1830 to 1840?
4. By how much did the slave population grow from 1830 to 1840?
5. Where did the information on this chart come from?
6. Between which years did the percentage of slaves increase the most?

By 1860, Tennessee had 20 times as many slaves as there were in 1800.

West | Middle | East

● Nashville
● Murfreesboro

What Do You Think ?

How do you think life in Tennessee would be different if the Grand Divisions had become separate states? If you had to choose a state capital for each new state, which cities would you choose? Why?

The main reason the General Assembly chose Nashville over Murfreesboro was because it was easier for people to travel to Nashville. Nashville was on the Cumberland River, which was deep enough for steamboats to travel. Murfreesboro was on the Stones River, which was too shallow for steamboats.

Another reason the General Assembly chose Nashville was because there was a hill in the center of town. A capitol building on top of the hill could be seen from all over the city.

The Three "States" of Tennessee

As the population of West Tennessee grew, competition between the Grand Divisions increased. The regions competed for government services, such as roads and bridges, but they also competed for the state capital.

The State of Frankland

People in East Tennessee and West Tennessee knew the state capital would be built in the middle of the state. But they did not want Middle Tennessee to get more services than they did. State senator Andrew Johnson asked the General Assembly to make East Tennessee a separate state, the state of Frankland.

The State of Jacksoniana

When people in West Tennessee learned of Johnson's request, they asked the General Assembly to do the same thing for their region. They wanted to call their new state Jacksoniana. The General Assembly refused to create three states, but the idea did not go away.

A Permanent Capital for Tennessee

Nine years had passed since the state constitution had said the General Assembly had to choose a capital city. Several towns wanted to become the state capital. One member of the General Assembly suggested the capital be located at the geographical center of the state. That was very close to Murfreesboro. After lengthy debate, the General Assembly settled on Nashville.

The State Capitol Building

William Strickland, a famous architect, designed the Tennessee state capitol building. He wanted it to look something like the Parthenon, a temple on a high hill in Greece. The Tennessee state capitol is also on a high hill. Many historians say our capitol building is Strickland's finest work.

Workers began work on the capitol on July 4, 1845. Several years later, the General Assembly began to meet there even though the building was not finished. When William Strickland died in 1854, the capitol was still not finished. Before he died, he asked to be buried in a wall of the capitol. The General Assembly granted Strickland's wish. He is buried in the northeastern wall of the capitol.

Workers placed the final stone in the capitol on March 19, 1859. It had taken 15 years and almost $1 million to complete. All of the building materials were from Tennessee.

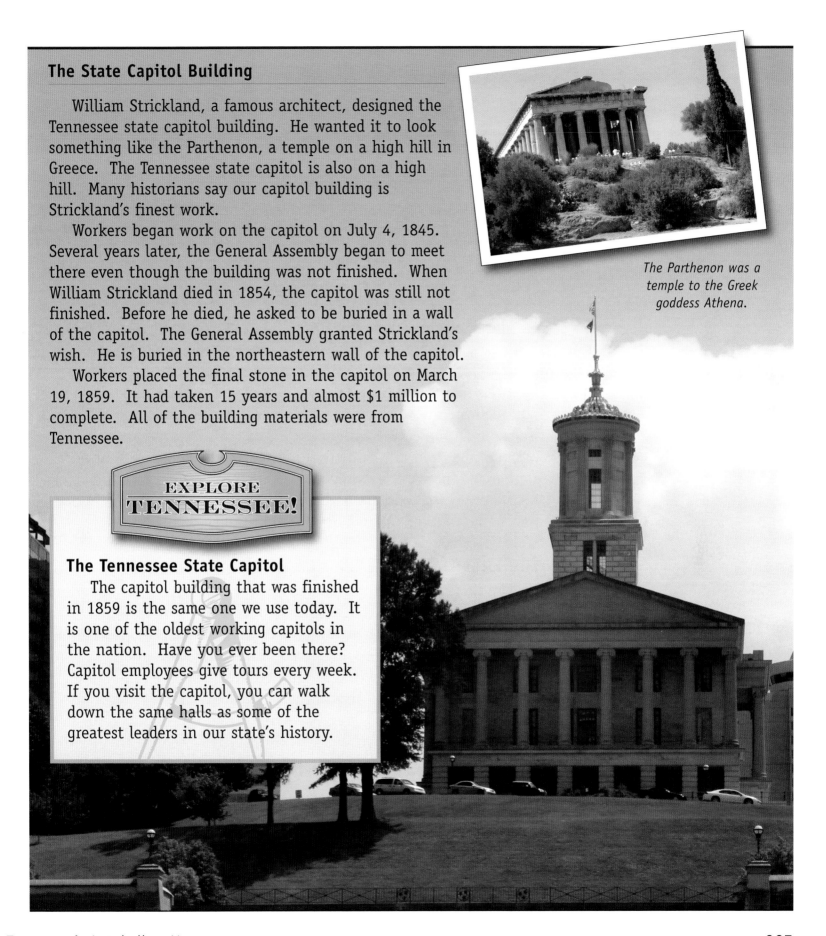

The Parthenon was a temple to the Greek goddess Athena.

EXPLORE TENNESSEE!

The Tennessee State Capitol

The capitol building that was finished in 1859 is the same one we use today. It is one of the oldest working capitols in the nation. Have you ever been there? Capitol employees give tours every week. If you visit the capitol, you can walk down the same halls as some of the greatest leaders in our state's history.

The Nashville and Chattanooga Railroad built this bridge across the Valley of Running-Water Creek.

Thousands of years ago, the very first tracks made for carts were carved in stone. The next type of tracks were built of wood. These were easier to make than carved stone tracks. But they often wore out or broke under the weight of heavy loads. When the first iron rails were built, people were thrilled. The iron rails carried train cars that weighed thousands of pounds, and they almost never wore out.

The Railroads Come to Tennessee

The first railroads in the United States began operating while Andrew Jackson was still president. Steam trains that ran on railroad tracks were the newest type of transportation. Workers built the tracks by laying heavy iron rails on the ground. Then they pounded the rails into place with spikes. Hour after hour, men laid tracks in all kinds of weather.

Soon the railroads came to Tennessee. The geography of our state made the work even harder. Some mountains were too steep for railroads, so workers had to dig tunnels through them. When they came to rivers, they had to build bridges.

The First Train

The first train to run in Tennessee was on the LaGrange and Memphis Railroad in 1842. It ran for only a few months, but people came from miles around to see it. This train helped people in other cities become more interested in building railroads.

Twelve years later, workers finished the Nashville and Chattanooga Railroad. It was the first railroad built entirely in Tennessee. Three years later, Nashville had a railroad to Louisville, Kentucky. Then railroad workers connected Knoxville to Virginia and several other eastern states. By 1861, Tennessee had more than 1,200 miles of train tracks.

What Do You Think?

When trains first appeared, people called the huge steam engines "iron horses." Why do you think people called them that? Do you think trains are like horses made of iron? Why or why not?

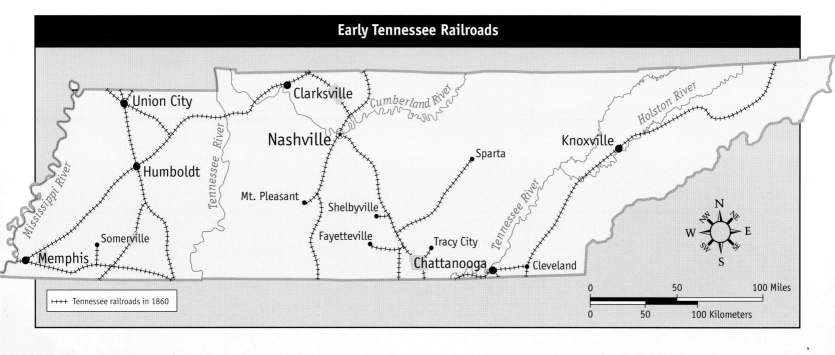

Early Tennessee Railroads

Union City

Clarksville

Cumberland River

Holston River

Nashville

Knoxville

Sparta

Tennessee River

Mississippi River

Humboldt

Mt. Pleasant

Shelbyville

Tennessee River

Somerville

Fayetteville

Tracy City

Memphis

Chattanooga

Cleveland

N
NW NE
W E
SW SE
S

┼┼┼ Tennessee railroads in 1860

0   50   100 Miles
0 50 100 Kilometers

This old photograph shows a train and many sets of tracks. Study the picture carefully to find clues that show which Tennessee city this is.

During the antebellum period, many women began questioning their lack of rights.

Women's Rights

During the antebellum period, women had only a few more rights than slaves. They could not vote. If they were married, they could not own property. Women were expected to spend their time taking care of their home and family.

Farm wives had a few more rights than women who lived in cities. Farmers and their wives worked as partners. As more people moved into towns, women lost much of their power. If a woman earned any money, she had to give it to her husband. Most men thought women were not as smart as men.

Some women began to resent their treatment as second-class citizens. They met together and talked about what they could do to win more rights.

2 MEMORY MASTER

1. What happened to Tennessee's population during the antebellum period?
2. What city finally became the state capital?
3. What is significant about the Nashville and Chattanooga Railroad?

Slavery, A National Issue

As the antebellum years wore on, more people fought to end slavery. Many Northerners thought the practice was very wrong. They went to meetings where people talked about the abolition of slavery. This kind of talk scared southern slave owners.

Before this time, Americans had always been able to compromise. They had worked together to solve problems. Now people were more loyal to the part of the country where they lived than they were to the nation. The United States became divided between slave states and free states. Southerners began talking about states' rights again. They didn't want the national government making decisions about things in their states.

What Do You Think?

Do you think the national government should have the right to make laws about things that happen within a state? Why or why not?

PEOPLE TO KNOW

John Bell
John C. Breckinridge
Jefferson Davis
Stephen A. Douglas
Isham Harris
Abraham Lincoln

PLACES TO LOCATE

South Carolina

WORDS TO UNDERSTAND

secede

Cotton was the most important crop in the South. Some called it the "white gold."

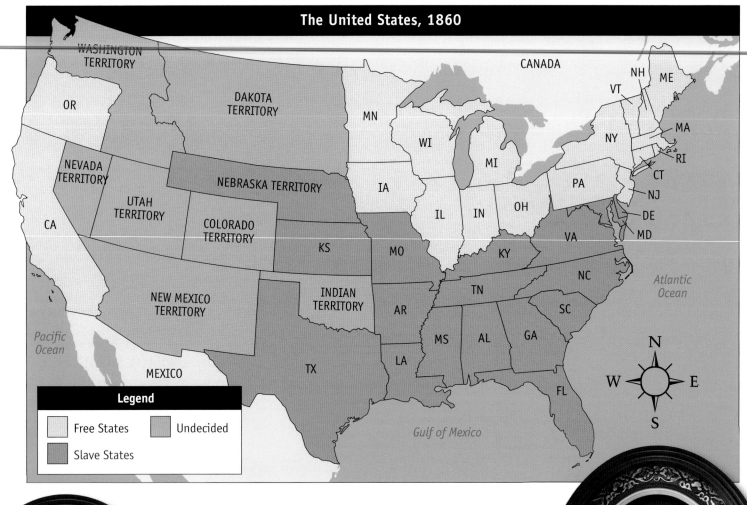

The United States, 1860

WASHINGTON TERRITORY

OR

NEVADA TERRITORY

UTAH TERRITORY

CA

COLORADO TERRITORY

NEW MEXICO TERRITORY

DAKOTA TERRITORY

NEBRASKA TERRITORY

KS

INDIAN TERRITORY

TX

CANADA

MN

WI

MI

IA

IL IN OH

MO

AR

LA

MS AL GA

FL

KY

TN

SC

NC

VA

PA

NY

NH ME

VT

MA

RI

CT

NJ

DE

MD

MEXICO

Pacific Ocean

Atlantic Ocean

Gulf of Mexico

N
W E
S

Legend

Free States

Undecided

Slave States

The Election of 1860

The Northerners who had been Whigs created a new political party called the Republican Party. The Republicans did not want slavery to spread outside the South. When it came time to elect a new president, they nominated Abraham Lincoln. Lincoln and the Republicans said they did not want to abolish slavery, but they did not want it to spread.

The Democratic Party divided over slavery. Northern Democrats and southern Democrats could not agree on a candidate. They nominated two different people for president: John C. Breckinridge and Stephen A. Douglas.

Abraham Lincoln

John C. Breckinridge

Stephen A. Douglas

John Bell and the CUP

Some people did not like any of the candidates. They decided to create a new political party, the Constitutional Union Party (CUP). Members of this party did not want to talk about slavery at all. They nominated John Bell, a U.S. senator from Tennessee. He owned many slaves, but he didn't want slavery to spread. He just wanted everyone to quit arguing about it.

During the campaign, John Bell's friends told people he was the only true national candidate. They said the other candidates were northern candidates or southern candidates. They said Bell was the only candidate who represented all parts of the nation.

John Bell

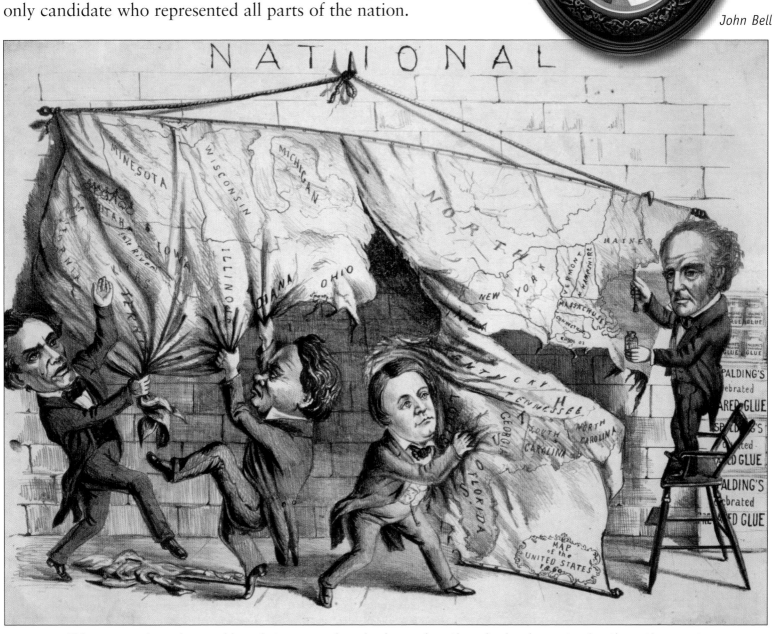

This cartoon shows how problems between northern leaders and southern leaders began tearing the nation apart.

Abraham Lincoln Wins!

Abraham Lincoln won the election even though the southern states refused to put his name on the voting ballot. Most Southerners did not believe him when he said he would not abolish slavery. They voted for John Breckinridge. John Bell, however, won the states of Tennessee, Kentucky, and Virginia.

South Carolina Secedes

When the southern states learned Abraham Lincoln had been elected, they talked about *seceding,* or leaving, the Union. One month after the election, the South Carolina General Assembly voted to do just that.

In February of 1861, representatives from South Carolina, Georgia, Florida, Alabama, Mississippi, Louisiana, and Texas met. They organized a new country called the Confederate States of America. They chose Jefferson Davis from Mississippi as their president.

Tennessee Divides

At the time the Confederacy was organized, eight slave states remained in the Union. Tennessee was one of those states. But many people who lived here, including Governor Isham Harris, wanted to join the Confederacy. Others, especially those in East Tennessee, did not want to secede. They wanted to remain part of the Union.

One of the people who did not want Tennessee to secede was Sam Houston. He said, "Let me tell you what is coming. After the sacrifice of countless millions [in] treasure and hundreds of thousands of lives, you may win Southern independence, but I doubt it. The North is determined to preserve this Union."

On February 9, 1861, the issue went before the people. By a very narrow margin, Tennesseans voted to stay in the Union. But it wasn't long before they changed their minds.

South Carolina

South Carolina was the first state to secede from the Union.

Tennessee Governor Isham Harris believed slavery should be allowed in the West because Southerners had fought to gain that land from Mexico.

The Confederates attacked Fort Sumter for more than 30 hours before U.S. soldiers surrendered.

The Civil War Begins

On April 12, southern Confederate soldiers attacked Fort Sumter, a Union fort in South Carolina. President Lincoln called for 10,000 Tennessee soldiers to crush the rebellion. When Governor Isham Harris received Lincoln's message, he wrote back, "Tennessee will not furnish a single man for purposes of [force] but 50,000 if necessary for the defense of our rights and those of our southern brothers." What Harris meant was that Tennessee would not help the Union. It would only help the Confederacy.

Tennessee Secedes

The state General Assembly met again. It asked Tennesseans to vote once more on the issue of leaving the Union. This time the vote was 104,913 to leave and 47,238 to stay. Most of the people who voted to stay were from East Tennessee.

A long and terrible civil war followed Tennessee's decision to leave the Union. It lasted four years. By the time the Civil War ended, every county in Tennessee had changed in some way. Every family in the state had been touched.

3 MEMORY MASTER

1. What is a compromise?
2. Who won the presidential election of 1860?
3. Why did South Carolina secede from the Union?

A TIMELINE of Slavery

1619: The first Africans arrive in Virginia as indentured servants.

1641: Massachusetts is the first colony to legalize slavery.

1682: Virginia declares that all black servants are slaves for life.

1688: The Quakers in Pennsylvania pass the first antislavery laws.

1691: South Carolina passes the first laws (codes) governing slaves.

1694: With the introduction of rice, the slave trade increases rapidly.

1705: The Virginia Slave Code defines black slaves as property.

1740: South Carolina passes the Negro Act. Slaves cannot leave the country, meet in groups, farm, earn money, or learn to read.

1775: The first abolition society forms in Pennsylvania.

1776: The Declaration of Independence states, "All men are created equal," but slavery remains legal in all 13 states.

1777: Vermont bans slavery. Over the next 25 years, Pennsylvania, Massachusetts, New Hampshire, Connecticut, Rhode Island, New York, and New Jersey also ban the practice.

1787–88: The U.S. Constitution does not address slavery directly, but it addresses three items associated with it:

1) Congress may pass laws against bringing new slaves into the country after 20 years.
2) The "three-fifths clause" states that all free people—including indentured servants—are to be counted in the census. Only three-fifths of all "other persons" are to be counted.
3) Article IV states that people "held to service or labor" in one state but who escape to another state must be returned to their owners.

1790: Congress allows slavery in the newly created Southwest Territory.

1793: Congress passes the Fugitive Slave Law.

1804: The Underground Railroad begins operating in Pennsylvania.

1820: Elihu Embree begins the abolitionist newspaper, *The Emancipator.*

1820–21: Congress admits the slave state of Missouri and the free state of Maine into the Union. Congress bans slavery north of the 36° 30' line of latitude in the Louisiana Territory.

1831: Nat Turner, a slave, leads a slave revolt in Virginia.

1833: William Lloyd Garrison and the Tappan brothers form the American Anti-Slavery Society.

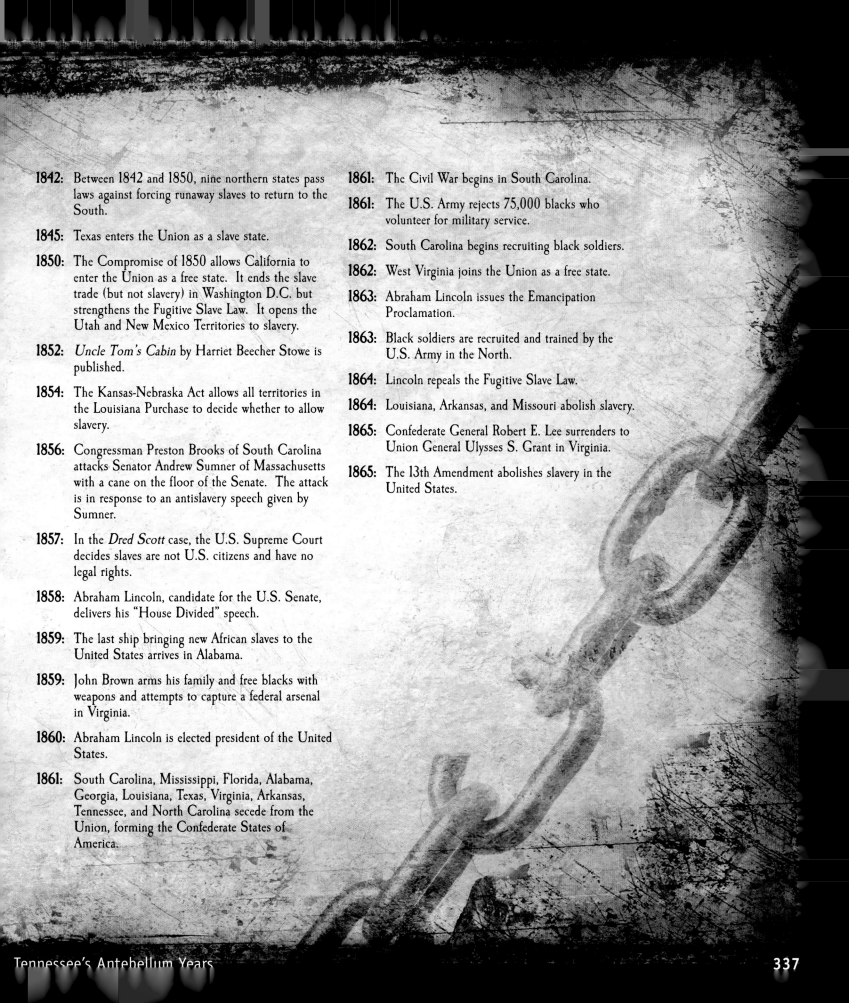

1842: Between 1842 and 1850, nine northern states pass laws against forcing runaway slaves to return to the South.

1845: Texas enters the Union as a slave state.

1850: The Compromise of 1850 allows California to enter the Union as a free state. It ends the slave trade (but not slavery) in Washington D.C. but strengthens the Fugitive Slave Law. It opens the Utah and New Mexico Territories to slavery.

1852: *Uncle Tom's Cabin* by Harriet Beecher Stowe is published.

1854: The Kansas-Nebraska Act allows all territories in the Louisiana Purchase to decide whether to allow slavery.

1856: Congressman Preston Brooks of South Carolina attacks Senator Andrew Sumner of Massachusetts with a cane on the floor of the Senate. The attack is in response to an antislavery speech given by Sumner.

1857: In the *Dred Scott* case, the U.S. Supreme Court decides slaves are not U.S. citizens and have no legal rights.

1858: Abraham Lincoln, candidate for the U.S. Senate, delivers his "House Divided" speech.

1859: The last ship bringing new African slaves to the United States arrives in Alabama.

1859: John Brown arms his family and free blacks with weapons and attempts to capture a federal arsenal in Virginia.

1860: Abraham Lincoln is elected president of the United States.

1861: South Carolina, Mississippi, Florida, Alabama, Georgia, Louisiana, Texas, Virginia, Arkansas, Tennessee, and North Carolina secede from the Union, forming the Confederate States of America.

1861: The Civil War begins in South Carolina.

1861: The U.S. Army rejects 75,000 blacks who volunteer for military service.

1862: South Carolina begins recruiting black soldiers.

1862: West Virginia joins the Union as a free state.

1863: Abraham Lincoln issues the Emancipation Proclamation.

1863: Black soldiers are recruited and trained by the U.S. Army in the North.

1864: Lincoln repeals the Fugitive Slave Law.

1864: Louisiana, Arkansas, and Missouri abolish slavery.

1865: Confederate General Robert E. Lee surrenders to Union General Ulysses S. Grant in Virginia.

1865: The 13th Amendment abolishes slavery in the United States.

Chapter 10 Review

What's the Point?

After Andrew Jackson completed his term as president, Tennessean James K. Polk became the new president. The United States fought and won a war against Mexico. California and the modern Southwest became part of the United States. The nation now stretched from ocean to ocean. The telegraph improved communication, and national debate about slavery increased. Compromise over slavery became very difficult as the population of Tennessee exploded. Nashville became the state capital. The railroad helped connect people and business. After Lincoln became president, South Carolina seceded. More states followed as the nation headed toward war.

Becoming Better Readers

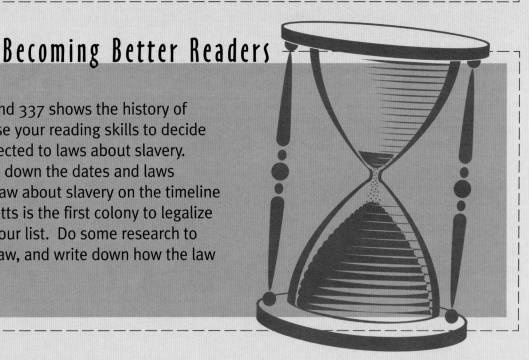

Slavery Laws

The timeline on pages 336 and 337 shows the history of slavery in the United States. Use your reading skills to decide which timeline events are connected to laws about slavery. Examine the timeline, and write down the dates and laws passed. For example, the first law about slavery on the timeline was in 1641 when "Massachusetts is the first colony to legalize slavery." Select one law from your list. Do some research to learn more about it. Read the law, and write down how the law changed the lives of slaves.

Climbing to Connections

Pre–Civil War Timeline

Use the timeline on pages 336 and 337 to complete the following questions:

1. Identify the beginning and ending dates of the timeline.
2. Explain which event was caused by Abraham Lincoln's election in 1860.
3. Examine the events and identify the date Tennessee showed whether it supported the North or the South.
4. Put these three events in order: *Uncle Tom's Cabin* is published, the Civil War begins in South Carolina, the Underground Railroad begins in Pennsylvania.
5. Select one event on the timeline. What if it had happened differently or not at all? How would history have changed?
6. Summarize how the Civil War affected families, the state of Tennessee, and the nation by writing one sentence about each.

Evaluation Station

The Many Faces of Andrew Jackson

In Chapter 9, Andrew Jackson was the symbol of a young, energetic nation. In this chapter, we read about how unhealthy Jackson was during and after his presidency. Compare these two views of Jackson. Make a Venn diagram like the one below. Describe Jackson before and after his presidency. Then evaluate the kind of example he sets for you today.

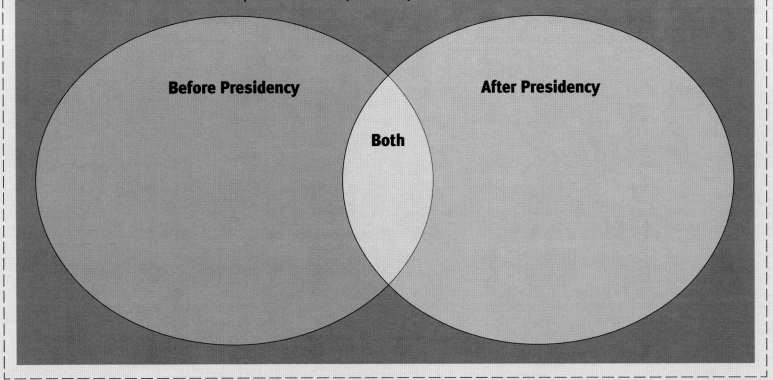

Before Presidency

Both

After Presidency

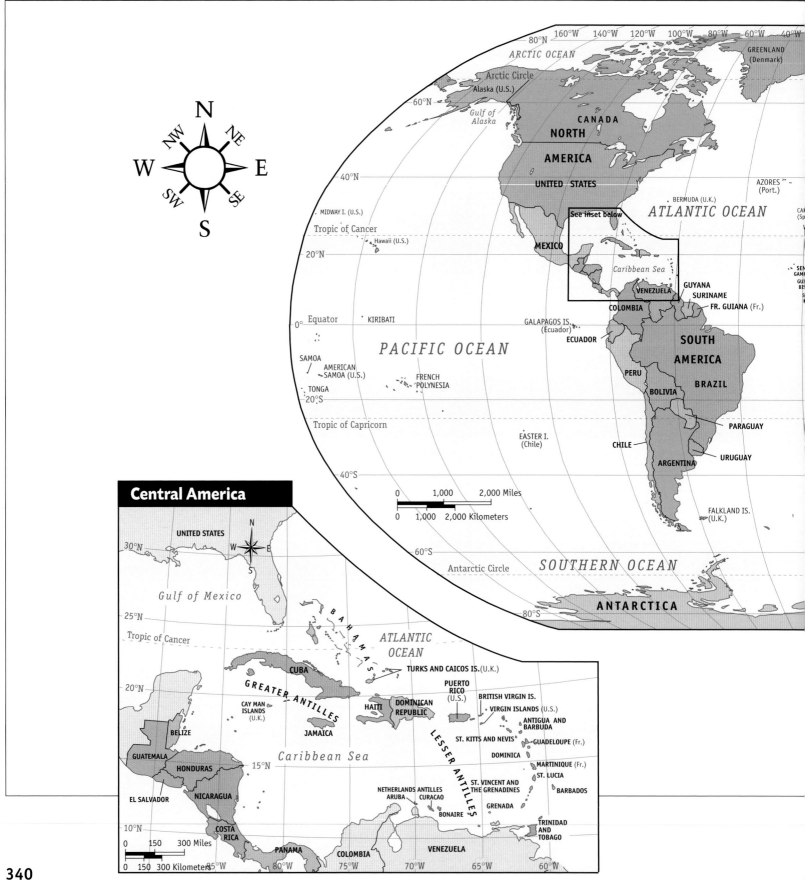

N
NW NE
W E
SW SE
S

ARCTIC OCEAN
Arctic Circle
Alaska (U.S.)
Gulf of Alaska
60°N
GREENLAND (Denmark)
CANADA
NORTH
AMERICA
UNITED STATES
40°N
AZORES (Port.)
BERMUDA (U.K.)
ATLANTIC OCEAN
MIDWAY I. (U.S.)
Tropic of Cancer
Hawaii (U.S.)
20°N
MEXICO
See inset below
Caribbean Sea
VENEZUELA
GUYANA
SURINAME
FR. GUIANA (Fr.)
COLOMBIA
SEN
GAM
GUI
BIS
KIRIBATI
0° Equator
GALAPAGOS IS. (Ecuador)
ECUADOR
SOUTH
AMERICA
SAMOA
AMERICAN SAMOA (U.S.)
PACIFIC OCEAN
PERU
BRAZIL
FRENCH POLYNESIA
BOLIVIA
TONGA
20°S
PARAGUAY
Tropic of Capricorn
EASTER I. (Chile)
CHILE
URUGUAY
ARGENTINA
40°S
0   1,000   2,000 Miles
0 1,000 2,000 Kilometers
FALKLAND IS. (U.K.)
60°S
Antarctic Circle
SOUTHERN OCEAN
80°S
ANTARCTICA

160°W 140°W 120°W 100°W 80°W 60°W 40°W
80°N

Central America

UNITED STATES
N
W   E
S
30°N
Gulf of Mexico
25°N
Tropic of Cancer
BAHAMAS
ATLANTIC OCEAN
CUBA
TURKS AND CAICOS IS. (U.K.)
20°N
PUERTO RICO (U.S.)
BRITISH VIRGIN IS.
GREATER ANTILLES
CAYMAN ISLANDS (U.K.)
HAITI
DOMINICAN REPUBLIC
VIRGIN ISLANDS (U.S.)
ANTIGUA AND BARBUDA
BELIZE
JAMAICA
ST. KITTS AND NEVIS
GUADELOUPE (Fr.)
GUATEMALA
Caribbean Sea
15°N
DOMINICA
MARTINIQUE (Fr.)
HONDURAS
ST. LUCIA
EL SALVADOR
NICARAGUA
ST. VINCENT AND THE GRENADINES
BARBADOS
LESSER ANTILLES
NETHERLANDS ANTILLES
ARUBA
CURACAO
GRENADA
BONAIRE
10°N
COSTA RICA
TRINIDAD AND TOBAGO
0   150   300 Miles
PANAMA
COLOMBIA
VENEZUELA
0 150 300 Kilometers
85°W   80°W   75°W   70°W   65°W   60°W

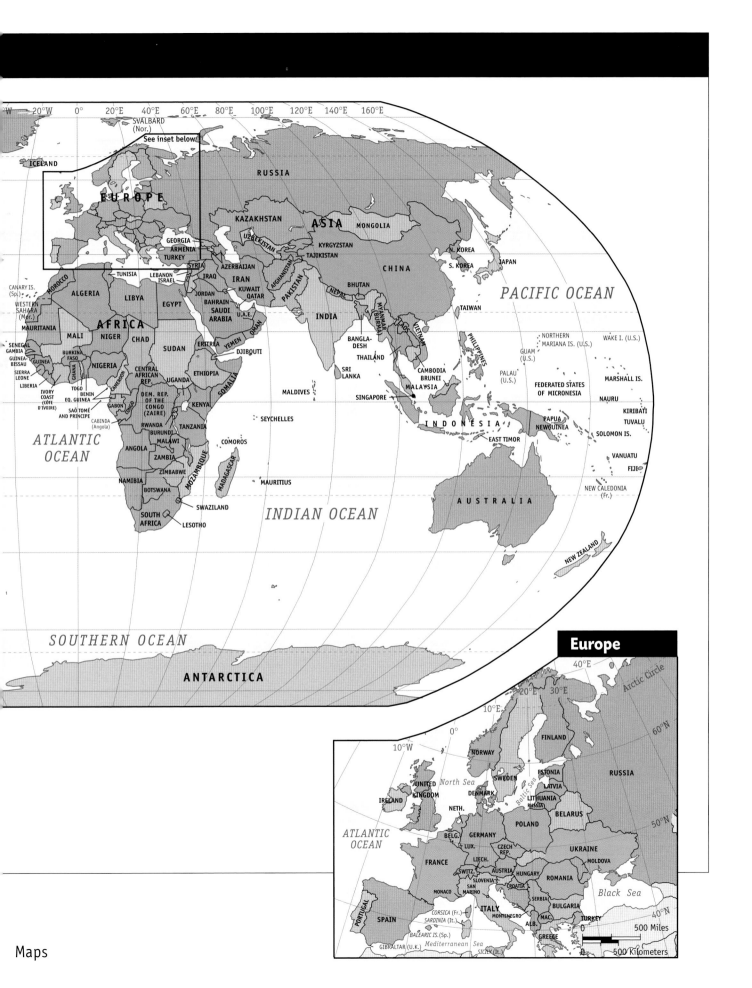

Europe

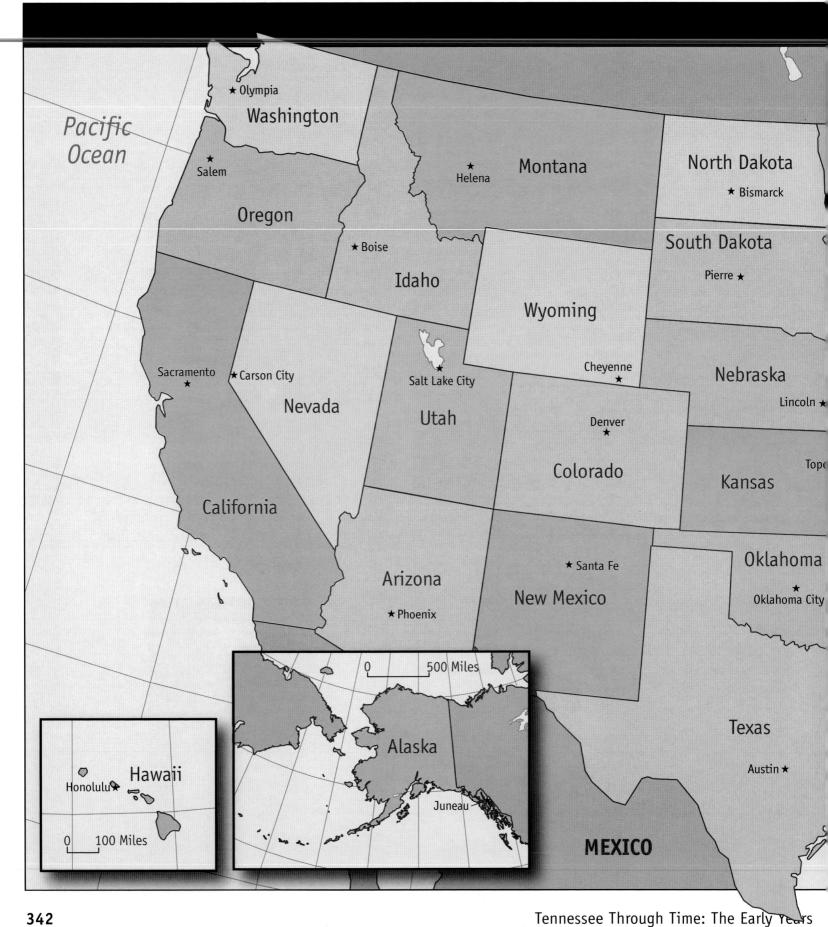

Pacific
Ocean

★ Olympia

Washington

Montana

★ Helena

North Dakota

★ Bismarck

Salem ★

Oregon

South Dakota

★ Boise

Pierre ★

Idaho

Wyoming

Sacramento ★ Carson City

★ Salt Lake City

Cheyenne
★

Nebraska

Nevada

Utah

Denver
★

Lincoln ★

California

Colorado

Kansas

Topeka

Arizona

Santa Fe ★

Oklahoma

★ Phoenix

New Mexico

★
Oklahoma City

0   500 Miles

Hawaii

Alaska

Texas

Honolulu ★

Juneau

Austin ★

0   100 Miles

MEXICO

Tennessee Through Time: The Early Years

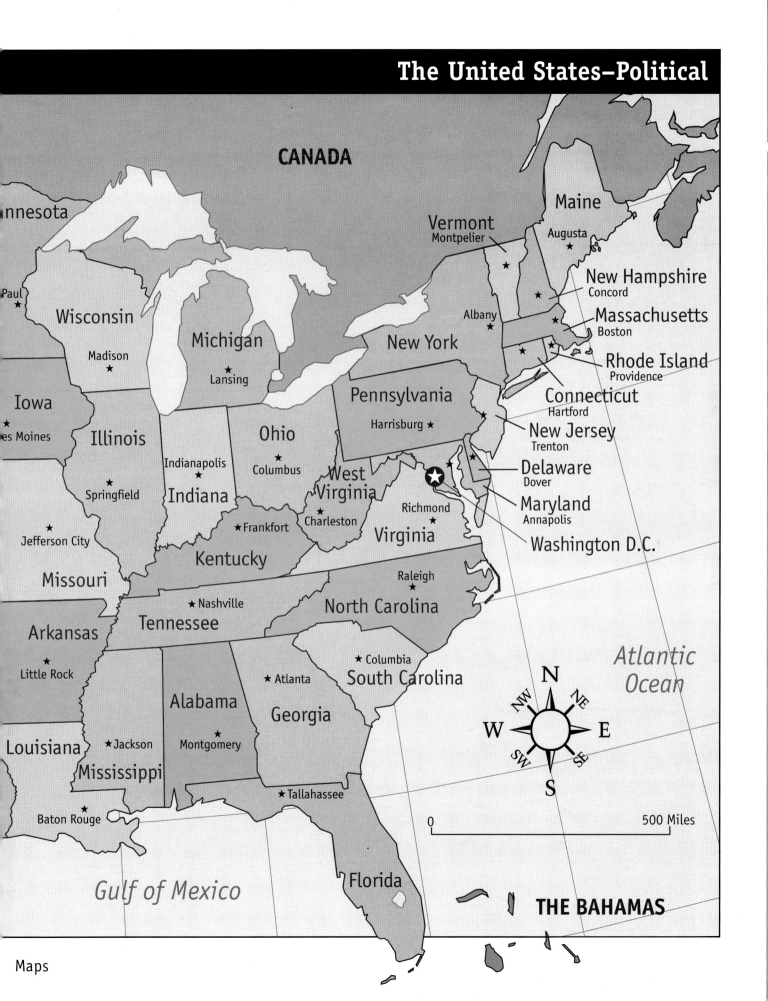

CANADA

Minnesota

Paul

Wisconsin

Madison ★

Iowa

es Moines

Illinois

Springfield ★

Jefferson City ★

Missouri

Arkansas

Little Rock ★

Louisiana

Baton Rouge ★

Mississippi

Jackson ★

Michigan

Lansing ★

Indianapolis ★

Indiana

Frankfort ★

Kentucky

Tennessee

★ Nashville

Alabama

Montgomery ★

Ohio

Columbus ★

West Virginia

Charleston ★

Vermont
Montpelier

Maine

Augusta ★

New Hampshire
Concord

Massachusetts
Boston

Albany ★

New York

Rhode Island
Providence

Pennsylvania

Harrisburg ★

Connecticut
Hartford

New Jersey
Trenton

Delaware
Dover

Maryland
Annapolis

Washington D.C.

Richmond ★

Virginia

Raleigh ★

North Carolina

Columbia ★

South Carolina

Atlanta ★

Georgia

Tallahassee ★

Florida

Gulf of Mexico

THE BAHAMAS

Atlantic
Ocean

N
NW NE
W E
SW SE
S

0   500 Miles

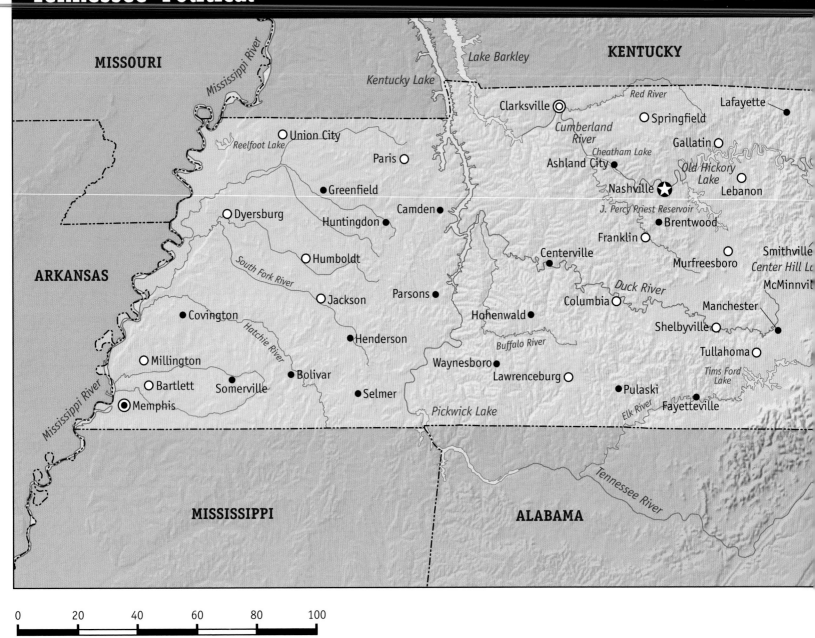

MISSOURI

Mississippi River

Lake Barkley

KENTUCKY

Kentucky Lake

Red River

Clarksville ◉

Lafayette ●

Springfield ○

Reelfoot Lake

Union City ○

Cumberland River

Gallatin ○

Paris ○

Cheatham Lake

Old Hickory Lake

Greenfield ●

Ashland City ●

Lebanon ○

Dyersburg ○

Camden ●

Nashville ★

J. Percy Priest Reservoir

Huntingdon ●

Brentwood ●

ARKANSAS

South Fork River

Humboldt ○

Franklin ○

Smithville ○

Centerville ●

Center Hill Lake

Murfreesboro ○

Jackson ○

Parsons ●

Columbia ○

Duck River

McMinnville

Covington ●

Hohenwald ●

Manchester ○

Hatchie River

Henderson ●

Buffalo River

Shelbyville ○

Millington ○

Waynesboro ●

Tullahoma ○

Mississippi River

Bartlett ○

Somerville ●

Bolivar ●

Lawrenceburg ○

Tims Ford Lake

Memphis ◉

Selmer ●

Pulaski ●

Pickwick Lake

Elk River

Fayetteville ●

MISSISSIPPI

ALABAMA

Tennessee River

0   20   40   60   80   100

Scale of Miles

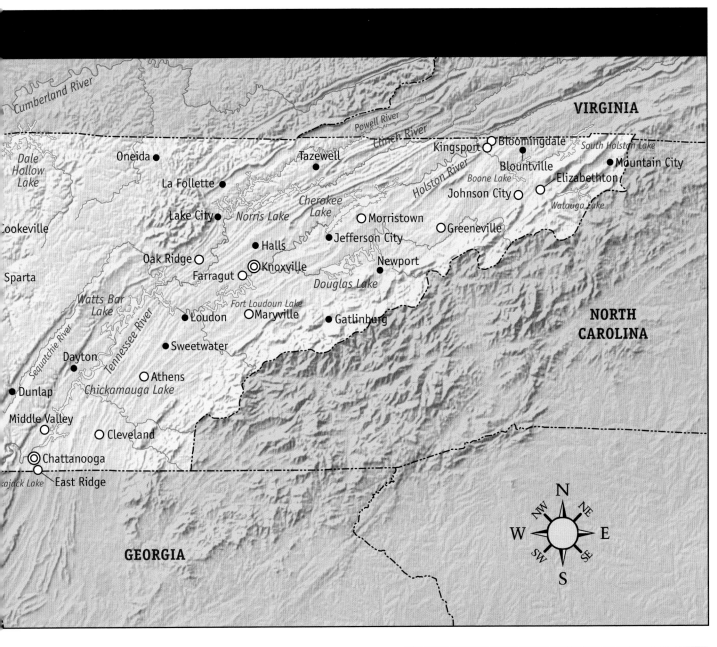

Cumberland River

VIRGINIA

Powell River

Limon River

Dale Hollow Lake

Oneida

Tazewell

Kingsport ● Bloomingdale

South Holston Lake

ookeville

La Follette

Holston River

Blountville

Mountain City

Boone Lake

Elizabethton

Cherokee Lake

Lake City

Norris Lake

Johnson City

Watauga Lake

Sparta

Morristown

Greeneville

Halls

Jefferson City

Oak Ridge

Newport

Farragut ◎ Knoxville

Douglas Lake

Watts Bar Lake

Fort Loudoun Lake

NORTH CAROLINA

Loudon

Maryville

Gatlinburg

Sweetwater

Dayton

Tennessee River

Sequatchie River

Athens

Chickamauga Lake

Dunlap

Middle Valley

Cleveland

Chattanooga

East Ridge

ajack Lake

GEORGIA

N
NW NE
W   E
SW SE
S

Legend		
✪ Capital	〜〜	River
◉ Major U.S. City		Lake
◎ Large City	– ··· –	State Border
○ Medium City		Mountains
● Small City or Town		

Counties and County Seats

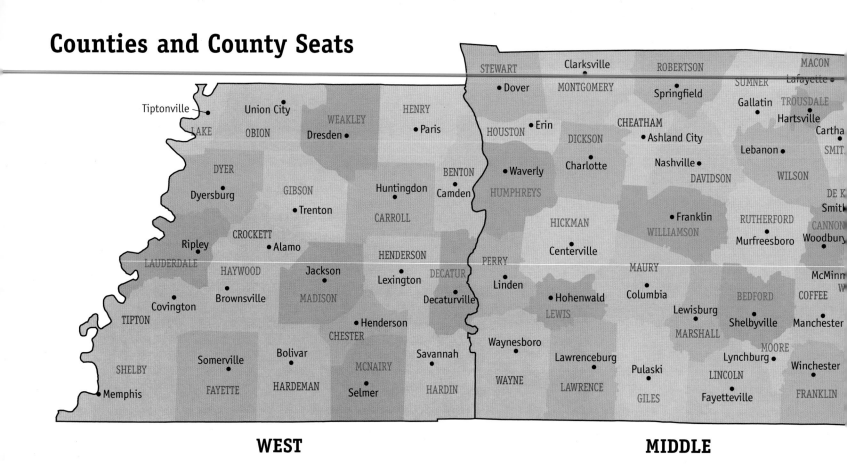

WEST

MIDDLE

Land Regions

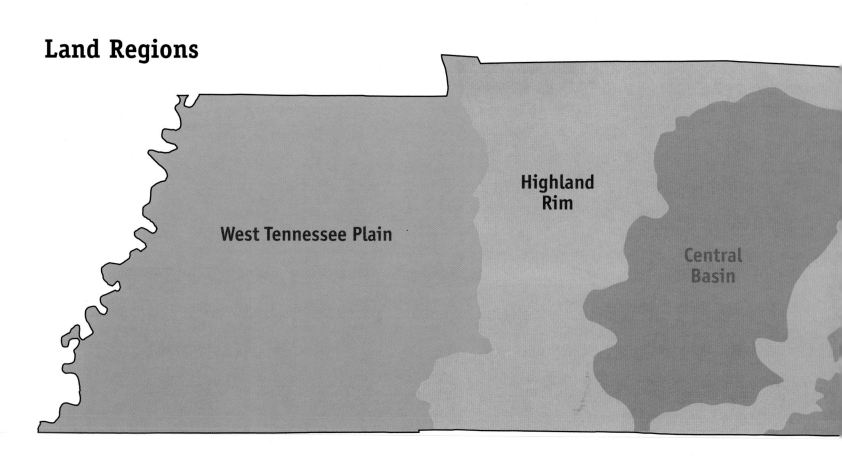

West Tennessee Plain

Highland Rim

Central Basin

Tennessee Through Time: The Early Years

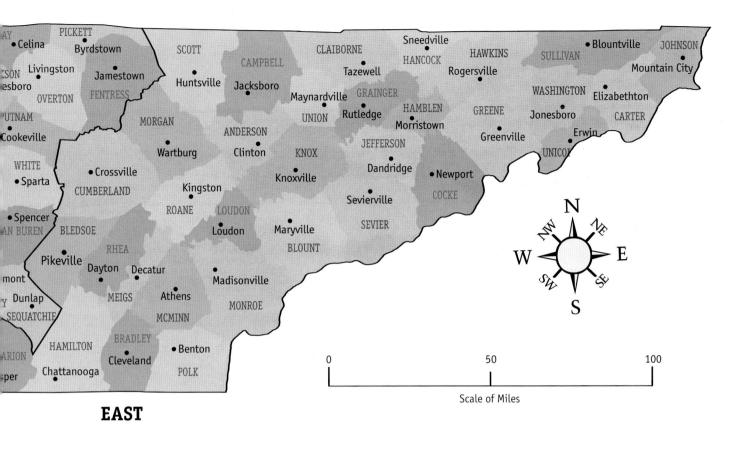

EAST

0   50   100

Scale of Miles

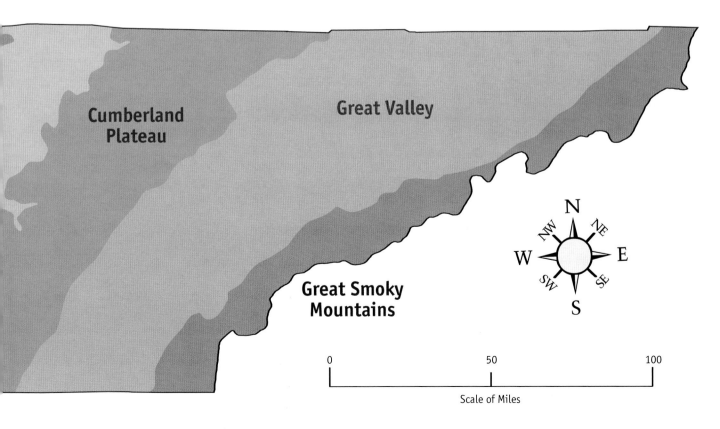

Cumberland Plateau

Great Valley

Great Smoky Mountains

0   50   100

Scale of Miles

Rivers

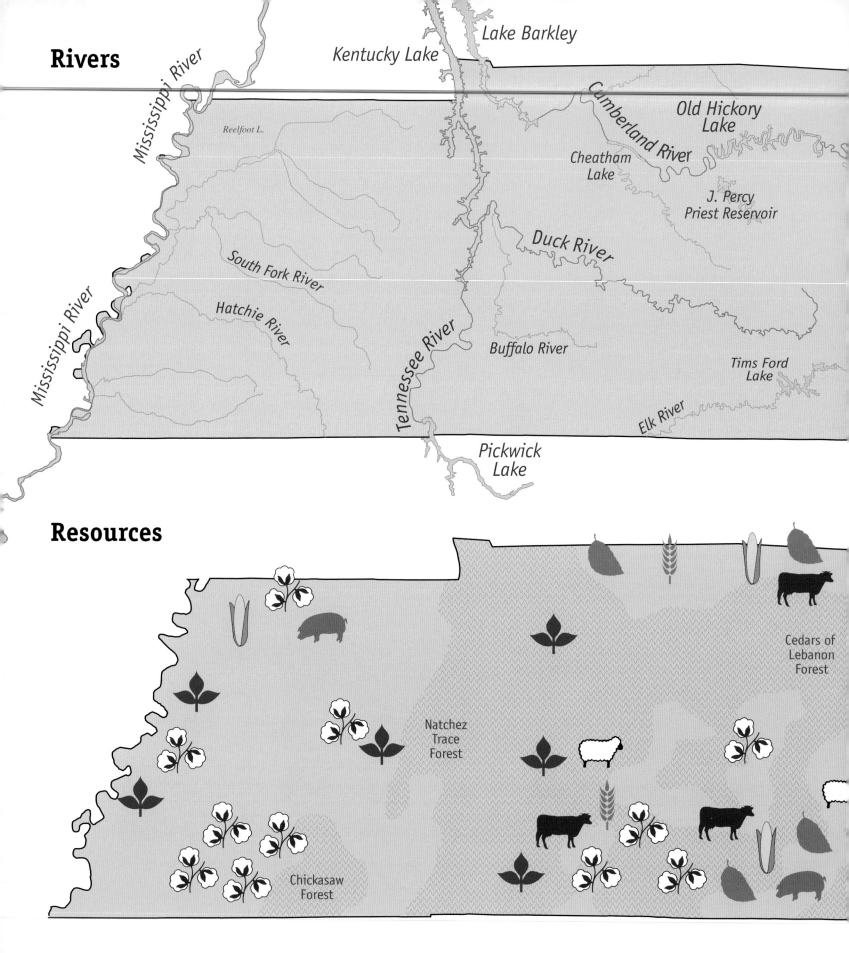

Resources

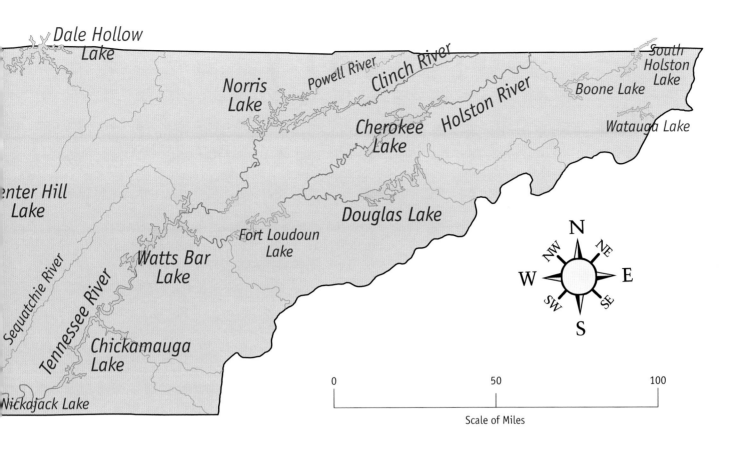

Dale Hollow Lake

Powell River

Clinch River

South Holston Lake

Norris Lake

Boone Lake

Cherokee Lake

Holston River

Watauga Lake

enter Hill Lake

Douglas Lake

Fort Loudoun Lake

Sequatchie River

Watts Bar Lake

Tennessee River

Chickamauga Lake

Nickajack Lake

N
NW   NE
W   E
SW   SE
S

0   50   100

Scale of Miles

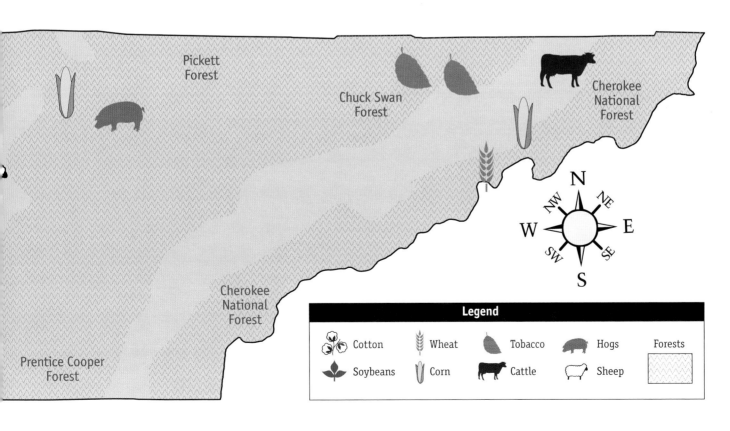

Pickett Forest

Chuck Swan Forest

Cherokee National Forest

Cherokee National Forest

Prentice Cooper Forest

N
NW   NE
W   E
SW   SE
S

Legend				
Cotton	Wheat	Tobacco	Hogs	Forests
Soybeans	Corn	Cattle	Sheep	

Maps

349

Glossary

The definitions listed here are for the **Words to Understand** as they are used in this textbook. The number in parenthesis following each word indicates the chapter in which the word first appears.

A

abolish (9): to put an end to something

abolitionist (9): a person who wanted to end slavery

absolute direction (2): the exact position of a place

absolute power (5): complete control

accent (2): a special way of speaking, usually regional

agriculture (1): farming; raising crops and animals

American Revolution (6): the war in which American colonists fought for independence from Great Britain

ambassador (7): someone sent to a foreign country to represent his or her native government

amendment (7): an adjustment, change, or revision

ancient civilization (3): a very old culture or society

antebellum (10): Latin for "before the war"

anthem (8): a song of praise to a country or cause

anti-Federalist (7): a colonist who did not support the Constitution

antislavery (9): opposed to slavery

archaeologist (3): a scientist who studies artifacts and the past

archaic (3): ancient; very old

Articles of Confederation (7): the first constitution of the 13 American states

artifact (1): an object made or used by people in the past

atlatl (3): a tool that aids in spear throwing

B

ballad (8): a song that tells a story

baptize (9): to participate in a religious ritual believed to cleanse spiritually; usually involves sprinkling or being immersed in water

barter (2): to trade

betray (6): to be disloyal

Bill of Rights (7): the first ten amendments to the U.S. Constitution

bluff (4): a high, steep coastline

boll (8): a rounded seed vessel or pod of a plant

boulder (2): a very large, rounded mass of rock

boundary (2): a border

boycott (6): to stop buying something specifically to make a point or to change a law

brand (5): to mark by burning

C

cabinet (7): a council composed of a leader's closest advisors

campaign (9): the period of time when candidates post signs, give speeches, and attend meetings to educate voters about their positions on political issues

cardinal directions (2): the four main geographic directions: north, south, east, and west

cede (7): to yield or give away

charter (5): a legal document granting permission to settle a piece of land

checks and balances (7): a system by which each branch of government limits the power of the other branches

chert (3): a soft rock used by Native Americans to make arrow and spear points

chief (3): the head or ruler of a tribe or clan

chiefdom (3): the land and people over which a chief rules

chinampa (3): an artificial island

chinking (8): dirt and mud used to fill gaps between logs in a log wall

chronometer (8): a timekeeping machine used to measure longitude at sea

chunkey (3): an old Cherokee game played with a circular rock and sticks

colonial (4): having to do with a colony or colonies

colony (4): a settlement controlled by a foreign government

commerce (1): the buying and selling of goods; business

communication (10): the exchange of information between persons

compete (4): to strive to win or gain advantage

compromise (7): an agreement reached when each side gives up part of what it desires

conductor (9): a person who helped slaves escape on the Underground Railroad

conquistador (4): a Spanish soldier who explored and defeated Indian civilizations in Central and South America

constitution (5): a document that outlines the ideas and laws of government

consumer (2): a person who buys goods or services

credit (5): the practice of buying things and paying for them over time

criticism (5): the practice of calling attention to things that are wrong; fault finding

criticize (7): to find fault with someone or something

cupboard (8): a cabinet with shelves used for storing dishes

D

debate (7): a discussion in which people with opposing ideas argue their points of view

debt (4): something (such as money, goods, or services) that is owed

delegate (6): a person chosen to act for others

democracy (5): government by the people

descendant (9): a person who comes from a specific ancestor

diverse (5): different; varied; such as people from different cultures or backgrounds

document (1): an official paper, letter, or form

dormant (2): inactive

duel (10): a formal fight

E

earthquake (2): a shaking or trembling of the earth

economics (2): the study of how people make, transport, buy, and sell goods and services

economic panic (9): a time when people stop buying goods and money becomes scarce

elevation (2): how high the land is above the level of the ocean

emancipate (9): to free or release

emigrant (9): a person who is moving from one country to another

employee (2): a person who works for wages for someone else

epidemic (9): an outbreak of a disease

equator (2): the geographic line around the middle of the earth; 0 degrees latitude

erosion (2): the wearing away of land by wind and water

evidence (1): proof

exchange (4): to barter or trade

executive branch (7): the branch of government that carries out the laws

expedition (4): a journey for a specific purpose

explorer (4): a person who visits and explores a new place

F

fault (2): a break or weak spot in the earth's crust

federal (7): central government

Federalist (7): colonists who supported the Constitution

fertile (2): rich, productive

fiber (8): a fine thread or string

fiddle (8): a violin

flax (8): a tall, thin plant that looked like wheat; fibers used to make cloth

G

generator (2): a machine that produces electricity

geography (2): the land, water, plants, animals, and people of a place

gin (8): short for engine; refers to a cotton gin

glacier (2): a large mass of ice

glossary (1): a list of words and definitions; usually found at the back of a book

goods (2): products that are made, bought, and sold

graffiti (7): writing or painting written illegally on public property

grid (2): a network of horizontal and parallel lines used for locating points on a map

grievance (6): a complaint against an unjust or unfair act

gristmill (9): a building that uses waterpower and a waterwheel to grind grain into flour

H

harmony (3): a condition in which there is agreement

hemisphere (2): half of the earth, usually divided by the equator or the prime meridian

historian (1): a person who studies history

historic (3): since written records have been kept

House of Burgesses (5): elected representatives that made laws for the colonies

human feature (2): things made by people

hunter-gatherer (3): a person who survives by hunting animals and gathering wild foods

hymn (8): a song of praise

I

immigrant (9): a person who has moved from one country to another country

immunity (4): resistance to disease

impressment (8): the act of forcing people to work for others

indentured servant (5): a person who worked for another person for a period of time in order to pay back a debt, usually the price of passage to the country

independent (6): not ruled by anyone else; acting on your own

index (1): an alphabetical listing of people, places, subjects, and events and their page numbers

Industrial Revolution (9): a time when business and industry developed rapidly

intermediate directions (2): the directions halfway between the cardinal directions; northeast (NE), southeast (SE), northwest (NW), and southwest (SW)

intolerable (5): impossible to tolerate; unbearable

irrigation (2): moving water from one place to another via canals, ditches, or sprinklers

J-K

judicial branch (7): the branch of government that interprets the laws

jury (7): a council that decides whether a person is guilty of breaking a law

keelboat (8): a flat-bottomed boat that could be rowed, sailed, poled, or towed

L

landfill (2): a place where tons of garbage is buried under layers of dirt

land speculator (5): a person who researches, buys, and sells land

latitude (2): geographical lines that run east and west; used for measuring distance from the equator

lava (2): hot melted rock from inside the earth

lease (6): a rental contract

legislative branch (7): the branch of government that makes the laws

legislature (7): the elected political leaders who make laws; the House and the Senate

long hunters (5): a hunter who stayed in the mountains for long periods of time

longitude (2): geographical lines that run north and south; used for measuring distance from the prime meridian

Louisiana Purchase (8): the Louisiana Territory, which the United States purchased from France

loyalist (6): a colonist who was loyal to Great Britain; did not support the American Revolution

M

mall (7): a large, public area

manifest destiny (10): the belief that the United States should expand its borders to the Pacific Ocean

manufacturing (2): making something from raw materials

manumission (9): the practice of freeing from slavery

market economy (2): an economic system in which decisions about buying and selling goods and services are made by buyers and sellers, not the government

mass production (9): the practice of making large quantities, usually with machinery

Mayflower Compact (5): an agreement written by the Pilgrims that established the first colonial government

militia (5): an army

Minutemen (6): colonial soldiers

mission (4): a religious settlement

moccasin (8): a shoe made of soft animal leather

motto (1): a slogan; words that describe a goal or idea

N-O

nation (3): a group of people connected by ties of blood or by common language, customs, traditions, or government

native (3): of or natural to a place or region

Native Americans (3): the first people to live in North America

navigate (4): to steer through water

oath of office (7): a promise made by an official before he or she takes office

oral history (1): spoken history; the stories of the past passed down through storytelling

ore (9): rock that contains minerals

overseer (9): a supervisor or manager

P

paleo (3): ancient; prehistoric; very old

Parliament (5): the legislature of Great Britain

Patriot (6): a person who wanted the thirteen colonies to be free from British rule

patroller (9): a person who searched for runaway slaves

periodical (7): a magazine or journal that is published in regular intervals

permanent (3): constant; not temporary

physical feature (2): natural landforms or characteristics of a place

pike (8): short for "turnpike"; roads between towns

Pilgrim (5): an English man or woman who traveled to North America on a religious journey and settled there

pillory (5): a wooden frame into which a person's head and hands were locked

plantation (4): a large farm

plate tectonics (2): the study of the folding and faulting of earth's crust

pole (8): to push or move with a long wood or metal pole

pollutant (2): substances that make the air or water dirty or unsafe

pollution (2): harmful substances in the environment

point of view (1): the way someone thinks; opinion; perspective

popular sovereignty (7): the idea that a state's power came from the people

pottery (1): ware, such as vases, pots, bowls, or plates, shaped from moist clay and hardened by heat

Preamble (7): the introduction to the U.S. Constitution

prehistoric (3): happening before written history

primary source (1): something made or written by someone who was there at the time; an original record

prime meridian (2): a geographic line from the North Pole to the South Pole running through Greenwich, England; 0 degrees longitude

principle (3): first, highest, or most important

privacy (7): being free from intrusion or disturbance in personal affairs

producer (2): a person who makes or sells goods or services

professional management (2): companies that help businesses organize and manage their business

profit (2): the amount of money left after expenses have been paid

Protestant (9): any non-Catholic Christian church

pueblo (4): a Native American village with homes built on top of each other

Puritan (5): a member of a Protestant religion who settled in North America

Q-R

Quaker (5): a member of a religious group called the Religious Society of Friends

quartering (6): providing housing for soldiers

ratify (7): to approve

recycle (2): to treat or process for reuse

reformer (9): a person who works for change

Regulators (6): a group of Scots Irish men in East Tennessee who want to separate from North Carolina

relative location (2): a description of place based on relation to other places or things

religion (3): a set of beliefs concerning the origin and purpose of life and the world

repeal (7): to cancel, rescind, or take back

represent (1): stand for

representative (5): a person elected to speak, act, or vote for other people

republican (7): a person who believes government should get its power from the people

reservoir (2): a place where water is stored for future use

retail (2): the business of obtaining goods from producers and selling them to consumers at a higher price

revival (9): a religious meeting intended to awake and revive the spirit of God in attendees

revolution (6): a time when a group overthrows and replaces its government

riot (6): a violent protest

rivalry (8): competition

S

sacrifice (3): the offering of an animal, plant, or human life to a higher power or god

salary (2): money paid to employees in exchange for work

scurvy (5): a disease caused by Vitamin C deficiency

secede (10): to withdraw formally

secondary source (1): something made or recorded after an event

separation of power (7): the dividing of governmental power amongst different branches

services (2): work done for money

shoals (6): a shallow and often dangerous section of a body of water

slavery (5): the practice of buying, selling, and owning human beings as though they were property

slogan (1): a catchword or catch phrase; a motto

smallpox (3): a deadly disease that spreads quickly

solid waste materials (2): garbage or things people don't want

spearhead (3): sharpened stones attached to sticks; used for hunting

station (6): a fort built by early settlers

station (7): a hiding place for runaway slaves

stowaway (4): a person who travels on a passenger carrier without paying a fare

strait (4): a channel of water that connects two larger bodies of water

~~supply and demand (2): a rule in economics that states that~~ the availability of something and buyers' desire for it affect how much it will cost

surrender (6): to give up

surveyor (5): a person who measures and surveys land

syllabary (9): a set of written symbols, each of which represents a syllable

symbol (1): something that represents or stands for something else

T

table of contents (1): a listing of a book's contents; usually at the front of the book

tall tale (8): a story about a person or event that is larger than life; usually teaches a lesson or moral

tax (6): money people pay to their government to pay for services

technology (1): the practice of using science and tools together

telegraph (10): a machine that sends coded messages over wires

timeline (1): a line that shows important events in the order in which they occurred

toll (8): a fee to use a road or bridge

trace (8): a path, trail, or road made by passing animals or ~~people~~

Trail of Tears (9): a trail Cherokee Indians traveled from the Southeast to Oklahoma Territory

traitor (6): a person who commits treason by betraying his or her country

treaty (4): an agreement

trial (7): a meeting held to decide a person's guilt or innocence

tsunami (2): a tidal wave

turbine (2): a machine that converts fluid into energy

tyranny (6): the cruel use of power

U-V-W

Underground Railroad (9): a system of escape routes and hiding places used by runaway slaves

volunteer (1): a person who offers to perform a service

wage (2): the amount of money paid to employees for each hour they work

war hawk (8): a congressman who wanted to go to war

westward expansion (10): the idea that the United States should expand its borders to the Pacific Ocean

Index

Credits

The following abbreviations were used for sources from which several images were obtained:

AJ – Adam Jones/www.adamjonesphoto.com
BSP – BigStockPhotos.com
BC – Bettmann/Corbis
DW – David Wright
GR – Gary Rasmussen
Granger – The Granger Collection, New York
iStock – iStockPhoto.com
JB – Jon Burton
LOC – Library of Congress Prints and Photographs Division
NARA – National Archives
NA – Neal Anderson
NWPA – North Wind Picture Archives
NYPL – Picture Collection, The Branch Libraries, The New York Public Library, Astor, Lenox and Tilden Foundations
SS – ShutterStock.com
TDT – Tennessee Department of Tourist Development
THS – Tennessee Historical Society
TSL – Tennessee State Library and Archives

All other photos and illustrations are in the public domain, royalty free or from the Gibbs Smith, Publisher archives.

Prelims: iv-vii LOC

Chapter One: 2-3 David Muench/Corbis; 4 (t) iStock/Bonnie Jacobs, (b) SS/Harris Shiffman; 8 Ariel Skelley/Corbis; 10 (t) The Museum of the Cherokee Indian/www.cherokee-nc.com; 11 (t) LOC, (c) TDT, (b) Tennessee State Museum; 12 DreamsTime/Paul Cowan; 14 SS/Johanna Goodyear; 15 (t) TDT, (b) TSL; 17 TSL; 18 (tl) ShutterPoint.com/Kristin Elmquist, (cl) SS/Dragan Trifunovic, (bl) SS/Tomasz Pietryszek, (bc) SS/Xavier Marchant; 18-19 US Fish and Wildlife Service; 19 (tl) SS/lidian, (tc) SS/Newton Page, (tr) iStock/Deborah Cheramie, (c) SS/Daniel Kvarfordt; 21 NASA.

Chapter Two: 24-25 AJ; 26 DreamsTime/Blair Howard; 34 SS/Olga Perevalova; 35 SS/A.S Zain; 37 Roger Ressmeyer/Corbis; 38-39 Craig C. Sheumaker/Panoramic Images/NGSImages.com; 39 TDT; 40 (t) SS/Billy Lobo H, (b) BigStockPhoto.com/Karla Caspari; 41 JB; 42 LOC; 43 TVA Cultural Resources; 44 (t) SS/Carole Gomez, (b) SS/Mary Bingham; 45 US Fish and Wildlife Service; 46 SS/J.Breedlove; 47 SS/Jaimie Duplass; 49 (t) GR; 51 iStock/Sean Locke; 52 SS/David Alexander Liu; 53 (b) 123RF.com/Dainis Derics; 54 TDT; 55 Gail Mooney/Corbis; 56 TDT.

Chapter Three: 60-61 Painting by Greg Harlin. Courtesy Frank H. McClung Museum, The University of Tennessee, Knoxville; 62 GR; 63 GR; 64 (b) SS/Krzysztof Nieciecki; 65 (t) GR, (b) NA; 66 Janis J Hansen; 67 Painting by Martin Pate, Newnan, GA Courtesy Southeast Archeological Center, National Park Service; 68 (t) GR; 69 (t) Tara Prindle, nativetech.org, (b) LOC; 70 (t) West Virginia Division of Culture and History, (b) GR; 71 (t) Courtesy Cahokia: City of the Sun, (b) Raymond Gehman/Corbis; 72 (t) SS/Elena Fernandez Zabelguelskaya, (b) SS/ Olga Gabay; 73 SS/RJ Lerich; 75 (t) Painting by Martin Pate, Newnan, GA Courtesy Southeast Archeological Center, National Park Service, (b) Courtesy of Cahokia: City of the Sun; 76 (t) SS/Elena Fernandez Zabelguelskaya, (b) Gianni Dagli Orti/Corbis; 77 (t) Gianni Dagli Orti/Corbis, (b) SS/Richard Welter; 79 (t) North Carolina Division of Travel and Tourism, (b) TSL; 80 GR; 81 (t) Courtesy of Cahokia: City of the Sun, (c) LOC, (b) Nebraska State Historical Society, Museum of Nebraska History Collections; 82 NA; 84 GR; 87 (t) TDT, (b) Janis J Hansen; 88 GR.

Chapter Four: 90-91 Picture Collection, The Branch Libraries, The New York Public Library, Astor, Lenox and Tilden Foundations; 93 NWPA; 94 BC; 96-98 LOC; 99 (t) LOC, (b) Paul Morley; 100 NWPA; 101-102 LOC; 103 BC; 104 (r) LOC; 105 (r) LOC; 106 SS/Mike Von Bergen, (inset) LOC; 107 Darby Erd, South Carolina State Museum; 108 (l) SS/Jubal Harshaw, (r) NWPA; 109 (b)

Blue Lantern Studio/Corbis; 110 Architect of the Capitol; 111 Print Collection, Miriam and Ira D. Wallach Division of Art, Prints and Photographs, The New York Public Library, Astor, Lenox and Tilden Foundations; 113 Richard Cummins; 114 (b) NYPL; 115 LOC; 117 BC; 118 NYPL.

Chapter Five: 122-123 DW; 124 BC; 125 (t) Richard T. Nowitz/Corbis, (b) LOC; 126-127 GR; 127 Nik Wheeler/Corbis; 128 (l) History of Maryland Slide Collection; 129 (r) NWPA; 131 LOC; 132 JB; 133 LOC; 134-135 Robert E. Goodier, A.W.S., W.H.S., Courtesy of PNC Bank, Delaware; 137 (t) NYPL; 138 (t) Granger; 139 GR; 140 (t) BC; 141 NWPA; 142 BC; 143 Granger; 145 NWPA; 147 NYPL; 149 The Museum of the Cherokee Indian/www.cherokee-nc.com; 150 Photography Collection, Miriam and Ira D. Wallach Division of Art, Prints and Photographs, The New York Public Library, Astor, Lenox and Tilden Foundations; 151 DW; 152 Ken Smith; 153 Granger; 154-155 DW; 156 LOC; 157 NWPA.

Chapter Six: 160-161 United States Capitol Historical Society; 164 BC; 165 NWPA; 167 Sycamore Shoals State Historic Area & The Carter Mansion; 171 (b) NWPA; 172 (t) NWPA; 174 NARA; 174-175 NWPA; 175 LOC; 176 LOC; 178 TSL; 181 Raymond Gehman/Corbis; 182 DW; 183 (t) West Nashville Founders' Museum, (b) BC; 185 Granger; 186 THS; 187 (t) THS, (r) West Nashville Founders' Museum; 188 TSM; 189 THS; 190 NWPA; 191 THS; 192-193 Architect of the Capitol, Painting by John Trumbull; 193 (tr) NARA (br) DW; 194 Granger.

Chapter Seven: 198-199 DW; 201 NARA; 202 Granger; 203 Peter Harholdt/Corbis; 204 LOC; 206-207 BC; 209 (t) United States Capitol Historical Society, (c) LOC; 213 JB; 214 NARA: 215 Independence National Historic Park; 216-217 LOC; 218 JB; 219 BC; 220 SS/Mladimir Ivanov; 221 LOC; 223 NARA; 224 (t) THS, (b) Rocky Mount Museum; 225 (l) LOC; 226 TDT; 227 TSL.

Chapter Eight: 230-231 Stapleton Collection/Corbis; 232 NWPA; 233 Virginia Historical Society; 234 GR; 235 TDT; 236 (t) NWPA, (b) SS/Martine Oger; 237 (b) SS/Laura Stone; 238 (t) LOC, (bl) SS/Serdar Yagci, (br) United States Mint; 241 BC; 242 NWPA; 243 SS/Mark Winfrey; 244 Granger; 245 (b) NWPA; 247 Granger 248 (tl, tr) LOC; 250-251 Gary R. Lucy Gallery; 251 (b) DW; 252 Gary R. Lucy Gallery; 253 Photo by Brian Crow, Provided by US DLM; 254 (bl) BC; 255 LOC; 256 (c) Granger, (b) SS/Sherry Yates Sowell; 257 (t) LOC, (b) NWPA; 258 Granger; 259 TSL; 261 NYPL; 262 Granger; 263 (c) Granger, (b) NWPA; 264 (l) LOC, (b) BC, (background) Smithsonian Institution/Corbis; 265 LOC; 266-267 LOC; 268 GR.

Chapter Nine: 270-271 LOC; 272 Corbis; 274 BC; 275 Travellers Rest Plantation and Museum; 276 TDT; 277 (l) TDT, (r) Granger; 278 (t) BC; 279 JB, (inset) SS/Phil Anthony; 280-281 Gary R. Lucy Gallery; 282 LOC; 283 Memphis/Shelby County Public Library Information Center; 284-285 LOC; 286 NWPA; 287 (l) THS, (r) LOC; 288 NWPA; 290 BC; 291 LOC; 292 (t) TDT, (b) LOC; 294 THS; 295 (t) Tennessee State Museum, (b) TSL; 296 (r) LOC; 297 (l) BC, (r) LOC; 298 LOC; 299 (c) Wisconsin Historical Society, (b) Granger; 300 (t) NARA, (b) NWPA; 301 Woolaroc Museum & Wildlife Preserve; 303 GR; 305 LOC.

Chapter Ten: 306-307 LOC; 308 LOC; 310 NYPL; 311 SS/Newton Page; 312 LOC; 313 TSL; 314 LOC; 316 (t) LOC, (b) Manuscripts, Archives and Rare Books Division, Schomburg Center for Research in Black Culture, The New York Public Library, Astor, Lenox and Tilden Foundations; 317 LOC; 318 (t) Kansas State Historical Society, (b) NARA; 319 Kansas State Historical Society; 320 (inset) LOC, (b) Granger; 321 (t, inset) LOC; 322 LOC; 324 Memphis/Shelby County Public Library Information Center; 325 LOC; 327 (inset) SS/Albert Barr, (b) SS/Pam Burley; 328 (t) LOC, (b) SS/Richard Foote; 329 LOC; 330-331 NWPA; 332-335 LOC.